# Race, Culture and Counselling

## Second Edition

# Race, Culture and Counselling

## The Ongoing Challenge

## Second Edition

*Colin Lago*

Open University Press

Open University Press
McGraw-Hill Education
McGraw-Hill House
Shoppenhangers Road
Maidenhead
Berkshire
England
SL6 2QL

email: enquiries@openup.co.uk
world wide web: www.openup.co.uk

and Two Penn Plaza, New York, NY 10121-2289, USA

First Edition Published 1996
Second Edition – First Published 2006

A catalogue record of this book is available from the British Library

ISBN-10: 0335 21694 3
ISBN-13: 978 0335 21694 9

Library of Congress Cataloging-in-Publication Data
CIP data applied for

Typeset by RefineCatch Limited, Bungay, Suffolk
Printed and bound by CPI Group (UK) Ltd, Croydon, CR0 4YY

# Contents

# Dedications

## The first edition

The writing of the first edition of this book was made possible by the generous support of the Alec Van Berchem Trust to whom we are deeply grateful.

We wish to dedicate this book to all of the people who struggle and strive to make this world a better place for us all to live in and to all of those who have nurtured and inspired us on our personal journeys and to those who have helped us towards writing this book.

Our gratitude also goes to our families who have supported our dreams and tolerated our absences and preoccupations caused by these concerns and the writing of this book.

Finally we wish to express our heartfelt thanks to Christine Davison, who has tirelessly typed and retyped many versions of the script.

## The second edition

This second edition is dedicated to:

Joyce, a much missed friend, colleague and co-trainer.

Gill, Becky and James for their continued support.

All those dedicated to the delivery of 'diversity sensitive' counselling and psychotherapy.

The many friends and colleagues who have actively supported me in writing this second edition.

The precious friends and colleagues who have contributed the new chapters in this second edition.

# List of tables and figures

## Tables

## Figures

# Acknowledgements

The authors would like to thank the following authors, journals and publishers for permission to reproduce copyright material that is detailed below. Although every effort has been made to trace copyright holders, the authors and publishers apologize in advance for any unintentional omission or neglect and will be pleased to insert the appropriate acknowledgement in any subsequent edition of this book.

American Counselling Association for extracts from Pedersen, P.B. (1987a) 'Ten frequent assumptions of cultural bias in counselling' and Sue, D.W. *et al.* (1992) 'Multicultural counselling competencies and standards: a call to the profession'.
John McLeod and Open University Press for passages from McLeod, J. (1993) *An Introduction to Counselling*.
Croom Helm for extracts from Tseng, W.S. in Cox, J.L. (1986) *Transcultural Psychiatry*.
Pluto Press for extracts from Fryer, P. (1984) *Staying Power: The History of Black People in Britain*.
Sage Publications for extracts from Krippner, S. and Jilek, W.G. in Ward, C.A. (1989) *Altered States of Consciousness and Mental Health: A Cross Cultural Perspective* and Hofstede, G. (1980b) *Culture's Consequences: International Differences in Work Related Values*.
Harbrinder Dhillon-Stevens for details of her PhD research and resulting production of interactive training DVDs.
*Counselling and Psychotherapy Journal*, BACP, for Chapter 14, previously published in 16(3), 2005.

# About the authors of the first edition

Colin Lago was Director of the Counselling Service at the University of Sheffield from 1987 to 2003. He was formerly a youth worker in the east end of London and a teacher in Jamaica. He is a white English man. The authors first met when they were both on the RACE sub-committee of the British Association for Counselling. Colin and Joyce have previously written together and co-produced a training video on the subjects considered within this book.

Joyce Thompson is a black Jamaican woman who has spent most of her life living and working in England. She migrated to England in 1956 and returned to live in semi-retirement in her native Jamaica in 1993. Joyce trained as a nurse, a teacher and as a counselling psychologist whilst in England. Both authors have been very active in the field of counselling, promoting the need for greater awareness and positive action in this area.

# Authorship of the second edition

After much consideration and with considerable reluctance, Joyce decided not to be actively involved in the production of this second edition. The distance of Jamaica from England (for convenient consultation purposes) and the need to enjoy her retirement whilst overseeing a move to a new house in Jamaica provided a more than sufficient rationale for her withdrawal from active involvement in this second edition. Her best wishes and 'blessings', however, continue to underpin this text. Colin Lago is therefore responsible for the following text, incorporating new materials, ideas, chapters and references. Colin now works as an independent practitioner, offering counselling, supervision and training. He continues to write, particularly in the field of diversity.

# Notes on contributors

**Shaindl Diamond** is a PhD student in the Counselling Psychology Program at the Ontario Institute for Studies in Education of the University of Toronto (OISE/UT). She received her undergraduate degree from Trent University in Women Studies and Psychology and her MA from OISE/UT in Counselling Psychology. Her academic interests include lesbian/gay/bisexual/transgender/queer psychology, multicultural psychology, critical psychology, anti-oppression and anti-racist education, feminist theory and equity studies.

**Joseph Roy Gillis** is an assistant professor at the Ontario Institute for Studies in Education at the University of Toronto in the Department of Adult Education and Counselling Psychology. His research and teaching interests include the development of a counselling model for hate crime survivors, attitudes toward sexual orientation diversity and teaching about sexual diversity in the classroom, sexual dysfunction in gay men, HIV prevention and safer sex fatigue, forensic psychology and psychological assessment. He has published broadly in those fields in academic journals and has presented his research to both community agencies and academic audiences. He also teaches a graduate level course on counselling issues for gay, lesbian, bisexual and transgendered individuals.

**Courtland C. Lee** is a professor and director of the Counsellor Education Program at the University of Maryland, College Park. His areas of research specialization include multicultural counselling and men's issues in counselling. He has written, edited or co-edited four books on multicultural counselling. He has also written three books on counselling African American male youth. In addition, he has written numerous articles and book chapters on counselling across cultures. Dr Lee is the former editor of the *Journal of Multicultural Counseling and Development* and serves on the advisory board of the *International Journal for the Advancement of Counselling*. He is a Past President of the American Counseling Association and the Association for Multicultural Counseling and Development, and a Fellow of the British Association for Counselling and Psychotherapy.

**Roy Moodley**, PhD, is Associate Professor in Counselling Psychology at the Ontario Institute for Studies in Education at the University of Toronto. Research and publication interests include traditional and cultural healing;

multicultural and diversity counselling; race, culture and ethnicity in psycho-therapy; and masculinities. Roy co-edited *Transforming Managers: Gendering Change in the Public Sector* (UCL Press/Taylor and Francis, 1999); *Carl Rogers Counsels a Black Client: Race and Culture in Person-Centred Counselling* (PCCS Books, 2004); *Integrating Traditional Healing Practices into Counseling and Psycho-therapy* (Sage Publications, 2005); and *Race, Culture and Psychotherapy: Critical Perspectives in Multicultural Practice* (Routledge, 2005).

**Gill Tuckwell** is a counsellor, supervisor and trainer who now works in private practice. Her interest and involvement in racial issues dates back some 35 years to her initial experiences as a teacher in an inner city school where she became aware of the need for schools to address issues of racial diversity. On moving into the counselling profession, Gill identified similar areas of concern, recog-nizing the challenge to counsellors to develop an understanding of racial dynamics in the counselling process. To this end, her book *Racial Identity, White Counsellors and Therapists* (Open University Press, 2002) was written to encourage white counsellors to explore the implications of their white identity and thus to become more racially aware as practitioners. Her contribution to the chapter in this book continues to focus on this area.

**Clemmont E. Vontress** received the BA Degree from Kentucky State Uni-versity in French and English in 1952 and the MS (1956) and the PhD (1965) in counselling from Indiana University, Bloomington, Indiana. One of the best known authorities on cross-cultural counselling, he is also known for articles, chapters and books on existential counselling and traditional healing. He has made several field trips to West Africa to study methods used by folk healers to treat patients complaining of physical, psychological, social and spiritual problems. He has also studied and written about ethno-psychiatry, an approach used for counselling immigrants from developing countries in France.

**Valerie Watson** is a qualified person-centred counsellor and supervisor and has experience of work in the independent and voluntary sector. In the past 20 years she has worked as a teacher, lecturer, trainer and external examiner in secondary and higher education and in a number of voluntary organizations including Victim Support. For the past 12 years Valerie has focused on counsel-ling and counsellor education with a personal and particular research interest in issues relating to ethnicity, race and culture. She has recently completed her thesis examining the training experiences of black counsellors in England. Currently, Valerie is a counsellor in the counselling service at the University of Nottingham.

# Foreword to the first edition

I am extremely honoured to write the foreword to this book. I first met the authors in the Fall of 1986, when we were involved in planning a bilateral conference on issues of cultural diversity and counselling in the United Kingdom and the United States. This conference spawned a professional collaboration that has established a trans-Atlantic exchange of ideas on multicultural counselling issues and practices. The authors have become respected colleagues and valued friends.

Through our collaborative efforts we have discovered that issues of race and culture are critically important and challenging to counselling. Scores of mental health professionals in both Great Britain and the United States seem to be ill prepared to provide culturally appropriate counselling services to a diverse population. Many are searching for new ways to intervene successfully into the lives of people from diverse cultural backgrounds. This search is made even more urgent by demographic projections that suggest that racial and cultural diversity will have an even greater impact on both of our societies in the next century.

This book, therefore, is not only timely, but critical to the future of counselling theory and practice in the United Kingdom and beyond. It is an excellent synthesis of traditional and contemporary ideas related to issues of race and culture in counselling. The authors have presented in this volume a brilliant and comprehensive examination of the complex and often vexing issues that must be addressed if counselling is to be empowering, as opposed to oppressive, for individuals from minority or disenfranchised groups. While the book in its entirety is profoundly important, several chapters are worthy of special note. These chapters, in particular, raise the level of scholarship on issues of race and culture in counselling in Great Britain into an important new dimension. They include the chapters dealing with: issues of race and power, cultural barriers to communication, indigenous approaches to helping, filmed cases, the culture of the counselling organization, supervision, training and research.

No doubt, many ideas presented in these chapters, and the remainder of the book will evoke strong feelings among readers. Some will become angry or defensive, whilst others will have their cultural ideas and experiences validated by the authors' arguments. No matter how you are personally affected, however, this book will challenge most of your assumptions about how to appropriately address the issues of counselling in a multicultural society. It will force you to move beyond your zone of professional comfort and assess your competence as a counsellor.

The work of Colin Lago and Joyce Thompson in this book makes a significant contribution to the literature on multicultural counselling. They have also helped to advance the theory base on counselling practice in the United Kingdom with their efforts. This book provides a major stimulus for the development or greater appreciation for the importance of cultural responsiveness in counsellor training and practice in Great Britain. It provides a new lens with which to view counselling theory and practice. The ideas presented here are an important effort in freeing counselling from the narrow confines of traditional thinking. Lago and Thompson's work provides a helping framework which allows for equal access and opportunities to all people regardless of race or culture.

*Courtland Lee*

# Introduction to the first edition

This book seeks to explore some of the major dimensions and subtleties underlying the issues of race and culture and how these might impact upon counselling and psychotherapy relationships. The authors have long been concerned about the nature of oppression and how discriminatory practices occur. Their professional experience within British society has exposed them directly to people who, because of their differing cultural and/or racial origins, have been discriminated against. They have previously worked together on training projects, writing tasks and the production of a training video on the subject addressed within this book.

Despite the British context within which and out of which this text has been written, many of the issues and concerns discussed here will be applicable to therapists in many other societies and cultures having culturally and racially different clients. The climate in which the contents of this book are set, and which is described more fully in Chapter 1, is a profoundly complex one in terms of history, population complexity, political perspectives and range of cultural identities and all this is compounded by discrimination and racism. Both counsellors and clients are participants in this climate and, as such, are prone to the multitude of complex forces and attitudes that shape people's lives.

Counsellors and psychotherapists have to acknowledge that their assumptions and beliefs about and attitudes towards those who are culturally and racially different may well be over-simplistic, judgemental and discriminatory. At worst, and as a consequence, therapeutic aims may well have anti-therapeutic outcomes. The dialogical approach of counselling and psychotherapy has now come of age alongside other healing approaches within many societies.

The challenges to counsellors are many:

- Do they understand the impact of their own past upon their assumptions about culture, identity, morals etc.?
- Do they understand the discriminatory nature and power imbalance of the relationship between dominant and minority groups in society and how such practices are perpetuated?
- Can they enhance their own learning about the groups from which clients come?
- Are they open to a wide range of challenging and perhaps contradictory views of the world expressed by clients?

- How might their theories and models of counselling be extended or modified to incorporate a wider range of understanding and response modes to clients?
- How might their way of being with clients recognize and address the societal and political implications (as well as the emotional and psychological implications) of the client's situation?

'Counsellors are trained to work in a sensitive, skilled and theoretically informed manner with individuals seeking help.' This is the opening sentence of Chapter 2. In order to work with culturally and racially different clients therapists will also require an understanding of how contemporary society works in relation to race, the exercise of power, the effects of discrimination, stereotyping, how ideologies sabotage policies, and so on. In short, counsellors require a structural awareness of society.

A broad overview of those engaged in the counselling profession would encompass many practitioners holding strongly humanitarian world views. However, counsellors are not necessarily aware of the nature or extent of the structural inequalities that so pejoratively affect black people's lives, nor are they clearly aware of their own position in those issues. For many white people who believe themselves to be tolerant, understanding, accepting (etc.) it is often very difficult to appreciate the multiplicity of mechanisms that exist in society that perpetuate systems of disadvantage amongst black people.

Chapter 3 opens with a quote stressing the complexity of the word 'culture' and continues with an examination of what differences in culture might mean. Despite very sincere attempts to understand clients' inner realities, counsellors, like all human beings, do respond initially on their own perceptual prejudicial criteria. The impact of visibility of, and then judgement of, difference might prevent any therapeutic progress whatsoever.

Fortunately it has been our experience that there are situations in which, while working with clients who have profoundly different cultural origins to ourselves, nevertheless a process of counselling has been helpful. Cultural difference itself is not necessarily a barrier to effective therapy though it can cause immense confusion as culture profoundly affects people's ways of being, their behaviour, their interpersonal relationships, their notions of meaning and so on.

When people share cultural origins and understandings, they share, often without any awareness, sufficient 'recipes' for understanding each other's present behaviour and predicting their future behaviour. Culturally different persons do not enjoy these shared assumptions, thus emphasizing the importance of therapists becoming culturally informed.

While communication constitutes part of the visible and audible aspects of people's behaviour, the inner origins of such messages come from the complex inner workings of their minds, their emotions, their memories, their relationships and so on. Within the context of this book, counsellors are being encouraged to understand more fully their inner complexities, and specifically their own cultural barriers to communication, the topic considered in Chapter 4. This chapter offers a very wide range of ideas concerning cultural differences in behaviour. This considerable range of information has deliberately been included to demonstrate the enormous extent of the potential behavioural differences that could occur between counsellors and their culturally different clients.

The relationship between language thought and experience is one of great complexity and is considered in Chapter 5. It is the authors' view that transcultural issues must not be reduced to the limiting interpretations of the function of language and language differences. They suggest that language has potential for infinite creativity and is subject to the speaker's capacity for ingenuity, invention and figurative, idiomatic and allusive expression. Taken from this philosophical stance, language always has the potential to express thought and to acknowledge experience. As counselling philosophy implicitly recognizes the potential for growth in people, it would seem an important component to view the nature of language within the counselling process as one that always has the potential of achieving its task of articulating and making understandable the clients 'agenda'.

The process of counselling, with its accent on acceptance, listening and dialogue, has the potential to provide people from minority groups or low-esteem positions with the opportunity to speak, practise, experiment with and thus create and develop their 'word', their symbols of meaning. Counselling, in this sense, contributes to a language and a confidence derived from clients' own explorations of their situation. This perspective demonstrates the complex relationship between language and power. If clients, through psychotherapy, develop their language, a confidence in their view of the world, much has been achieved. On the other hand, therapists must pay attention to their use of language and its potential negative effects upon clients. Also, counsellors must take responsibility for interacting in the language requested by the client.

Counsellors are significantly influenced in the ways they approach, reflect upon and predict the outcome of their work by the tutorial and theoretical influences they were exposed to whilst in training or in post. Many of the current theories of therapy are rooted, historically, in central European and North American cultures. Chapter 6 offers an explanation of some of these and subsequently presents some critiques when they are compared with non-western approaches.

The writings of western therapists frequently feature metaphoric concepts such as process, rhythm, dance and journey, in attempting to describe their work. Positive inferences may be drawn from these perspectives in relation to therapists' interest in and capacity of openness towards other cultures, disciplines and belief systems. The nature of people who become psychotherapists is extremely fascinating and further complicates the relationship between theory, practice and culture as embedded in the persona of the counsellor. The ways in which people cope, attempt to solve their problems and seek assistance are shaped by the social and cultural norms and the symbolic meaning within their culture. In addition, differences also exist between cultures on what is even deemed as problematic.

A matrix of healing approaches first mentioned in Chapter 1 is reintroduced in Chapter 7 and offers a conceptual model for understanding a complete range of helping interventions. This section introduces the reader to a wide range of non-Eurocentric healing methods and reminds us that, long before western medicine recognized the fact, African traditional healers had taken the position that ecology and interpersonal relations affect people's health. Healers around the world have shaped and developed 'spontaneous experiences' to arrive at highly elaborated healing systems. Meditation traditions, drum- and dance-related trance-inducing systems and healing practices employing psychedelic drugs are well-known examples. Most western therapies have an individual emphasis; the healing forms described in Chapter 7 have much more a community or family focus. We have to recognize the breadth and complexity of the spectrum of healing approaches embedded in all societies and note that each have their validity within the cultural frameworks from which they originate. In addition, there are often similarities between the forms of activity used by different cultures, e.g. trance states, though the rituals may be differently structured.

Chapter 8 offers a series of transcripts taken from transcultural counselling interviews that may be used for training and discussion purposes.

Historically the literature on transcultural counselling has substantially ignored organizational and systemic issues. Chapter 9 attempts to confront this vacuum by considering the nature of the organizational context within which counselling takes place. The location within which the therapy takes place might be, for some clients, as important as the therapy itself. All cultures have conventions influenced by both codes and practices related to hospitality. These conventions influence the design and layout of buildings as well as informing interpersonal behaviours. This whole chapter is concerned with stimulating a consideration of how counselling organizations can create the conditions (physical, psychological and emotional) within which successful therapy can occur.

Supervision, training and research are the subjects of the final three chapters. Each of these facets that prepare, support and underpin therapist practice have immense significance for the development of transculturally sensitive and skilled therapists. These elements subsume a deep concern for ethical and effective therapeutic practice to all clients living in multicultural and multiracial societies. We are concerned that counselling and psychotherapy does not become a further oppressive or damaging instrument of society but that it continues to aspire to be an appropriately liberating and therapeutic force for any troubled individuals, families or groups seeking psychological help and emotional support.

We have deliberately used various terms interchangably within this book in relation to the helping or therapeutic process. We are cognizant of the current debate about differences between counselling and psychotherapy. Our concern here, whatever these differences are, is to address all who aspire, through the skills of listening, relating and dialogue, to assist others' suffering. We hope that the various terms used, e.g. counsellor, counselling, psycho-therapist, therapist, psychotherapy etc., facilitate easy reading. There are also a range of terms used in the book to describe the activity of counselling a client from another racial or cultural background. In recent times these terms have included cross-cultural, intercultural, transcultural and multicultural. In most instances we have used the latter conventions of transcultural, a term increasingly popular in British literature, and multicultural, a term current in the United States. Similarly, we have used terms such as 'culturally different', 'racially different', 'black' and 'white' as variously descriptive of counsellors and clients. Where we have used the terms 'black' and 'white' we intend these to be interpreted in their political sense where blackness is used to describe those who are not the traditional power holders or members of a dominant majority group in a society. Language can age very quickly and connotative meanings may thus swing from having positive to negative effects. Consequently we have erred from giving precise definitions and interpretations of these terms but rather encourage the reader to appreciate our attempts to address the lived complexity of such helping relationships, whatever the current definitions are.

*Colin Lago and Joyce Thompson*

# About the book

This book seeks to explore some of the major dimensions and subtleties underlying the issues of race and culture and how these might impact upon counselling/psychotherapeutic relationships. It is an attempt to contribute to the literature that urges awareness, understanding and acceptance between people of different cultural, racial and linguistic origins.

The dimensions of race and culture are extremely complex and have many consequences in therapy. Wherever persons of different races and cultures come together in a counselling relationship, some of their interactions will be an unknown quantity, each may experience discomfort and fear and the results, for both parties, might be negative.

This is not a book of case studies, neither is it a cookbook manual of 'how to do it'. Rather, it articulates a range of issues that are pertinent to therapists who live and work in a multiracial society and also addresses the challenges posed to trainers, supervisors and researchers of counselling and psychotherapy.

# Introduction to the second edition

Almost a decade has passed since the first edition of this book was published. In these intervening years there have been significant events, frequently and profoundly traumatic for those involved, in the UK, Europe and the rest of the world. Often, these have reflected and focused attention upon race relations, intercultural (mis)-understanding, political and religious differences. The context within which the first edition was written now seems to be more sharpened than ever by these recent 'major' events, events that have and will continue to impact upon many people, some of whom may become clients of counsellors and psychotherapists, both now and a long time into the future.

Within this category, I am including the attack on the Twin Towers in New York (11 September 2001), the preceding strands of international political and military activity that gave birth to this attack (over more than a decade) and the resulting development of the 'war on terror'. One direct outcome of this international incident was the rise in 'Islamaphobia' across the western world, leading to serious transgressions of what is considered 'decent' behaviour by any modern state towards those of perceived Islamic beliefs. Given the profound interconnectedness of the world, such an apparently distant event from the UK nevertheless became transposed into the experience of psychotherapy clients (of Asian and middle Eastern ethnicities) expressing considerable anxiety and fear about their safety from aggression. 'Following 11 September, it seemed that overnight', one young doctor told me, 'I experienced hostility from some of my patients, hostility which hadn't been there before. In addition, new racist graffiti suddenly appeared in the hospital toilets. I became very anxious indeed and found it hard to concentrate on my work.' From discussions with American, Canadian, French, German and Austrian colleagues I am aware of similar discriminatory behaviours occurring in those countries, similarly impacting upon particular groups, some of whom are therapy clients.

Another such event was the expansion of the European Union to include new member states during 2004. This gave rise to grossly exaggerated media reportage on the likely impact of increased and unrestricted immigration to the UK as well as other 'more prosperous' European countries. Herman Ouseley, formerly Chairman of the Commission for Racial Equality (1993–2000) wrote an article in the *Guardian* newspaper entitled 'Forget this phoney debate; we need to confront racism' (10 April 2004). He reported that:

During the six-month period up to February 2004, 1509 articles on immigration and asylum appeared in the tabloid newspapers and 1254 in the broadsheets. Reporting in the Daily Express (365), the Sun (332), and the Daily Mail (330) became increasingly hysterical as the papers battled to outdo each other. The speculation about the likely migration to Britain from Eastern Europe after accession in May was typical: the first headline on 18 January (2004) suggested that 100,000 gypsies were expected to seek entry; the next day another newspaper quadrupled the number; by day three a third newspaper announced that '1.5 million Gypsies were on their way!'

Ouseley goes on to add that there were no corrections, challenges or repudiations; no Press Complaints Commission investigation into standards and accuracy; no consideration for the damage done to race relations in the UK. The powerful role of the media in shaping and influencing public opinion in the field of race relations was briefly alluded to in the first edition. The above report only confirms its continuing role as a significant influence in the everyday world we each inhabit – an influence that impacts upon therapists and clients alike.

Rather more dramatically, worldwide it is estimated that:

- between 1990 and 1999, 2 billion people had been affected and traumatized by world disasters, conflicts and wars;
- 56,000 people were killed annually;
- in 1999, 80,000 people were killed;
- there were 13.75 million refugees in 1999;
- in this same decade there were 452 conflict situations;
- by the year 2000, 4000 people were being killed weekly; and
- there were 21 million displaced persons.

Within the UK, following the murder of a young black man, Stephen Lawrence, the government instituted a public enquiry under the chairmanship of Sir William Macpherson. The report was published in 1999. It highlighted widespread racism both within the police force and in other public institutions. The Macpherson Report was the first government report to acknowledge the existence of institutional racism and, as a consequence, legislation was introduced amending the 1976 Race Relations Act to extend the scope of anti-racist legislation, and making it a statutory obligation for public bodies actively to promote racial equality (Home Office 2001).

Despite the critical importance of these developments, Fernando (2003) also cites more recent events (the reports on racial violence in three northern UK cities, the publication of the immigration white paper (Home Office 2002) and the introduction of a requirement that new migrants should swear an oath of allegiance to Britain) which continue to obscure the many manifestations of and responsibilities for racism under other guises.

At the time of writing (early Spring 2005), the world is reeling with the dire consequences of the tsunami wave that emanated from an undersea earthquake to devastate extensive coastal regions of Indonesia, Sri Lanka, India, Thailand and other territories in the Indian Ocean. Already, over 150,000 people have been reported dead in these regions. Massive international aid programmes have been implemented to assist the survivors and to commence the extensive repairs required to restore some semblance of life as it was before. However, given the sheer size and multinational impact of this disaster, the resulting psychological and emotional trauma in survivors and their relatives is likely to continue for many, many years.

To this list of 'events' in the last decade since the first edition was published could be added many more, just as damaging and having as great an impact on those involved as the events that have been noted above. The sheer size of the human population worldwide affected by incidents of war, nature, politics, revolution, terrorism and so on is enormous. We may add to the above by considering all those who live in settled communities who are members of minority groups (ethnic, religious, cultural) and who thus may be subject to discriminatory behaviours from the majority population. In addition, 'majority' populations are in a continuous state of flux in relation to issues of identity and diversity. Beyond all the above categories, there is also that percentage of the population at large that will require therapy from therapists who are sensitive to, informed about and skilled in the issues of diversity and identity.

In brief, the underlying rationale for this text has been strengthened since the first publication a decade ago, both internationally as well as locally within the United Kingdom. Urgent attention continues to need to be brought to this specialist field of 'diversity' within counselling and psychotherapy. In the previous edition, terms such as 'transcultural' and 'multicultural' were frequently used, reflecting the terminology that was then in common use. 'Diversity' has now become the embracing conceptual term within the profession and beyond, and is rather more broadly related to a wide range of groups (including those in cultural, racial and ethnic minority groups) in society deemed as diverse from the mainstream population. A working definition of 'diversity' has recently been developed by the British Association for Counselling and Psychotherapy (BACP Equality and Diversity Forum, 2005) and is now included in Chapter 1.

Though the first edition, and to a very great extent this second edition, focuses on the specific areas of 'race', culture and ethnicity as signifiers of oppression and discrimination, the author is aware of the complexities of multiple diversity and multiple oppression. Previous writings by Moodley (2003a) and Dhillon-Stevens (2004b) are now extended through the inclusion of the new chapter by Shaindl Lin Diamond and Joseph Roy Gillis (Chapter 16). They offer the values of poststructural analysis to assist the conceptualization of others and their differences and diversities. Indeed, this chapter includes an articulate and succinct quote by Sue (2001) that, for me, expressed something I have become concerned about in the new adoption of diversity as a generic term. That is, in Sue's words,

> This stance is not intended to negate the importance of the many cultural dimensions to human identity but notes the greater discomfort that many psychologists experience in dealing with issues of race rather than other sociodemographic differences. As a result, race becomes less salient and allows us to avoid addressing problems of racial prejudice, racial discrimination, and systemic racial oppression.
>
> (p. 792)

The issues considered within this chapter combined with the overall focus of the book constitute, I hope, an inclusive and complementary embracing of this complex field.

In addition to trying to update the original text, which itself has proved a considerable difficulty, a series of new chapters have been added. The challenge of updating the text has been the sense of being caught between the importance of recognizing the integrity of the first edition, leading to a tendency to 'tweak' the script appropriately and the realization that, were I involved in writing this again, (I think) it would be completely different! I am grateful to the friends and colleagues who offered a contemporary critique of the first edition, thus facilitating my own internal debates as to what needed to be changed and modified. As a consequence of their feedback, and respecting this frustration and the tension between maintaining the integrity of the first edition and wishing to offer a contemporary text, I was delighted and am grateful to Hannah Cooper and her colleagues at Open University Press who were open to the idea of the inclusion of six new chapters in this second edition.

Language, as noted in Chapter 5, is a powerful and complex medium. The author has attempted to maintain a respectful, sensitive and contemporary vocabulary within this second edition. To avoid the stylistically acceptable though somewhat cumbersome use of 'his/her', the gender prepositions have been used alternatively throughout the text.

The new contributions to the text constitute a potent development to this field of professional therapeutic aspiration and application. Respected writers, hailing from different ethnic, cultural and 'racial' origins, from Canada (Moodley, Diamond and Gillis), the United States (Lee, Vontress) and the UK (Tuckwell, Watson), have contributed significantly to what I hope will be the usefulness of this text to those who consult it. To those contributors I must also record my thanks for their continued support, commitment and efficiency in returning their scripts on time!

Courtland Lee, in Chapter 12, offers a synthesis of the models of identity development. At the time of writing the first edition, these models were only just seeping into this author's consciousness, but I could see, then, the tremendous value they held in stimulating systematic reflection by therapists on their identity and its relationship to their work with clients.

Val Watson, in Chapter 13, has provided us with the alarming evidence she collected during her doctoral research on the experience of black counselling trainees and practitioners on counselling and psychotherapy training courses in the UK. One need go no further than this chapter to appreciate the motivating rationale for this whole text. Life experience is substantially determined by our cultural, ethnic and 'racial' heritage. This chapter constitutes an urgent call to all therapy trainers to review their curricula and training practices.

The subject matter of Chapters 14 and 15 (by myself and Gill Tuckwell respectively) reflects on the nature and implications of whiteness as a signifier of dominant and majority status. In much of the writing related to diversity and difference, there has been less explicit attention focused upon the role of the dominant majority, yet the majority of therapists are likely to hail from this group within society. Difference and diversity exist only as they relate to this 'dominant' group. For substantial and beneficial changes to occur within society and within individual practitioners, members of this group have to reflect on their relative 'racialized' identity as it stands alongside other identities, rather than view it from the opaque powerful position it has occupied for so long – a position of being and defining the 'norm', the 'normal', the 'standard'.

Finally, in Chapter 17 Roy Moodley and Clemmont Vontress critically reappraise the research efforts that have been dedicated to informing professional practice in transcultural therapy and point to possible new avenues for exploration.

Writing this Introduction to the second edition has taken place in my home in Sheffield. In completing this piece, a memory has just flitted across my brain that took me back to sitting on the balcony of Joyce's home in Jamaica when we completed the first draft over a decade ago. Joyce has continued to be a great and dear friend and this book is dedicated to her.

*Colin Lago*

# 1  The climate, the context and the challenge

## The climate: the multicultural and multiracial nature of society today

> Britain has always had ethnic minorities. People with diverse histories, cultures, beliefs and languages have settled here since the beginnings of recorded time.
>
> (CRE Fact Sheet, Revised 1999)

The multicultural and multiracial composition of British society today is enormously complex. Inevitably, any systematic analysis of a population will rest upon the nature of how people and groups are categorized and to what extent they enjoy temporary or permanent residence.

Let us consider some of these complexities. Whilst living in Leicester during the 1980s the author came across a survey of city residents that revealed 43 different countries of origin in that one city alone. At Sheffield University, where the author worked previously, there were 3846 international students in 2003/04 coming from 116 countries. Indeed, in terms of international students, it was estimated that between 80,000 and 100,000 temporarily resided in Britain to pursue higher education in the late 1980s and early 1990s (Morgan and Bo 1993). This figure has now risen to approximately 319,000 in 2003 (Dudley 2004).

As stated above, categorization of different groups in society is a problem-strewn activity. Skellington and Morris (1992) include a complete chapter in their book on the 'construction of racial data'. They point out that racial categories or racial groups do not exist as objective biological facts in any meaningful way. The scientific study of human beings has been unable to identify significant characteristics that can be found in some groups of people but not in others that would allow us to delineate distinct racial groups. Such studies have not found any differences of ability or intelligence. Tuckwell (2002) also considers this question more fully and notes that despite the absence of significant differentiating characteristics, 'race' continues to be a complex social and political phenomenon (pp. 8–27).

Skellington and Morris (1992) suggest that nationalities of origin might be a more reliable measure to use in that these reflect a legal status; however, such measures do not account for groups that are legally and residentially British. Even the national census changed the way it categorized people between the 1971 and 1992 surveys.

In April 1991 there were nearly four million people resident in the UK who were born elsewhere, 7.3 per cent of the population (Sanders 1994). At the 1991 census, just over three million people in Britain did not classify themselves as white. Approximately, half of this group were South Asian (i.e. of Indian, Pakistani and Bangladeshi descent), and 30 per cent were of black African and Caribbean descent (CRE 1999).

The term 'immigrant' has for many become synonymous with being black. However, the majority of immigrants are white, from Eire, the old Commonwealth (Australia, New Zealand and Canada) and from other European countries. The 1981 census revealed that 3.4 million people in Britain were born overseas and of those 1.9 million were white. Owen's analysis of the 1991 census reveals that 61 per cent of immigrants are white (Owen 1992–95). The same source reveals that the Southern Irish still form the largest category of non-native residents, though their numbers had dropped by 12 per cent between 1981 and 1991. During this period the number of British residents born in Bangladesh had increased by 116 per cent, those born in Japan by 130 per cent and Turkey by 125 per cent. The survey also noted that just over 28,000 Japanese were now resident in this country.

Table 1.1 shows the ethnic composition of the population of Great Britain, 1991. The CRE Fact Sheet from which this data is taken notes that

> The ethnic group question in the 1991 census does not yield complete data on Britain's very diverse ethnic minority groups, both white and non-white. The term 'ethnic minority' is generally used to refer to those who did not tick the 'white' category. This fact sheet distinguishes between white and non-white ethnic minorities. The ethnic categories used are those in the study or survey quoted.

Skellington and Morris (1992), using figures taken from the Labour Force Surveys, indicate that almost one person in 20 living in Great Britain belongs to a minority ethnic group. For the period 1986–88, these surveys estimated the minority ethnic group population to be 2.58 million or 4.7 per cent of the total British population (p. 36). Projections towards the end of the twentieth century indicated that the proportion of black people in the total population of Britain would stabilize at around 6 per cent (p. 48).

**Table 1.1**   Ethnic composition of the population of Great Britain – 1991

|  | Number | Percentage of total population | Percentage born in UK |
|---|---|---|---|
| Total population | 54,888,844 | 100.0 | 93 |
| White | 51,873,794 | 94.5 | 96 |
| Ethnic minorities | 3,015,050 | 5.5 | 48 |
| Black Caribbean | 499,964 | 0.9 | 53 |
| Black African | 212,362 | 0.4 | 36 |
| Black Other | 178,401 | 0.3 | 84 |
| Indian | 840,255 | 1.5 | 42 |
| Pakistani | 476,555 | 0.9 | 50 |
| Bangladeshi | 162,835 | 0.3 | 37 |
| Chinese | 156,938 | 0.3 | 28 |
| Other Asian | 197,534 | 0.4 | 22 |
| Other–Other | 290,206 | 0.5 | 40 |

Source: CRE 1999

Political unrest in several parts of the world significantly increased the incidence of asylum seeking during the late 1990s and early years of this new century. The top ten countries of origin of asylum seekers in the first three-quarters of 2003 were Somalia, Iraq, Zimbabwe, China, Iran, Afghanistan, India, Turkey, Pakistan and Congo (Migration Watch UK 2004).

In terms of both culture and race, the above snapshot of contemporary Britain serves to reveal a population that has a myriad of origins and a huge range of ethnicities and subcultures. As we shall see later, these groups experience differential life opportunities and realities within Great Britain.

## A brief historical perspective

### Emigration trends

Whilst these early sections of Chapter 1 attempt to provide an overview of the rich multicultural, multiethnic and multiracial nature of the UK, thus providing the contextual nature within which this book is situated, little attention ever seems to have been given to the very considerable patterns of migration from these shores over many centuries. Indeed, the Migration Watch UK website notes that Britain *'is a nation of emigrants, not of immigrants! Since the Middle Ages our people have spread to all corners of the globe; the country's dominant migration experience has been to send people abroad, rather than to receive them from overseas. The balance did not change until the early 1980's.'* It goes on to note:

There are no direct data worth mentioning until the 19th Century, but indirect estimates suggest a net emigration of between 5,000 to 7,000 people per year from the 16th Century to the end of the 18th Century . . . By the end of the 19th Century we know from direct data that up to 90,000 persons per year were leaving Britain . . . Over 11 million British people emigrated across the Atlantic from 1815 to 1930 . . . There has been a steady net outflow of British citizens during this period (the 1990's) peaking at 91,000 in 2002. Indeed in that year there was a net overall migration from the UK.

(Migration Watch UK 2001: 1)

### Immigration trends

'Britain has always been a mixed society, a nation peopled by migrants, from the Bronze Age and Neolithic migrants who travelled to north west Europe five thousand years ago, to the refugees from eastern Europe and Africa arriving in Britain today' (CRE 2004). Bragg traces the origins of the English language back to the fifth century with the arrival of Germanic warrior tribes. More exactly, this group was composed of several different tribes including the Saxons, the Angles and the Jutes (Bragg 2003: 1–3). Other significant groups to have arrived and lived in Britain before and after then include the Romans, the Vikings and the Normans.

Native West Africans probably first appeared in London in 1554 (Jordan 1982). This was before we had potatoes, tobacco or tea and ten years before Shakespeare was born (Fryer 1984). Their presence reflected the developing trading opportunities at that time between Britain and West Africa. Some West Africans were brought to London to develop their language skills in order to assist the trading process and some were sold as household servants. The predominant purpose of these contacts was that of trading, as extensive English participation in the slave trade did not develop until well into the seventeenth century.

By the middle of the eighteenth century, however, Britain had become the leading slave-trading nation in the world and the centre of what was known as the triangular trade. Her ships carried manufactured goods to West Africa, transported slaves to the New World and brought back sugar, tobacco and cotton to Britain. In 1757, in the month of July, 175 ships with cargo worth £2m docked in British ports. In terms of population, by 1770 in London alone there were 18,000 black slaves, forming nearly 3 per cent of an estimated population of 650,000 (Hiro 1971).

Jordan (1982) and Hiro (1971) elucidate several dimensions that reflect white people's perceptions of black people from historical accounts that continue to be perpetuated today, several hundred years later. These include notions such as 'skin colour, religion, savage behaviour, libidinous men, black people as workhorses' and so on. The attitudes that fuel contemporary prejudice often have a very long history.

Approximately 100,000 Huguenots arrived from France in the seventeenth century and a similar number of Jews in the late nineteenth century (Migration Watch UK 2004). The last two centuries have also seen considerable immigration from Ireland and other European countries.

During the nineteenth century the largest group of immigrants to settle in England were the Irish. By 1841 there were more than 400,000 living in England, Scotland and Wales and the 1851 census showed that there were 727,326 Irish immigrants in Britain (Rees 1982: 75).

Britain experienced considerable Jewish immigration in the decades preceding the First World War. An estimated Jewish population of some 60,000 in 1880 had increased to approximately 300,000 by 1920 (Rees 1982). This population is now estimated at 285,000 (CRE 1999).

Just after the Second World War a sizeable number of Polish immigrants (120,000) were accepted into Britain under the Polish Resettlement Act of 1947. Rees (1982) notes that this Act was one of the few constructive legislative initiatives in the field of immigration, a field that has been dominated by ways to keep people out (specifically black people) rather than allowing them in. Other frequently represented national groups immigrating at this time were Lithuanians, Ukrainians, Latvians and Yugoslavs (approximately 100,000), though their treatment by the authorities was substantially different and indeed deficient to the Poles referred to above (Rees 1982: 82).

The largest groups of postwar economic immigrants (1948 onwards) came from the poorer Commonwealth territories of the Caribbean, the Indian subcontinent, the Mediterranean and the Far East. Under the British Nationality Act of 1948 citizens of the British Commonwealth were allowed to enter Britain freely, to find work, to settle and to bring their families. Indeed, many chose to take this option as a result of employer and government-led recruitment schemes.

However, successive immigration policies since the 1960s have significantly reduced the immigration possibilities of persons specifically from the New Commonwealth and Pakistan (i.e. predominantly black people).

> Immigrants represent a declining proportion of Britain's minority ethnic group population. Nine out of every ten minority ethnic group children aged under 5 were born in the UK. In 1984, the third PSI survey estimated that 40% of Britain's black population was British born; moreover PSI further estimated that 50% of those who came to Britain as immigrants had lived in Britain for over 15 years.
>
> (Brown 1984)

More recent statistics taken from the Home Office (Heath *et al.* 2004) revealed that:

- the total number of work permit holders and dependents admitted to the UK in 2003 was 119,000;
- 64,390 persons were removed or departed voluntarily from the UK in the same period;
- applications for asylum, excluding dependents, fell by 41 per cent in 2003 to 49,405. Nationalities accounting for the most applicants were Somali, Iraqi, Chinese, Zimbabwean and Iranian.

(Heath *et al.* 2004)

### Disadvantage, discrimination and racism

Towards the end of 1993 a public survey was conducted on racial harmony in Britain. One in every four white Britons, it found, would not wish to have a non-white person living next door to them. Arabs, Pakistanis, Africans, West Indians and Jews were cited as groups of people Britons would not wish to have as their neighbours (reported in *RACE* Newsletter 1993).

In 1984 the first British Social Attitudes survey described a British society that was seen by more than 90 per cent of the adult population to be racially prejudiced against its black and Asian members (Jowell *et al.* 1984). More than one-third classified themselves as racially prejudiced; 42 per cent also thought racial prejudice would be worse in five years' time.

In 1992 the Runnymede Trust and the National Opinion Poll produced the findings of the largest national study of attitudes to racism since the mid-1980s and found that two out of every three white people thought Britain was a very or fairly racist society compared to four out of five Afro-Caribbeans and 56 per cent of Asians.

The *Observer* newspaper published a (12-page special edition) feature on 'Race in Britain' (25 November 2001). Containing both articles and survey analyses, this special edition addressed many perspectives of contemporary life in Britain today. Amongst the findings it reported were the following:

- Identity: 61 per cent surveyed reported that as long as someone felt British, they were British regardless of colour.
- A surprising 72 per cent of Britons were unable to name three ethnic minority Britons they admired, while 55 per cent could not name a single one.
- Politics: In response to the question 'Is the government's record on race relations good/bad/indifferent?' a striking aspect here was that non-white Britons were almost twice as likely as white Britons to

believe the government's race relations record was good (50 per cent compared to 28 per cent).

- Personal: 60 per cent of the respondents indicated they had close friends from a different ethnic background. Fifty-seven per cent of white Britons made this claim and the figures rose to 84 per cent of ethnic minority Britons. There were regional, gender and age differences in the responses where those in the south-east were most likely and those in Scotland least likely to have a different ethnic friend. Younger people generally and men also figured highly.
- Post 11 September (2001): Generally, this survey noted a marked shift in attitude before and after 'September 11' on the question of whether race relations were improving. When the same question was asked two weeks prior to the attacks, 33 per cent said they were improving and only 21 per cent said they had got worse. This situation changed afterwards to only 27 per cent favouring the 'improvement' perception and 36 per cent deeming it to be worse.

Moving from these recent sets of findings to a slightly more historical perspective, much evidence can be found of aggressive behaviour towards non-white groups in the United Kingdom. In 1919, for example, there was a series of attacks on black people in the dock areas of Britain – Cardiff, Glasgow, Liverpool, Hull, Manchester and London. In the 1940s there were attacks in Liverpool (1948), Deptford (1949) and Birmingham (1949). In the late 1950s black people became a particular target for racist white youths. The 1960s brought 'paki-bashing' and attacks by white 'skinheads'. The 1970s saw racial violence and harassment escalate. Evidence suggests that the situation worsened in the 1980s (Skellington and Morris 1992) and indeed the number of reported attacks rose to 8779 in 1993, an increase of nearly 1000 over the previous year. By the year 2000 police recorded 25,100 racially aggravated offences. Unreported incidents are estimated to be as high as 150,000 (*Guardian*, 18 March 1994). This figure was substantially increased by estimates provided by the British Crime Survey, which cited 280,000 racially motivated incidents in 1999. Research by the Institute of Race Relations showed that in the last decade over 50 people had been killed in racial attacks (IRR News 2002).

The Home Affairs Committee in its 1986 report, *Racial Attacks and Harassment*, accepted as its starting point that '*the most shameful and dispiriting aspects of race relations in Britain is the incidence of racial attacks and harassment*' (Home Affairs Committee 1986: 22). In relation to racial violence, half of all victims know their attackers. It is estimated that children or young people cause half of all attacks and 20 per cent involve neighbours (IRR News 2002).

Sadly, the adjectives used by the Home Affairs Committee (see above) to describe race relations in this country ('shameful' and 'dispiriting') apply to all aspects of socio-cultural life. Accounts and reports of disadvantage, discrimination and racism are repeated with nauseating frequency. The issues are rife in housing, immigration, health, education, the media, criminal justice, social services and the labour market as the following paragraphs demonstrate.

### Immigration

At the end of the sixteenth century Queen Elizabeth I issued a decree 'to rid this land of all blackamoors'. That sentiment has been a strong influence in much of the immigration policy of the last hundred years. Indeed, Skellington and Morris assert that 'understanding immigration policy is central to understanding racism in British society' (1992: 50). Many governments have passed a variety of laws that have 'provided a legal framework for the institutionalization of racism' (Allen 1973). Many of these laws have underpinned the equation between blackness and notions of 'second class' and 'undesirable'. This has led on to the notion that 'black people are in themselves a problem and the fewer we have of them the better' (Ben-Tovim and Gabriel 1982). Just one example of immigration law practice, as determined in part by the various laws and the attitudes exacerbated by them, is given below.

In 1990 the refusal rate for Guayanese visitors to Britain was 1 in 87 compared, for example, with 1 in 3600 for Norwegians (Skellington and Morris 1992). A similar startling differential was discovered in 1982 when a comparison was drawn between visitors from Ghana who were 250 times as likely to be refused permission to enter the UK than a passenger from Sweden (Mactaggart and Gostin 1983). Indeed, the United Kingdom Immigration Advisory Service also found that, on immigration statistics published for 1985, a New Zealander was 333 times as likely to be admitted to the UK than someone from Ghana.

### Unemployment and housing

The publication in 1977 of David Smith's report, *Racial Disadvantage in Britain*, marked an important milestone in understanding the extent and nature of discriminatory behaviour against 'black' groups in this country. Smith's report provided evidence of the following points:

- as total unemployment rises, unemployment of minorities rises more steeply (p. 69);
- all minority groups had penetrated comparatively little into non-manual jobs (p. 73);
- the earnings of minority men are lower than those of white men (p. 84);
- Asians and West Indians tend to live in accommodation of a much

lower quality, from a structural point of view, than that occupied by whites (p. 230).

Fifteen years later unemployment among ethnic minorities was estimated at 22 per cent in 1993, compared with 10 per cent among white workers. Between the summers of 1992 and 1993 black unemployment rose 3 per cent but for whites it was 1 per cent; among women the difference was even greater (*Guardian* 1994).

### The media

In the realm of the media, several major studies appeared in the late 1970s and 1980s that indicated the extent to which 'people have derived from the media a perception of the coloured population as a threat and a problem, a conception more conducive to the development of hostility towards them than acceptance' (Hartmann and Husband 1974: 208).

Troyna's later study (1981) of local media (newspaper, radio) also revealed that far more attention was paid by the press to the manifestations of racial conflict and tension than on the scarcity of social resources, which underlie the reasons for this conflict.

### Other aspects

Other readily accessible research findings in this area are to be found in the book by Skellington and Morris (1992). They cover the incidence of violence and harassment (physical and mental), social services and welfare benefits, housing, the criminal justice system, education and the labour market. Points such as the following are made:

- The number of racially motivated incidents in England and Wales in 1990 was 6359 (p. 63).
- Blackness and poverty are more correlated than they were some years ago . . . the conditions of the black poor are deteriorating (p. 67).
- Various research studies reveal a higher incidence of diagnosis of schizophrenia amongst the black population compared with whites and suggest that black people tend to receive harsher forms of medication than equivalent white groups (p. 82).
- Discrimination is also revealed in the NHS employment practices, right through from the appointment of consultant doctors through to ancillary workers (p. 83).
- Evidence suggests that black minority ethnic groups are under-represented as clients receiving the preventative and supportive elements of social services provision, but over-represented in those aspects of social services activity that involve social control functions and/or institutionalization (p. 87).

- Differential figures between blacks and whites were also revealed in studies on the legal system, in jury composition (p. 104), the magistracy (p. 105), solicitors and barristers (p. 106) and probation officers (p. 107).
- In 1989, the Director of the Prison Reform Trust claimed that if white people were jailed at the same rate as black people, the total prison population of the UK would be 300,000. It is under 50,000 (p. 107).
- The incidence of school suspensions and expulsions was significantly higher for Afro-Caribbean pupils than others (p. 122).

The above trends continue to be evident today. Evidence published by the Institute of Race Relations (2002) noted that:

- In 2000–01 police recorded 25,100 racially aggravated offences.
- In the same year all racist incidents recorded by the police in England and Wales totalled 53,090.
- More alarmingly, the British Crime Survey suggested a probable under-reporting of racist attacks and estimated that there were 280,000 racially motivated incidents in 1999, 98,000 of these (i.e. 35 per cent) were against black, Indian, Pakistani and Bangladeshi people (who comprise just 7 per cent of the population).
- Their research shows that in the last ten years, there had been over 50 people killed in racial attacks.

### Summing up

The climate, then, in which the contents of this book are set is a profoundly complex one in terms of history, population complexity, political perspectives, a huge range of cultural and ethnic identities and all compounded by discrimination and racism. Both counsellors and clients are participants in this climate and, as such, are prone to the multitude of complex social and political forces and attitudes that shape people's lives. The contents alone indicate that any overly simplistic assumptions about the nature of British society and the people who live within it just cannot be made. Counsellors and psychotherapists have to acknowledge that their assumptions and beliefs about and attitudes towards those who are culturally and racially different may well be over-simplistic, judgemental and discriminatory. At worst, and as a consequence, therapeutic work may well have anti-therapeutic outcomes.

## The context: the acceptance of therapy and the challenge of diversity

What she needs is a good listening to
(From an advertisement on behalf of the National Society
for the Prevention of Cruelty to Children)

The previous section offered the reader an introduction to the complexity of today's multicultural, multiracial society, a society that has also experienced in the last three to four decades a substantial attitudinal shift towards the greater acceptance of counselling and psychotherapy.

A range of data is presented in the following pages charting this general development, a development that is leading towards a new professional helping infrastructure within society. As counselling/psychotherapy becomes increasingly embedded in society the authors fear that it may, at worst, become like all other areas of intervention in people's lives (mentioned in the previous pages) discriminatory and racist in practice. However, this is anticipating the contents of the final section of this chapter. Let us return to the situation of counselling today and chart some of its developments.

### The development of counselling

The opening quotation above was used by the NSPCC in their advertising during the Spring of 1994. Some years previously both the Midland Bank and the Labour Party coined the use of the term 'listening' within their slogans and advertising literature. The Labour Party thus became 'the listening party' and the Midland 'the listening bank'. It is suggested here that such advertising terminology was no accident but an attempt to create an ideological perspective based upon trends recognizable as current in society and emanating directly from the therapeutic disciplines.

Listening, of course, is a central activity in counselling and psychotherapy. So is empathy. As a technical concept that owes much of its origins to the development of the work of Dr Carl Rogers in client-centred therapy, over 20 different definitions have now been developed, including an extensive treatment of it by Rogers himself. Not lagging far behind, marketing personnel appended the term to a range of beauty products, including that of Empathy shampoo!

Similarly, at about the same time, a security company developed the logo 'Securicor Cares'. Care of others, in the general sense, is embodied within the concept of counselling. 'Care' also is a mnemonic for Rogers's core therapeutic conditions of counselling.

CA – communicated authenticity (congruence, genuineness)

R – regard (acceptance, warmth)

E – empathy

However interesting, ironic and humorous the above examples may be, they do give an indication of the impact of ideas derived from counselling and psychotherapy upon society during the decade from 1985 onwards.

Certainly, a research survey conducted on behalf of the Royal College of Psychiatrists in 1991 revealed that 85 per cent of the 2000 respondents believed that depression was caused by life events and that counselling, not medication, was the most appropriate form of assistance. Such a sizeable proportion again indicates the extent to which the public has adopted some of the belief systems of counsellors and psychotherapists themselves.

In September 2004, the British Association for Counselling and Psychotherapy published the results of a survey on attitudes to therapy conducted on its behalf by the Future Foundation (BACP 2004a). A total of 1008 people were surveyed. The following points demonstrate some key findings from this report.

- Counselling and psychotherapy are now considered acceptable and valuable forms of treatment for a wide range of different circumstances by the majority of British people – 63 per cent agree that they know someone who could benefit from counselling and psychotherapy.
- 21 per cent of the sample interviewed had personally experienced some form of counselling and psychotherapy.
- There was a widespread acceptance of life crises as reasons for seeking therapy. For example, 82 per cent of the sample believed that terminal illness was an acceptable trigger for seeking therapy, and 70 per cent for bereavement. Among the committed 'therapees' (those who had had therapy) there was acceptance of a wide range of reasons for seeking therapy including: developmental (to learn more about yourself), phobias, and general malaise.
- 45 per cent of employees expressed a desire for the opportunity to avail themselves of confidential counselling provided by their employer.

### Significant landmarks

Of course, it is somewhat difficult to accurately chart the key points of this historical development of attitude change towards the talking therapies. However, some of the following will have provided contributory milestones on this journey.

First, the enormous influence of Sigmund Freud's work. Though dating back to the turn of the twentieth century, the significance and impact of psychoanalysis and psychoanalytic thought over the last hundred years has been very considerable indeed. Not only have these early ideas contributed to theories of personality and theories of therapy, they have permeated disciplines such as literature, art, philosophy, psychology, sociology, organizational development and many more. As a consequence, the ideas and concepts themselves have become part of everyday language, e.g. Freudian slips, the unconscious, the significance of dreams, defence mechanisms, projection, free association, the ego and so on. (A very readable account of Freud's work can be found in Jacobs 1992.)

Second, the formation of the National Marriage Guidance Council. The council first opened its doors in 1938, in response to the rising divorce figures at that time. The founder, Dr Herbert Gray, was convinced that relationships were taking a significant strain on life in the twentieth century. As news of its work spread, the Council received many hundreds of requests from troubled couples and, from an earlier emphasis on research and education, counselling emerged as the main service. A small London office opened in 1943 and in the ensuing five years over 8000 clients were seen. By 1988 there were 160 centres offering almost a quarter of a million interviews per year. Sadly, marriages were still breaking down at the rate of 160,000 divorces per year and waiting lists to see a counsellor grew to almost 10,000 with queues of up to six months in the worst affected areas.

Reorganized and relaunched in 1988 under the name Relate (which embraced a commitment to all kinds of couple relationships), counsellors now work from a variety of community buildings, bringing the number of locations up to over 400 across the country. Relate is a vigorous national organization often consulted by the media and is active in training over 400 counsellors a year. It helps an average of 750 relationships every day (Relate 1992).

Third, the Samaritans, founded in 1953 by the Reverend Chad Varah. The first centre was run from the crypt of his church, St Stephen Wallbrook, in London. He responded to what he perceived to be a need for people to talk about things that may be unacceptable under normal circumstances, e.g. relationship problems, job worries, sexual difficulties, suicide, depression etc.

The biggest branch of the Samaritans is in Central London, though there are now over 200 branches throughout the UK. Two and a half thousand volunteers take approximately two and a quarter million phone calls per year. One example of a local branch (Sheffield) reveals that over 200 volunteers take about 24,000 phone calls each year.

Fourth, the establishment and development of the British Association for Counselling and Psychotherapy (BACP). Formed in 1977, the British Association for Counselling grew out of the Standing Conference for the Advancement of Counselling, which was inaugurated in 1970 with the help of the National Council of Voluntary Organizations. In 1978 the headquarters moved from London to Rugby where it continues to base its operations.

Membership of the Association grew from 1300 in 1977 to 11,400 in 1994 (as reported in the first edition of this book). Membership in 2005 now stands at approximately 22,000. In September 2000, the Association formally recognized that it no longer represented just counselling but also psychotherapy and consequently changed its name to the British Association for Counselling and Psychotherapy (BACP).

> BACP is the largest and broadest body within the sector. Through its work BACP ensures that it meets its remit of public protection whilst also developing and informing its members. Its work with large and small organisations within the sector ranges from advising schools on how to set up a counselling service, assisting the NHS on service provision, working with voluntary agencies and supporting independent practitioners. BACP participates in the development of counselling and psychotherapy at an international level.
>
> (BACP website)

The Association has been a significant leader (often in association with other professional membership organizations in the field) in representing the world of the talking therapies. The following items represent some of its recent contributions to the sector:

- The *Ethical Framework for Good Practice*. This completely revised version was published in 2002 and provides a core frame of reference for members for use in their relations with clients, colleagues, fellow members and the wider community (BACP 2002).
- Publications include a monthly journal for members (*Counselling and Psychotherapy Journal*), a quarterly research journal, books, pamphlets, reports and guidelines. BACP also publishes a *Counselling and Psychotherapy Resources Directory* and a *Training Directory*.
- The Association has Accreditation and Recognition schemes for therapists, supervisors, trainers, training courses and organizations.
- A busy programme of conferences, seminars, workshops and other training events is run each year providing continuing professional development opportunities for its members.
- BACP receives on average 5000–6000 enquiries each month.
- BACP operates specialist divisions and forums that focus on informing members and the public in the following areas: children and young people, healthcare, workplace, higher and further education, spiritual and pastoral, independent group practice, equality and diversity and the voluntary sector.
- Recent initiatives have included the commissioning of the national attitude survey to counselling and psychotherapy (Future Foundation

2004) and the development of a teaching resource for students aged 14–16 entitled *Exploring Mental Health* (BACP 2004b).

- The earlier 'RACE' division of the Association (which had been dedicated to the exploration and dissemination of good therapeutic practice in a multiracial/multicultural society) has more recently evolved into the 'Equality and Diversity Forum'.
- BACP has enthusiastically embodied the concepts of 'managing diversity' (NCVO 2003) and has consequently instituted a major staff training initiative in this area.
- In addition, 'diversity' has been the chosen theme for its regional consultations held throughout the UK in 2004/05.
- The 'Equality and Diversity Forum' has created a working definition for 'diversity' that may well change over time, but nevertheless represents an exposition of the term that has come to be used popularly, but often without any accurate sense of detailed meaning. (This definition is offered later in the chapter.)
- BACP formally recognized the work of the Terence Higgins Trust in their pioneering work offering culturally sensitive counselling services to the African community in London by presenting an 'Outstanding Contribution' award in 2004.

A cursory internet search of other counselling and psychotherapy organizations in the UK revealed a further 45 organizations, some of which constituted more general membership bodies whilst others reflected particular theoretical perspectives and/or fields of application.

Fifth, increased training opportunities. The early 1970s saw the establishment of the first full-time courses of counselling training at London, Swansea and Keele universities. Since then, formalized training courses, both full-time and part-time, have mushroomed considerably and are run by a wide range of organizations that include universities, colleges and independent training institutes. The current *Training in Counselling and Psychotherapy Directory* published by BACP (2005) lists over 350 organizations in the UK offering, between them, over 1200 training courses. A wide range of courses are now offered that range from short introductions to the subject right through to masters degrees and doctorates.

Sixth, the more recent explosion of counselling literature. This phenomenon has been most marked since about 1980. In addition to the publication of a substantial number of new books on the subject, there have also been wide-ranging newspaper articles, regular columns by therapists and articles written by clients themselves. Television and radio programmes have also proliferated in this time, often focusing upon causes of psychological distress and appropriate forms of treatment.

Seventh, development of theory. Running parallel to this wide-ranging development of interest has been the extraordinary development of theoretical perspectives for practitioners. Only a few years ago the number of 'brand name' therapies had risen to 481 in the United States alone (Karasu *et al*. 1984)! More recently there have been books published, such as the one by Palmer and Satoru (2000), offering an explanatory text to 23 different current therapeutic approaches.

Eighth, allied to and as a consequence of the various factors depicted above there has also been a significant expansion in the number of voluntary and statutory organizations offering counselling to the community. In addition, many specialist agencies concerned with counselling, mental health and minority groups have emerged and developed across the UK. One example is Nafsiyat, an Intercultural Therapy Centre. Nafsiyat was set up in London in 1983 to provide a specialist psychotherapy service to black and other ethnic and cultural minorities (Kareem and Littlewood 1992: 14). The word Nafsiyat was coined from three ancient languages, the syllables meaning mind, body and soul.

Jafar Kareem, an Indian trained in psychodynamic psychotherapy, conceived the idea of a specialist centre that would offer psychotherapy to black and ethnic minority people out of his experiences of working as a psychotherapist in the National Health Service. Concerned to offer a form of therapy that was relevant and pertinent to clients, Nafsiyat aimed to offer a form of dynamic psychotherapy which was not necessarily tied to one theoretical orientation but which derived its strength from various analytical, sociological and medical formulations. Kareem defined Intercultural Therapy as follows:

> A form of dynamic psychotherapy that takes into account the whole being of the patient – not only the individual concepts and constructs as presented to the therapist but also the patient's communal life experience in the world – both past and present. The very fact of being from another culture involves both conscious and unconscious assumptions, both in the patient and in the therapist. I believe that for the successful outcome of therapy it is essential to address these conscious and unconscious assumptions from the beginning.
>
> (Kareem 1978)

The pioneering work of Nafsiyat in the UK has been considerable, not only in its development and delivery of intercultural therapy but also in its contributions to training and research in this field. From being just one of a handful of agencies dedicated to working with ethnic minorities in the UK in the 1970s and 1980s, many other organizations have now been established. A search on the internet in the Spring of 2005 offered over 410,000 results for 'black mental health', over 18,000 results for 'black mental health organizations' and over 4000 results for 'transcultural therapy'.

It seems as if the various influences outlined above have significantly affected, indeed confronted, the cultural stereotype of the 'stiff upper lip' so long prevalent in Britain. As 'talking about one's troubles' rather than burying such issues of concern has become much more acceptable, so too have opportunities developed for people to work in groups, either facilitator-led or self-help.

The above examples give an indication of the variety of ways in which the theoretical and therapeutic ideas originating at the turn of the twentieth century have had an enormous impact upon attitudes and responses to mental health issues in society today. In turn, these have influenced the development of a wide range of organizations offering counselling, in a variety of settings for general use, particular populations and specific disorders. Despite this considerable development, however, it is important to point out that a substantial proportion of counselling in Britain continues to be conducted in the voluntary sector, though an increasing number of posts have been created in statutory and commercial organizations in the last decade. Counsellors from the varying cultural/racial/ethnic groups within society have emerged in slightly larger numbers in the last two decades, thereby facilitating some more choice for people seeking counselling. This situation, however, still requires much more development. The training costs of becoming a therapist these days are very considerable and students from poorer backgrounds are substantially disenfranchized from embarking on such training. In addition, Watson's recent doctoral research (2004) on the training experiences of black students on counselling/psychotherapy courses graphically reveals the complex challenges they face in becoming qualified. (See the later chapter by Val Watson for further details.)

### Squaring the circle

Tseng and Hsu (1979) have noted that four dominant modes of helping have always existed in all cultures. Putting it slightly differently, they note that the cultural modes of exploration and intervention in the area of personal distress proceed from the four reference points of natural, supernatural, medico-physiological and socio-psychological.

In diagrammatic form:

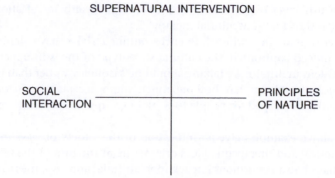

Figure 1.1   Four healing interventions.

Transformed into nouns for healing methods the matrix looks like this:

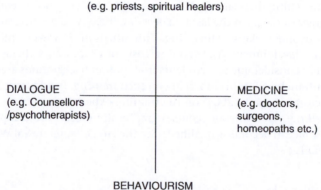

Figure 1.2   Four healing functions.

Historically, in many societies, it is possible that the healers (wise elders, shamans, witch doctors, priests etc.) embodied all four modes depicted above in their healing powers. A healer, for example, may have listened to the troubled person's story (dialogue), appealed to the gods for help through prayer and ritual (spirituality), given the person berries or potions to take (medicine) and finally recommended certain exercises or penance activities (behaviourism).

The sophisticated development of professional specialisms specifically in the last century has seen these particular helping activities develop into quite different and separate disciplines. Of course, each form of helping depends on communication and dialogue. However, Freud warned as early as 1904 that communication and dialogue could not be left to chance (Jones 1959). The emergence of counselling, underpinned by research activity since the 1940s, has meant that considerable attention has been devoted to this particular aspect of human helping behaviour. As a result counsellors and psychotherapists have become more knowledgeable and specialized in this area.

Doctors and priests have long enjoyed the established roles of helpers in the community. The rather more recent advent of behaviourism and different counselling approaches in this country has meant that there has been a 'squaring of the circle' of completing the spectrum of healing methods. However, unlike previous traditional societies, each of these activities is now carried out by different personnel using a wide variety of theoretical and practical intervention styles to assist troubled people.

Notwithstanding the above variations, it is argued that the dialogical approach of counselling and psychotherapy has now achieved some equivalency with other approaches and acceptability with the public at large. This spread of interest, supported by the huge increase in literature, training courses and media exposure, has led many allied professions such as teaching, nursing, social work and so on to adopt counselling skills as a vital component in their daily work.

Counselling and psychotherapy has come of age.

## Diversity

Whilst this book focuses specifically upon the consideration of the impact of cultural, ethnic and racial identities and issues upon the therapeutic endeavour, it is most important to acknowledge the changing climate, concepts and terminologies pertaining generally to this field of application. Authors such as Moodley (2003a, 2003b), Diamond and Gillis (in this volume) and Lago and Smith (2003) have acknowledged the complex interplay of factors such as gender, class, age, race, ethnicity and sexual orientation upon therapeutic practice. The term 'diversity' aspires to embrace the breadth and range of these issues as demonstrated below by the current working definition generated by the BACP Equality and Diversity Forum.

> Within the context of BACP's Equality and Diversity Strategy, our commitment to diversity is:
> A principled stand which recognises, values and responds to the natural diversity of human life and experience, and does not view difference from the majority cultures as inherently pathological or problematic. This requires the application of a critical perspective to

unspoken or unexamined norms, as well as a commitment to social inclusion and to treating people with fairness and respect.

A commitment to diversity ensures that differences are viewed as part of normal human variation. It requires recognition of power, privilege, disadvantage and oppression and challenges notions of supremacy.

There are particular groups, which are privileged in UK society. These groups represent the often unexamined norm from which 'difference' is defined.

This document then offers group categories of the 'advantaged/norm' and the 'disadvantaged/different', the former listing white people, heterosexual people, able-bodied people, men and people of working (income-generating) age and the latter listing black and minority ethnic people, lesbian, gay and bisexual people, disabled people, women, young people and older people, unemployed people.

This working definition continues:

> Consideration also needs to be given to unconscious or unacknow-ledged notions of supremacy linked with advantaged/privileged groups. For example, an unexamined notion of white supremacy can lead to a situation where white cultural values, and the state of being white, are imagined to be the norm, and any variation from this norm is automatically viewed as problematic or pathological. This sense of supremacy can be evidenced in prejudice, stereotyping, discrimin-ation, exclusion, which can occur at an individual, organisational/ institutional and societal level.
>
> BACP recognises that specific efforts may need to be made to ensure equality of opportunity and appropriateness of services for the following groups, because of a history of disadvantage: Black and minority ethnic people, disabled people, lesbian, gay, bisexual and transgendered people, refugees and asylum seekers, older and younger people.
>
> The issues are not the same for these groups, and their experience of discrimination and social exclusion may be significantly different . . . Engaging actively with issues of diversity does not mean 'treating everyone the same'. It involves recognising and valuing the unique and distinct qualities which exist between individuals and groups. This involves responding appropriately to difference and diversity by ensuring services are available to all who may wish to access them on an equitable and accessible basis.
>
> (BACP 2005)

Diversity embodies the postmodernist view of multiple identity, a view that is supported by emerging writings in the therapeutic fields of narrative, existential and client-centred therapy (e.g. see Cooper *et al.* 2004).

## The challenge

> Every worker in the mental health field should be trained to recognise the ways in which their own cultural upbringing is likely to have affected their perceptions of the problems which their clients bring . . .
>
> (Murphy 1986: 179)

The very pertinent quote above effectively highlights the essence of one of the most important points emerging from this whole chapter. That is, the profound and often unconscious impact of our own cultural heritage upon our attitudes and perceptions towards others, especially those who are racially and culturally different from us. One challenge that emerges from this, for counsellors, is that of their willingness and capacity to explore their cultural and racial origins in order to try to understand better their own cultural identity, beliefs and value systems. As part of this they also need to become more aware of their attitudes towards other groups and cultures, of their stereotypes and their assumptions.

It could be argued that in its broadest sense all counselling is 'cross-cultural' in that it embodies two persons who by definition have already had differing backgrounds and thus to a certain extent have their own unique identities (cultures). However, within the field of transcultural counselling (where, literally, the two participants hail from differing ethnic, cultural, spiritual backgrounds), the potential 'differentness' of the other (in terms of appearance, sound, dress, values and so on) is likely to have an additional impact upon the counsellor. Inevitably the counsellor will make assumptions in both scenarios. However, the assumptions made in transcultural counselling, as we shall see later in this book, may have much more serious implications and consequences.

Additionally, it is argued that the counsellor requires an understanding of the political processes in society that continue to perpetuate racist and discriminatory processes. An understanding of these mechanisms is necessary in order for the counsellor at least to avoid recreating them within his or her therapeutic practice. Ideally, such knowledge will inform the counsellor's work and will contribute to informed, relevant and creative responses to the client and his or her concerns.

Contemporary critiques of counselling and psychotherapy have acknowledged that increasingly these professional activities have emphasized the nature of individual and personal pathology and isolated them from social and political concerns (Hillmann and Ventura 1992; Orbach 1993; Lago 1994).

In summarizing the various perspectives above we believe that the challenge to counsellors is a multifaceted one:

- Do they understand the impact of their own past upon their assumptions about culture, identity, morals and so on?
- Do they understand the discriminatory nature and power imbalance of the relationship between dominant and minority groups in society and how such practices are perpetuated?
- Can they enhance their own learning about the groups from which clients come?
- Are they open to a wide range of challenging and perhaps contradictory views of the world expressed by clients?
- How might their theories/models of counselling be extended or modified to incorporate a wider range of understanding and response modes to clients?
- How might their way of being with clients recognize and address the societal and political implications (as well as the emotional and psychological implications) of the clients' situation?
- Do they have any awareness at all of the discriminatory life experiences that many clients will have experienced and are likely to have internalized?

> So I would see counsellors having a socially activist role in Britain as well, encouraging British society to look not only at what you are doing to yourselves . . . but what you are doing to other people in the world. British counsellors could benefit from being exposed to conditions in a developing country because of the stark and therefore . . . more visible tensions there, and this might help them to understand their own country better.
>
> (Swart in Dryden 1990: 317)

# 2 Issues of race and power

Given that relations between black and white groups over several centuries have been typified by oppression, exploitation and discrimination, how might contemporary relationships within counselling be transformed into creative (rather than further damaging) experiences?

(Lago and Thompson 1989a: 208)

What is evident, then, is that racism is an ideology which is continually changing, being challenged, interrupted and reconstructed, and which often appears in contradictory forms. As such, its reproduction in schools and elsewhere can be expected to be complex, multi-faceted and historically specific . . . specific forms of racism can be expected to change, and inherited racist discourses are likely to be re-constituted. New circumstances are likely to lead to new formulations of racism.

(Troyna 1993: 15)

## Introduction

Counsellors are trained to work in a sensitive, skilled and theoretically informed manner with individuals seeking help. The process of their work is dependent upon the quality of the relationship that develops between them and their clients. A considerable amount of time during their training, quite appropriately, is devoted to understanding individual psychology and pathology and the processes of healing through dialogue. They emerge thus influenced from their training and then engage in counselling practice that further reinforces their understanding of individual human beings. Their primary focus becomes that of individuals and their pathologies and difficulties.

The intention of this chapter, which we believe is central not only to this text but to any counselling engagement, is that counsellors need also to have a systematic structural understanding of society. Our contention is that racism, for example, functions as pathology of and in society. At worst a counsellor's over-concentrated focus on individual pathology might deprive her of important understandings of the client's world, understandings that could be applied usefully in the counselling encounter.

We have previously asserted that:

- In order to understand relationships between black and white people today, knowledge of the history between differing racial groups is required.
- Counsellors will also require an understanding of how contemporary society works in relation to race, the exercise of power, the effects of discrimination, stereotyping, how ideologies sabotage policies and so on. In short, counsellors require a structural awareness of society.
- Counsellors require a personal awareness of where they stand in relation to these issues.

(Lago and Thompson 1989a: 207)

This chapter considers each of these aspects in turn.

Van Dijk (1993) in his multinational study of the racist discourse of elite groups in society recognized that 'much elite text and talk about minorities may occasionally seem to express tolerance, understanding, acceptance or humanitarian world views, although such discourse is contradicted by a situation of structural inequality largely caused or condoned by these elites' (p. 6).

A broad overview of those engaged in the counselling profession would encompass many practitioners holding the various humanitarian world views referred to above. Indeed, it would be somewhat alarming if counsellors did not espouse such philosophic concerns for their fellow beings, as they have often entered the profession as an expression of their own caring. However, we contend that, very much like the elite groups Van Dijk refers to above, counsellors are not necessarily aware of the nature or extent of the structural inequalities that so pejoratively affect black people's lives, nor are they clearly aware of their own position in those issues. If not actively involved in the various modes of oppression their involvement in the problem of racism is characterized by unawareness, passivity, blind acceptance and indifference.

## The profound effects of history on the rise of racism

> Her Majestie understanding that there are of late divers blackamoores brought into this realme, of which kinde of people there are allready

here to manie . . . Her Majesty's pleasure therefore ys that those kinde
of people should be sent forth of the lande . . .
(From an open letter sent by Queen Elizabeth I on 11 July 1596 to
mayors and sheriffs in different towns; cited in Fryer 1984: 10)

In the first chapter we have already begun to describe the multiracial
nature of British society. We drew reference to the historical perspective, offering brief data on when and why various groupings from other cultures and
societies came to live in Britain. Popular memory often relates only to the
so-called 'waves' of immigration that occurred in the 1960s.

Interestingly, Fryer (1984) points out that there were Africans in Britain
before the English came here. They were soldiers in the Roman Imperial Army
that occupied the southern part of our island for three and a half centuries.
Among the troops defending Hadrian's Wall in the third century AD was a division of Moors. Fryer quotes other instances of African presence long before the
sixteenth century, the time referred to in Chapter 1. In terms of continuous black
presence, however, we have to date that from about the mid-sixteenth century.

Fryer's scholarly work provides an extraordinarily detailed and substantial
account of the historical, political and social dimensions of Britain's relationship with black people in the last 500 years. Van Dijk talks about this period as

> [a] time when (European) elites have engaged in the predominant
> practice of derogation, inferiorization, exploitation, subjugation and
> occasional genocide of non-Europeans. These others were variously
> seen and treated as barbarians, savages, infidels, semi-animals, mon-
> sters, slaves, subordinates, 'niggers' (and related racist words), wet-
> backs, guest workers, insurgents, terrorists, economic refugees or
> many other categories combining the concept of threat, inferiority,
> alien origin, appearance and culture.
>
> (Van Dijk 1993: 52)

This section of the chapter draws heavily on Fryer's seminal work and readers
are recommended to consult its extensive coverage of these issues. Consequently, where we have quoted from this particular work we have only
recorded page numbers.

The origins of racism in Britain are closely intertwined with the historical
data recording early contacts between Britons and other (specifically black)
cultures. The move from racial prejudice ('essentially irrational and . . . in large
measure sub-conscious') towards racialism ('a rationalized ideology based
upon what is purported to be irrefutable scientific fact') was drawn by Charles
Lyons (1975) in his review of black–white relations between 1530 and 1860.

The ancient myths of Africa and Africans derived from travellers' tales
already held great sway in the sixteenth and seventeenth centuries. The

formation and retention of racially prejudiced views is especially persistent, Fryer argues (1984: 153), in communities that are ethnically homogeneous, geographically isolated, technically backward or socially conservative, and where the knowledge and political power is concentrated in the hands of an elite. Such communities feel threatened by national or racial differences and their prejudices enhance group cohesion. England in the sixteenth and seventeenth centuries was a classic instance of such a community, though its geographical isolation was rapidly being overcome and its technology was about to leap forward.

Fryer argues that racial prejudice is largely transmitted by word of mouth and is often 'scrappy and self-contradictory' (p. 134). Racism, by contrast, he asserts, is transmitted largely through the written word and becomes relatively systematic, acquiring a pseudo-scientific veneer that glosses over its irrationalities and enables it to claim intellectual respectability. The most important aspect of these distinctions, however, is the realization that the primary functions of racial prejudice are cultural and psychological. The primary functions of racism, however, are economic and political.

This distinction was acutely observed and recorded by Morgan Godwyn in 1680 when he pointed out the economic basis and role of plantocracy racism. Fryer extracts the following five key points from the text of Godwyn's book.

1   Racist ideology was created by planters and slave merchants out of 'avarice'.
2   It was, initially, furtively spread.
3   Historically, by 1680 it had become respectable enough for its propagators in England to come into the open.
4   Opponents of racism were, as yet, few and uninfluential. There was little resistance.
5   One of the functions of racism was to justify the planters and merchants in their own eyes as well as in the eyes of society.

Finally, Godwyn also proposed that the planters were prepared to say anything that would safeguard their profits. As Fryer points out, 'Godwyn was the first to analyse racism as a class ideology and even after 300 years neither his analysis nor his language has lost its cutting edge' (p. 148).

An extraordinary range of eighteenth- and nineteenth-century writers, famous for their contributions to liberalism, literature, philosophy and politics, actually contributed significantly to the spread of racist views through their various writings. Such luminaries included:

• Sir William Petty, founder of modern political economy and one of the founders of the Royal Society (Fryer, p. 151);
• John Locke, philosopher (p. 151);

- David Hume, philosopher (p. 152);
- William Knox, provost-marshal of the British colony of Georgia and author of religious tracts (p. 154);
- Edward Long, justice of the Vice-Admiralty Court and author of the *History of Jamaica* in 1774. 'Long's peculiar talent lay in linking a scientific-sounding assertion of black inferiority – he was the first pseudo-scientific racist – with a defence of black slavery . . .' (p. 157).

The above list, however, only provides a snapshot into contemporary thought in the eighteenth and nineteenth centuries. Indeed, Charles Lawrence describes racism, by the 1770s, as being firmly established in Britain as a 'principal handmaiden of the slave trade and slavery' (foreword in Hammon and Jablow 1970).

Despite the end of the British slave trade in 1807 and slavery in 1833, racism was not then, and never has been since, dispensed with. Fryer notes that it was now too valuable as a component in the rise of the British Empire. 'The culminating stage in the rise of English racism was the development of a strident pseudo-scientific mythology of race that would become the most important ingredient in British imperial theory' (Fryer p. 165). The various government policies embodied in Britain's relationship with countries in its Empire were dominated by racist perspectives, leading Fryer to conclude that 'the golden age of the British Empire was the golden age of British racism too' (p. 165).

We cannot even gain a sense of reassurance from the above accounts that racism was a minority and crazy view during this time. 'Virtually every scientist and intellectual in nineteenth century Britain took it for granted that only people with white skin were capable of thinking and governing . . . Only in the last thirty or forty years has racism lost intellectual respectability' (p. 169).

Inevitably, a range of contending schools of pseudo-scientific racist thought had developed over this period, but they were all agreed on one essential point – that black people were outsiders, that they were forever barred from high office, from important posts in law and medicine in church and state and from any important voice in their own affairs. Despite vigorous attempts in recent years in education, training and equal opportunities legislation to eradicate these attitudes, their existence in society is still highly prevalent, as evidenced by a huge range of research studies demonstrating disadvantage and discrimination (Smith 1977; Skellington and Morris 1992).

An organic connection was also made in the nineteenth century between the attitude of the British ruling class to the peoples of its colonies and the attitude it took to the poor at home (p. 169). This interconnectedness of issues surrounding 'race' and 'class' has been much explored and debated in contemporary sociology. This very potent combination of factors embodied in the categories of race, class and economics continues to have a huge impact upon the relationships between groups of people in Britain today – between the rich and poor, employed and jobless, powerful and powerless, white and black, resident and immigrant, and so on. These issues are not just of passing concern to social scientists and therefore worth studying. They have a very real impact upon the direct, daily experience of black people's lives in Britain.

This section has attempted to capture, in just a few pages, the very serious, punitive and extensive range of attitudes, behaviours and practices that were formed over several centuries to justify inhuman, disrespectful and colonial domination of black peoples. Counsellors must take note of the impact such historical relations may have on any therapy relationships they develop in the present. This section is developed further, later in the chapter.

## Towards a structural awareness: racism, power and powerlessness (definitions and practices)

For many white people who believe themselves to be tolerant, understanding, accepting and so on, it is often very difficult to appreciate the multiplicity of mechanisms that exist in society that perpetuate systems of disadvantage amongst black people. As Troyna (1993) has so elegantly described in the opening quotation to this chapter, the ideology of racism is an immensely complex and changing phenomenon, and consequently racist practices become less visible and less specific, and are therefore more difficult to notice and comprehend. The value of social science research outcomes in this field is that they serve to point up the fact that, sadly, despite changes in legislation and working practices, the systems of disadvantage and racism continue.

### Racism: definitions

Judy Katz (1978), in her very useful handbook for anti-racism training, provides the following definitions of racism:

1   A belief that human races have distinctive characteristics that deter-
    mine their respective cultures, usually involving the idea that one's
    own race is superior and has the right to rule others.
2   A policy of enforcing such asserted rights.
3   A system of government and society based upon it.
              (Random House Dictionary of the English Language 1967)

To these definitions may be added:

4   Perpetuation of belief in the superiority of the white race.

5    Prejudice plus power.

The final definition used above, though perhaps apparently simplistic, does contain a readily accessible formula for analysis of issues and events. If one views things from a prejudiced perspective and has the power to act out those views, the outcome is going to be racist. (See also the definitions listed in the Appendix.)

### Racism in counselling and psychotherapy

Ponterotto and Pedersen (1993) include a table developed by Ridley (1989: 61) demonstrating the 'varieties of racism in counselling'. Ridley offers examples of overt (intentional) and covert (intentional and unintentional) racism within both the individual and institutional counselling settings.

He thus lists as an overt individual intentional racist act the example of a therapist who, believing that racial/ethnic minority groups are in some way inferior, refuses to see them as clients. Similarly, a counselling agency openly denying access to its services to racial/ethnic minority clientele would be guilty of (overt) institutional racism. At the covert level of institutional racism, Ridley offers the example of a counselling agency deliberately setting fees too high for most lower- and middle-income minority families, thus effectively excluding them from therapy. An example of unintentional institutional racism would be where an agency employs standardized psychological tests without considering their validity in relation to culturally diverse clients. British equivalents of this practice might include the usage of questionnaires employed by some agencies to assess levels of client psychological distress upon entry to the service. Such questionnaires may well not have been tested for applicability with different client groups.

In circumstances where counselling and psychotherapy agencies see proportionately fewer clients from minority groups than are represented within their locale, then it is incumbent upon them to explore why and how this situation exists. In what ways might the service be deemed to be overtly, covertly or unintentionally racist? What links does it forge with the different elements of the local population to ensure accurate communication of its services? What is happening at the point of referral into the service? Are referring agencies themselves not picking up the need or are they referring elsewhere to other forms of help and treatment? The exercise detailed in the next section might be usefully employed within agency staff training and awareness raising days to enhance necessary reflection on the patterns of service usage and hopefully to stimulate new initiatives and practices designed to ensure a more equitable service delivery across the local population.

Returning to the examples offered by Ridley (introduced above), practices of individual covert racism would include a senior colleague referring minority group clients to other colleagues or trainees within the service because of their own social discomfort but claiming they were too busy.

At the unintentional level, counsellors might judge clients' lateness as a sign of disrespect or their patterns of eye contact as suspicious or evidence of resistance to the process. Continuous and honest self-reflections enhanced by good supervision are required by practitioners to monitor carefully their inter-actions with clients from minority groups. Similarly, agencies also need to monitor their work closely and strive to maximize their potential of sensitive service delivery across the populations they serve.

## An exercise to explore how racism works in the organization

Katz also includes in her book a training exercise that enables white people to explore the subtleties of those disadvantaging mechanisms within organiza-tions. She invites participants to design a racist community (Katz 1978: 46). The goals of the exercise are listed as:

1 To identify the key elements of racism.
2 To discover how racism functions in our society.

Training groups are invited to create, on flip chart paper, their design of a racist community or organization. Groups may wish to produce a community that is blatantly and overtly racist or one that is much more subtle.

The designs must take into account and define the various elements of any working community such as the following: the make-up and constitution of the community, identification of the decision makers and how decisions are made, who controls the money, how formal and informal policies are created, and so on.

After the designs have been created the groups are invited to consider and discuss three major elements: first, the key elements of a racist community; second, a comparison of the designed community with real communities, and third, the issue that only whites have the power to oppress black people in this country and that black people do not have the power to oppress whites.

### A racist counselling organization

This exercise can also be specifically applied to organizations. A counselling agency, designed by these criteria, might look something like the following.

**Name of organization**: 'We listen and we care'

**Aims of organization**: To provide counselling to anyone in the local community who requests it or is referred.

**Organizational structure**:

1 *Management committee*. This group was initially brought together by the present director (details below) who had tried for some years to get this organization 'off the ground'. The management committee is thus comprised of local dignitaries chosen initially for their reputation of concern for people in the community combined with their positions of standing (e.g. town councillors, directors/ employers of local companies, senior staff from allied projects/services and so on). Both their concern and their access to sources of funding and other staffing provisions were criteria in their selection.

2 *Director*. The director is a highly qualified and experienced therapist. Having had a successful career in private practice in London (to which he had commuted) he had chosen to retire early. However, as a consequence of hearing about different local experiences and appreciating the lack of local counselling resources he initiated discussions, which led to the eventual formation of the project. After funding and premises had been successfully located it was only a natural outcome that he was appointed as director of the project. He negotiated a three-day contract only, as he did not wish to become embroiled in full-time work again.

3 *Counsellors*. There are two part-time paid counsellors and the rest are voluntary. The part-time paid counsellors, because they are qualified and experienced, also provide in-house training and supervision to the volunteers. At present there are ten volunteers.

One of the part-time paid counsellors is a former trainee of the director. The other part-time colleague, appropriately professionally qualified, had worked in a similar project in another town before moving to this area.

The volunteer counsellors have been selected by a panel involving the director and the two part-time paid counsellors through interview. In some cases the candidates have been students on one of the local counselling courses and are thus already partially trained. The other candidates have been selected for their perceived sensitivity and receptivity to others, combined with their availability to attend the in-house training courses and provide voluntary provision.

4 *Secretarial and reception staff*. Reception is provided by a team of ten volunteers who work one afternoon or one evening per week. In most cases they have been located through 'friends of friends'. Most administrative and secretarial work is carried out by the director who is assisted occasionally by a retired secretary who previously had been a personal assistant to the managing director of a local firm. (The managing director, incidentally, is on the management committee.)

**Agency funding**: Funding to pay the salaries, heating, lighting, rent and all other expenses is principally obtained from fundraising efforts and grants from the local authority and trust funds.

Clients are expected to pay a 'nominal contribution' set at a minimum of £5.00 per session, and where appropriate, in consultation with the counsellors, are invited to contribute more.

**Decision making/policy setting**: All major decisions and policies are created and set by the director in consultation with the management committee. The two part-time counsellors meet the director weekly to monitor trends, discuss current issues and dilemmas and in general oversee the clinical work of the counselling team.

---

This brief description of an agency could, of course, be considerably expanded. However, there is enough material above for us to consider the implications of the question in the exercise earlier: 'What are the key elements that make this agency racist?' The specific racist implications are printed in brackets and bold type at the end of each of the following statements.

### Aims of organization
The statement is all embracing and rather grand. However, as an ideology what are the contradictions it conceals?

1  Despite the open statement, patterns of client usage reveal that a disproportionate number of clients come from the area immediately surrounding the agency and the middle-class suburbs. Black clients are under-represented compared with their population size in the town. **(Is client usage monitored? How are actions taken to ensure that the agency is seen to cater for all?)**

2  This situation might arise through a range of elements including directories of local resources, and who hears about the agency from the director's local talks. **(Who initiates advertising? Where is it displayed? Where does the director give speeches?)**

3  How are clients referred to the agency, who refers clients, how can they self-refer etc? **(Referrals rely on the knowledge base and disposition of their referrers.)**

4  How welcoming to all clients is the service? **(Receptionist behaviours and sensitivities can significantly affect the clientele of the service. Are there any black receptionists?)**

5  What is the effect of the locale in which the agency is located? **(The location of an agency will have effects upon its usage.)**

*Management committee*
This is comprised of local dignitaries who already hold office in various commercial, civil and political organizations in the area. As a body,

1    What is their racial composition?
2    Are they fully sensitive to the needs of all elements of the local community?
3    Their selection is subject to who the director knows and who they themselves might recommend. (**Friends of friends and word of mouth are both restrictive mechanisms.**)

*The director*
Received a very expensive analytic training many years before. Such training, inevitably, is only accessible, in the majority of cases, where candidates come from backgrounds of personal wealth and are acceptable to selection committees or training institutes. (**Both these factors discriminate against the likelihood of black people attaining such life opportunities.**) Also, having been the instigator of the idea of the project he automatically became its director after obtaining the funding. No other choice was considered. (**This ensured that no other candidates were considered for the post, a denial of equal opportunity recruitment practice.**)

*Part-time counsellors*
One of these had been a trainee of the director and thus this previous contact had clearly influenced the appointment (**selection of people already in the system**). The other colleague had previous experience in a similar organization. (**Previous experience, although in many cases helpful, also implies previous attitudes, unthinking acceptance of working practices gained from elsewhere and a closed response to new challenges.**)

*The volunteer counsellors*
The volunteer counsellors have variously been students of the senior counsellors (**trained in the same mould, already schooled in the subtle power relationships of student/teacher, which is then replicated in the paid/ voluntary skilled/less skilled division of labour in the agency. Inevitably these elements lead to restrictive styles of counselling practice and a perpetuation of the status quo of previous power differentials**).

*The reception staff*
Located predominantly through a system of friends of friends. (**Who knows whom? Who is considered OK? How are such criteria decided? What are the grounds for selection?**)

*Client fees*
Could all clients pay these? (**On what criteria do the counsellors decide how much the clients should pay? Are these criteria set by agency policy etc?**)

*Decision making/policy setting*
Within the practices of how decisions and policies are made within the agency, how does the whole gamut of issues relating to service delivery to minority groups become considered and acted upon?

**Brief summary**

The inclusivity of these processes ensures, through no malign intention, that certain issues are seldom if ever taken into account. So all the questions relating to any discriminatory practice might never be considered. Also, when the ideology of the agency is that 'we counsel all', how dare it be accused of biased delivery?

## Exploring personal attitudes

The thrust of this book is towards the encouragement of all those who work as therapists to develop an ongoing commitment towards the exploration of their thoughts, attitudes and practices (both personal and professional) in relation to minority groups in society as well as minority group clients they see. There are a range of methods and questionnaires through which this process may be pursued and some of these are listed and detailed below.

---

## 'My most challenging client'

In quiet reflection, imagine what sort of person, coming from a completely different/diverse background to yourself, might be your most challenging client if they were to come into your office now. (This exercise invites you to reflect on the immediate affective, behavioural, cognitive responses you might experience upon first meeting a client. At this stage you are not invited to consider the issues a client might bring that would cause you challenge.)

Define those particular elements of the other's identity that are different to your own. Explore individually (either through reflective writing or thinking) or with others your initial responses to this imagined challenging client. What are your thoughts, feelings and reactions to this person? Where might some of these reactions come from in your past? What might you do to consider these further? How might you work on these identifiable judgemental reactions?

---

This exercise is inspired in part by work developed by Janis Galway (1989) and is featured in Lago and Barty 2003: 156/160. In its original form, participants are invited first to define the various elements that constitute their identity, such as ethnicity, race, age, class, gender, education, urban/rural, family status, education, religion, occupation and so on. Second, they are invited to consider an imaginary client who differs considerably in each of their identity statuses. Having drawn up these contrasting and therefore challenging identities of self and a completely different 'other', participants are invited to consider, within three areas of their practice, what they would now require to respond knowledgeably and sensitively to this 'challenging' client and his or her identity composition. The three areas they are invited to consider are:

- Knowledge – what new knowledge would they require to work with this person?
- Attitudes – what new attitudes, feelings or viewpoints would work with this person require?
- Skills – what new skills or performance competencies might be needed?

(This tripartite composition of characteristics – beliefs and attitudes, knowledge and skills – parallels the format developed by Sue *et al.* (1992) in their key recommendations for multiculturally skilled counsellor characteristics. See the later chapter on the training of therapists for more details.)

## Assessment of prejudice

Ponterotto and Pedersen (1993) list several racism and prejudice scales (pp. 137–45) and include two appendices (pp. 156–63) that have been developed within the United States. Unfortunately, the author is not aware of any work that has been carried out in the UK to modify these instruments for a British application. Nevertheless, some of these are listed briefly below as resources for reference, personal reflection and consideration.

- *Modern Racism Scale*. Developed by McConahey in 1986, this scale is designed to measure white people's racial attitudes towards black people. Described as a brief instrument consisting of six or seven items worded along a four- or five-point Likert-type format. A modified version has been developed by Jacobson (1985) and is termed the *New Racism Scale*.
- *Institutional Racism Scale*. This was developed to assess how individuals construed institutional racism, engaged in anti-racism and viewed organizational commitment to the reduction of racism. Developed by

Barbarin and Gilbert (1981: 147) the IRS is described as a carefully thought-out and constructed instrument.

- *Situational Attitude Scale* (Sedlacek and Brooks 1970). This was originally designed to measure attitudes of whites towards blacks in various social and personal contexts.
- *Quick Discrimination Index*. This instrument was designed to measure subtle racial prejudice and sexism and was developed by Ponterotto *et al.* in 1993. It was developed in response to the authors' concerns that many of the existing instruments included items that were easily discernible as prejudice measures and therefore subject to 'social desirability contamination'. That is, that respondents might answer in socially acceptable ways rather than in ways that accurately reflected their thoughts and feelings.
- *Black Racial Identity/Consciousness*. Ponterotto and Pedersen list three self-report instruments in this category. They are the African Self-Consciousness Scale (Baldwin and Bell 1985), the Developmental Inventory of Black Consciousness (Milliones 1980) and the Racial Identity Attitude Scale (Parham and Helms 1981; Helms 1990).
- *White Racial Identity/ Consciousness*. Developed also by Helms (1990) the White Racial Identity Attitude Scale is described by Ponterotto and Pedersen as the only widely used instrument in this category. This is described as a multidimensional instrument measuring attitudes consistent with Helms's White Identity Stages. (See the later chapters on research (Chapter 11) and identity development by Courtland Lee (Chapter 12) for an exposition of the identity development models.)

D'Andrea and Daniels (1992) published an 'Affective, Behavioural, Cognitive Model of Racism' which featured five key stages. Briefly, these are:

- One: 'Affective–Impulsive'. They describe persons at this stage demonstrating a cognitive style that reflects simple, hostile and often illogical thinking about persons from different racial and ethnic groups.
- Two: 'Dualistic–Rational'. Persons operating from this second stage are driven by a strong cognitive orientation from which they rationalize justification for separation between racial groups.
- Three: 'Early Multiplistic Libertarian'. Persons at this stage frequently possess a general liberal world view. Interestingly, though, the dominant intellectual character of this stage of racism often goes hand in hand with a generally apathetic affective modality.
- Four: 'Principled Libertarian'. Persons at this stage manifest not only overt disgust for racism but feel compelled to address this social ill both in personal and professional ways.

- Five: 'Principled Activistic–Integrative Perspective'. In addition to the qualities of the previous stage persons at this stage distinguish themselves primarily by the manifestation of a committed behavioural disposition to reduce the level of racism.

An exploration and considered reflection of this full model (each stage is described much more fully with references to likely affective, behavioural and cognitive functions) would offer a considerable range of thought-provoking ideas and give an indication of the areas for growth, attitude and action necessary to enhance a less prejudiced/racist perspective.

Finally, within this brief section addressing structured methods for the enhancement of self-awareness with respect to prejudice and racism are two exercises described in Katz (1978: 155–63). The first, under the title of 'Exploration of Racist Attitudes', provides a list of 30 statements which, when scored for present or previous attitudes held, invites participants to consider, through discussion, their understanding of why particular statements are racist and to consider on which myths these attitudes are based. The second, entitled 'Assessing One's Understanding of Individual Racism', provides a short text that participants are required to explore for assumptions, noting those with which they agree.

The above models all offer opportunities for the enhancement of therapists' awareness within the specific domains of prejudice and racism.

## The dynamics of the white counsellor–black client counselling partnership

In our chapter on 'Counselling and Race' (in Lago and Thompson 1989a), we developed a matrix of counselling pairings as indicated in Figure 2.1.

| White client<br>Black counsellor | White counsellor<br>Black client |
|---|---|
| White client<br>White counsellor | Black counsellor<br>Black client |

**Figure 2.1**  Matrix of counsellor dyads.

This diagram then acted as a base for exploration of the different issues, elements and dynamics potentially present in each of the pairings in the figure. For the purposes of this chapter, however, we will concentrate here on the white counsellor/black client interactions. From the above-mentioned chapter we wrote the following:

> A series of questions can assist us in addressing, briefly the issues for a white counsellor with a black client: how structurally aware of society is the counsellor? Do they have an understanding of the myriad of disadvantaging mechanisms that exist in contemporary society in relation to black people? What class background are they from? What experience of black people have they had? And what effects, perceptions, and attitudes have these left upon the counsellor?
>
> From experience gained by the authors whilst involved in training groups, it seems reasonable to state that many white people are quite unable to cope with radical black-perspectives and black people's pain and anger, specifically in relation to racism. Rogers (1978) has noted this phenomenon and suggests that white people who are effective in responding to oppressed groups seem to learn two attitudes. One is the realization and ownership of the fact that 'I think white'. The other is the ability to respond empathically, to be able to enter into the black person's world of hate, bitterness, and resentment, and to know that world as an understandable, acceptable part of reality. To achieve this ability Rogers (1978) suggests that the white persons themselves need to listen to their own feelings of anger at unjust situations. This is clearly something that could most usefully be done in training and therapy, in order that the fullest opportunities for personal learning may be gained.
>
> From the perspective of power, this combination of white counsellor with black client has a potential danger, namely a perpetuation of the notion of white superiority. The white person, as the counsellor in this situation, has the power. The sensitive handling of that power is absolutely crucial. For example, white counsellors have to work out ways of enhancing their own sensitivity and knowledge of client groups beyond the counselling framework. The pursuit of this knowledge, however justified that might be within the counselling process, could be perceived as an unethical abuse of their power. Black clients so used would have every right to experience further anger and a sense of injustice.
>
> (Lago and Thompson 1989a: 211–12)

The various aspects mentioned above all relate to the potential complexity of any relationship between black and white people. At worst it is a relationship overloaded, burdened and profoundly affected by the past, generally speaking, and by the past lives of the two people engaging in the counselling relationship specifically.

To add to the seriousness and weight of the above, Carotenuto reminds us of the very inequality of power inherent in any therapeutic relationship. He says:

> We often tend to conceal the fact that no other profession involves a greater inequality of power than the psychotherapists' in which one of the two poles is always, by definition, psychologically weaker than the other. For reasons intrinsic and structural to the psychological field, when a person is overwhelmed by suffering or convinced that his/her rational dimension, which up to that moment had qualified them as a human being, has failed, asks someone stronger than them to save them, then he/she places that person in a position of power and superiority. This could also be why we undertake this profession; it is the only one that allows us to deal always with weaker individuals, in partial identification with the omnipotent figure of saviour offering a hand to the suffering.
>
> (Carotenuto 1992)

These various dimensions of power, alluded to above, have been coherently described by Gillian Proctor (2002) in her book on the dynamics of power in counselling. She notes that the components of power embodied by the therapist are threefold. These are: role power (so succinctly defined in the statement by Carotenuto above); social power (the power distribution with respect to the structural positions in society of the therapist and the client); and historical power (the impact of both their histories upon their own sense of personal power).

This final section on the power imbalance in therapy combined with the various historical origins and contemporary mechanisms of racism described earlier in the chapter serve to confront all therapists with the immensely delicate and challenging task transcultural counselling poses. Counsellors need to be acutely aware of these issues and where they stand in relation to them, both as persons in society and as therapists.

# 3   Towards understanding culture

> An individual cannot, through introspection and self-examination, understand himself or the forces that mould his life, without understanding his culture.
>
> (Thomas and Sillen 1972)

> The general culture of a nation affects how people think, feel, and behave in that country. Theories of social behaviour and personality are usually culture specific, because theorists see events in terms of their own life experiences and times. Their personality is usually the product of a single culture. Their perceptions of the world around them are influenced by their native culture, which may act as blinders. They are unable to see or understand cultural differences outside their immediate view. The recognition of this problem contributed to the emergence of cross-cultural counselling in the last quarter of the 20th Century. Since the beginning of the Civil Rights Movement in the United States, much attention has been given to considering the usefulness of available psychotherapeutic theories for counseling minority group clients . . .
>
> (Moodley *et al.* 2004: Foreword)

## Culture: a complex word and concept

> Culture is one of the two or three most complicated words in the English language.

This quote, to be found in Raymond Williams's book *Keywords* (1983), not only tells us something about the importance of the word but also hints at the multiplicity of its definitions and its manifestations. It has been estimated that, by the early 1960s, there were in excess of 160 different definitions of culture in the social science literature!

Williams devotes six pages of his book to this keyword, 'culture'. Incidentally, a further three pages are given over to the word 'racial'. This factor alone, we believe, indicates the potential enormity of the task not only that we take on in trying to write this book but for any counsellor embarking upon a process of counselling with someone who is culturally or racially different. The words themselves (culture, racial) have immense realms of meaning and diverse usages in history. As culture is one of three keywords in the title of this book it seems appropriate to outline some of the historical usages, implications and connotations of the word and then move towards an explicit statement of how we see this concept. There is no doubt that, perhaps on reflection of the huge number of academic definitions mentioned above, we all probably have slightly different understandings and thus uses of the word. Though this range of usage can offer subtlety and complexity of meaning it can also create immense misunderstanding.

Following the lines quoted above, Williams in his introductory paragraph proceeds thus:

> Culture is one of the two or three most complicated words in the English language. This is so partly because of its intricate historical development, in several European languages, but mainly because it has now come to be used for important concepts in several distinct intellectual disciplines and in several distinct and incompatible systems of thought.
>
> (Williams 1983: 87)

Having Latin origins, the word 'colere' had a range of meanings: inhabit, cultivate, protect, honour with worship. By the early fifteenth century, the word culture had passed into English with primary meanings then in husbandry, the tending of natural growth. Williams goes on to say that 'culture, in all its early uses, was a noun of process: the tending of something, basically crops and animals' (1983: 87). Through a slightly different linguistic route, by a century later the term had developed an important next stage of meaning, by metaphor, and was extended to the process of human development.

Culture, as an independent noun, was not important, according to Williams, before the late eighteenth and early nineteenth centuries. Connotative, metaphorical and linked terms such as 'civility', 'cultivation' and 'cultivated' were all being developed at this time, thus laying a basis for some of the modern complexities referred to earlier.

The developments associated with 'culture' in the French and German languages also have to be recognized. The term 'couture', the original French name for culture, has obviously since developed its own very specialized meanings in the world of fashion, Williams argues. In France, culture became linked to the noun 'civilization' by the mid-eighteenth century (p. 89). In German, the term 'cultur' (late eighteenth century) and later 'kultur' (nineteenth century) was mainly used as a synonym (as in the French) for civilization, first in the abstract sense of a general process of becoming 'civilized' or 'cultivated'; second, in the sense established by eighteenth-century universal historians, as a description of the secular process of human development.

Williams (1983) informs us that there was then a decisive change of use in Herder. In his unfinished *Ideas on the Philosophy of the History of Mankind* (1784–91) he wrote of cultur: 'Nothing is more indeterminate than this word, and nothing more deceptive than its application to all nations and periods.' He attacked the assumption of the universal histories that 'civilization' or 'culture', the historical self-development of humanity, was what we would now call a unilinear process, leading to the high and dominant point of eighteenth-century culture. Indeed, he attacked what he called European subjugation and domination of the four quarters of the globe, and wrote:

> Men of all the quarters of the globe, who have perished over the ages, you have not lived solely to manure the earth with your ashes, so that at the end of time your prosperity should be made happy by European culture. The very thought of a superior European culture is a blatant insult to the majesty of Nature.

The very radical tone of this quote, now written some 200 years ago, contains philosophic values that are certainly implied and indeed made explicit in other parts of this book. For example, the belief that cultures are different, not deficient. All cultures are sufficient unto themselves. Also, it confronts the false superiority assumed in much of western colonial thinking and practices, a false superiority and prejudice that has its historical roots in phenomena such as the triangular slave trade and the colonialization of other countries.

Originally influenced by G.F. Klemm's *General Cultural History of Mankind* in Germany (1843–52), which traced human development from savagery through domestication to freedom, the work of an American anthropologist, Morgan, traces comparable stages commencing with Ancient Society and culminating in Civilization. This was directly followed in English by Tyler in *Primitive Culture* (1870). It is along this line of reference that the dominant sense of the word in modern social sciences has to be traced. Along the way the term folk culture had become introduced as a way of emphasizing national and traditional cultures. It was also used at this time to distinguish between things human and the mechanical, inhuman, abstractly related concepts emerging out of industrial development.

We can easily distinguish now, Williams writes (p. 90), the sense which depends on a literal continuity of physical process, as now in 'sugar beet culture' or, in the specialized physical application in bacteriology since the 1880s, 'germ culture'. However, once this physical definition has been surpassed, three broad active categories of usage have to be recognized. They are, first, the independent and abstract noun which describes a general process of intellectual, spiritual and aesthetic development from the eighteenth century; second, the independent noun, whether used generally or specifically, which indicates a particular way of life, whether of a people, a period, a group, or humanity in general; and third, the independent and abstract noun which describes the works and practices of intellectual, especially artistic, activity. This can often be one of the most widespread uses of the term – culture as music, literature, painting, sculpture, theatre and films, though in fact this usage is a relatively late addition.

This variety of usages and connotative meanings indicates a complex argument about the relations between general human development and a particular way of life and between both and the works and practices of art and intelligence (Williams, p. 91). A classic difference apparently exists between the disciplines of archaeology and cultural anthropology when reference to culture is primarily to material production, while in history and cultural studies the reference is primarily to signifying or symbolic systems.

Williams continues:

> The anthropological use is common in the German, Scandinavian and Slavonic language groups, but it is distinctly subordinate to the senses of art and learning, or of a general process of human development in Italian and French. Between languages as within a language, the range and complexity of sense and reference indicate both difference of intellectual position and some blurring or overlapping. These variations, of whatever kind, necessarily involve alternative views of the activities, relationships and processes which this complex word indicates. The complexity is not finally in the word but in the problems which its variations of use significantly indicate.
>
> (1983: 91)

The above passages represent our attempt to precis Raymond Williams's extended considerations of the word 'culture'. As they stand above we can already begin to see what a potent and difficult concept it is that we are touching upon when we simply refer to the word 'culture'. And yet, with all of this meaning, Williams provides us with further 'stings in the tail' by first noting other developments of the term, such as culture vulture, cultural (adjectival use becoming common in the 1890s), sub-culture, culturalism etc. and second, acknowledging how the term has attracted hostility, in English: 'It is significant that virtually all the hostility has been connected with uses involving claims to superior knowledge' (1983: 92).

Interestingly, in their chapter on 'The Scope and Methods of Cross-Cultural Research', Frijda and Johoda chose to avoid the task of defining culture. 'Like most psychologists we are not anxious to dispel the illusion . . . that we know what we mean by this concept . . .' (1969). Unlike Frijda and Johoda, we will attempt to offer some operational definitions that we hope will inform our usage of the term within the overall context of this book.

## Culture: some further thoughts and working definitions

Gert Hofstede, an international management consultant, has defined culture as 'the collective mental programming of a people in an environment' (1980b). In short, it applies to every facet of behaviour, interpersonal relations, ways of thinking, feeling, speaking and so on. This definition then is not related simply either to the artefacts of culture (that might include such items as music, art and architectural designs), or to its usage as a term inferring deficiency, but rather is focused directly on how people understand how they should live and behave within their own grouping.

When we think of culture in relation to people's behaviour, there is a great temptation to consider exotic or foreign cultures. We often fail to see ourselves as being products of cultures, of our upbringing and our locale. We can so easily assume the stance of apparently neutral outside observers, judging quite coolly and at a distance what others do and how they do it!

For example, in considering greetings behaviour, what do you think when observing men greeting each other by kissing on both cheeks as opposed to shaking hands? Or how might you react if someone, in being introduced to you, bowed from a distance when you might have expected a handshake or kiss? We might have a whole myriad of reactions, but it is important to acknowledge that these very reactions are programmed by our own culturally determined views of the world. We cannot but judge others upon the criteria that we hold to be true, polite and appropriate. Consequently, in any transcultural counselling encounter a situation develops in which two people may be judging each other by two sets of quite different criteria. Further, it is likely that both parties will not recognize this and, even if they did, would not satisfactorily be able to articulate why it was that they behaved how they had!

Ruth Benedict (1968) has examined the arbitrary nature of culture and notes that all over the world, since the beginning of human history, it can be shown that people have been able to adopt the cultures of others. She states that there is nothing in the biological structure of people that makes this process difficult. People are not committed in detail by their biological constitution to any particular variety of behaviours. The great diversity of social solutions that people have worked out in different cultures are all equally possible on the basis of their original endowment. She thus asserts that culture is not a biologically transmitted complex. By implication, then, it is a socially transmitted one.

## Responding to the inner or the outer?

The point has already been made in both this and the previous chapter that in any encounter between two visibly different persons, one judges the other based upon one's own criteria which are pre-established and in some part are stimulated by how the other person looks and behaves. Refining this somewhat further and based on Benedict's findings above, let us consider a counselling session where a white therapist is consulted by a black client. At worst, the white therapist might respond in all sorts of ways to the visibility of difference, the black skin, failing completely to recognize the inner 'being' of the client that may be profoundly rooted in the same culture as the therapist. Only difference will be seen, the similarity of culture perhaps going unrecognized.

Of course, this is one of several key issues that are being addressed in this book. The above paragraph presents this issue very starkly. The lived experience of counselling interviews is considerably more complex than this, though, at worst, the outcome might rest upon this initial impact of visibility of difference.

An analogy with the wider world of counselling is pertinent here. Counsellors are trained to listen to their clients and to respond to what it is they hear and sense of the client's inner world. Trained counsellors become sensitive to the fact that what clients present (indeed what we all, most often, present to the outside world) are their defence systems. What we see, therefore, from the outside, are manifestations of people's defence systems. If counsellors can suspend their judgements of what they see and rather attend to what they hear, what the client has to say about their inner world, they come closer to understanding the person inside the bodily mask they are seeing. Counsellors and therapists are trained and sensitized to this purpose. Notwithstanding all of this, however, all human beings, counsellors included, do respond to and judge others, initially, on their own perceptual prejudicial criteria. This first point of contact, then, between culturally and racially different counselling pairings is profoundly crucial and will impact upon what might ensue between the two persons and whether the process will be deemed to have been therapeutically useful.

## Culture and the individual

We have recognized above that culture is socially transmitted and profoundly affects our ways of seeing and thinking about the world, of understanding relationships among people, things and events, of establishing preferences and purposes, and of carrying out actions and pursuing goals.

From a sociological perspective, Bourdieu (1976) describes culture as not merely being a common code or even a common catalogue of answers to recurring problems; he asserts that it is a 'common set of previously assimilated master plans from which, by an act of invention, similar to that involved in the writing of music, an infinite number of individual patterns directly applicable to specific situations are generated'.

Later in the same chapter Bourdieu investigates the role of social institutions (in this case the school) in establishing masterplans of thought in consciousness and in transmitting the (cultural) unconscious, thus producing individuals equipped with the unconscious system (or deeply buried) masterplan that constitutes their culture.

Bourdieu's phrase (above), 'an act of invention', could apply to acts of behaviour within a situation. That act of behaviour, depending upon the person, could conceivably be one from within a very wide range of potential behaviours culturally acceptable (or not) for that situation. The choice of that behaviour is likely to be the result of the complex factors that constitute the cultural background and the personality of the actor, and personality, as Yeaxlee (1925) reminds us, 'is not static but dynamic . . . it is perpetually receptive and creative'.

For many years this realization has remained a fundamental problem for the disciplines of psychology and sociology: the relation between the individual and the social order. Ruth Benedict (1968) writes that

> no culture yet observed has been able to eradicate the differences in the temperaments of the persons who compose it. It is always a give-and-take.
>     The problem of the individual is not clarified by stressing the antagonism between culture and the individual, but by stressing their mutual reinforcement. This rapport is so close that it is not possible to discuss patterns of culture without considering specifically their relations to individual psychology.
>
> (Benedict 1968: 183)

This realization is important and takes us beyond the findings of Kardiner and Linton who, in an extensive joint study (Kardiner and Linton 1947; Kardiner 1959) reflecting anthropological and psychoanalytic origins, convincingly demonstrated that each culture tends to create and is supported by a 'basic personality type' composed of the complex personality characteristics that are congenial with the total range of institutions . . . within a given culture.

This development, then, (in our account above) of the complex relationship between individual personality and culture further complicates the dynamics of any transcultural counselling partnership. The dynamic interplay between the two factors (personality and culture) which is manifested in all people's behaviour removes any possibility for simplistic predictions of others' behaviour and any assumptions about what they believe, think, what their guiding constructs are, and so on.

It has been our experience that there are situations in which, with clients having profoundly different cultural origins to ourselves, nevertheless a process of counselling has been helpful. Our hypothesis, in these circumstances, is that the personality traits within the clients have been open and conducive to our counselling style and approach. Despite the enormous cultural gulf, and all the differences that implies, successful therapeutic work has occurred.

## Cultural understanding: the demands on the counsellor

> White culture is such a dominant norm that it acts as an invisible veil that prevents people from seeing counselling as a potentially biased system.
>
> (Katz 1985)

This chapter has concentrated so far upon an extended discussion of the term 'culture' and continued with offering several definitions that are operationally consistent with the way in which the notion of culture is being used in this text. Culture profoundly affects people's ways of being, their behaviour, their interpersonal relationships, their notions of meaning and so on.

Valentine (1968), within her definition of culture, embodies a requirement of any outsider, in our case the counsellor, to understand that: 'the culture of a particular people or other social body is everything one must learn in order to behave in ways that are recognizable, predictable and understandable to those people'.

Reflecting upon the above paragraph, Valentine's statements throw down a considerable challenge. She says 'everything one must learn'. How does the counsellor learn? By listening to the client? Self-evidently this represents a therapist's core activity. However, in listening, what is heard will be the presentation of the dilemma or problem presently being experienced by the client, mediated through his personality type and style and influenced by his cultural origins. Only tangentially, therefore, might the counsellor gather a cultural understanding of the client.

By attending to the client's behaviour? If the client scratches her nose or constantly stares at the counsellor, for example, is she behaving culturally appropriately, or personally reacting to the stress of the environment, or simply responding to physiological demands at this time (her nose itches or she may be concentrating). Again, the counsellor may only have intuitions of cultural phenomena affecting the client and indeed these intuitions may be quite inaccurate.

By asking the client? If you, as client, were asked 'about your culture', what would you say? How would you describe it, what aspects would you concentrate upon? Any description you gave, also, would be partial and extremely limited. Also, such questions from the counsellor could indicate to you as client that the counsellor is really concerned to understand and help you. However, such questions could cause you to resent the counsellor's inquisitiveness and curiosity or leave you feeling that he was more interested in your culture, your differentness, than in you and the difficulties you are presently facing. Emotionally, your response might be one of mistrust of motive and possible withdrawal from the counselling. An underlying fear, sometimes expressed by members of minority groups, is that 'the counsellor only wants to know because she wants to find out about us, and I am aware there are many occasions, historically, where such knowledge has been used against me or my forebears'.

Asking, then, though apparently the most obvious strategy, might have considerable implications for the client's perception and trust of the counsellor and will not necessarily yield the information the counsellor feels he requires. The tension between valuable encounter and engagement with the client (on the one hand), as compared to 'invasion' of the client (on the other), is a subtle yet critical element in the building (or not) of enhanced understanding between counsellor and client.

By consulting other sources of information? These might be through books, films, attending training courses and through conversations with other people. These demands certainly put pressures on counsellors to engage in a considerable amount of extra work outside their counselling activity. Given the huge number and variety of cultures in Britain alone, it would be impossible for any counsellor to accumulate such knowledge. A more realistic perspective might be for counsellors to try to begin to get to know something of those specific cultures from which their clients most regularly come.

This whole section advocates that the counsellor needs to be culturally informed. However, the responses to each question above, on how the counsellor might know more, lead to further complexities.

One training mechanism developed in the United States to fulfil such purposes is called a 'Culturegram'.[1] This is a regularly updated, written description, about three pages in length, offering details of some principal characteristics of a culture. The Centre that produces them has culturegrams now for a huge range of cultures in the world. Such sources of information might be useful, for example, to a student counsellor seeing many international students from certain countries or to a counsellor who works with recently arrived refugees. In these cases, the counsellor and client do come from distinctly different cultures and appropriate information exists in this readily accessible form.

However, there are quite distinct limits on the precise nature and interpretation of this information. It could be argued that what is written reflects more the position of the (culturally different) author than the culture described. Phenomena described from an outsider's cultural perspective may be understood quite differently from within the insider's frame of reference. Also, though perhaps broad cultural tendencies may be describable, the extent to which they are acceptable as truth and therefore applicable to the complete range of personalities within that culture has to be seriously questioned.

Any descriptions of another culture will always be limited. It is certainly likely that such descriptions would not encompass the range of data that significantly affects different aspects of interpersonal behaviour featured in the next chapter. Counsellors will still be short of information that they consider might be useful to them, i.e. insights into how clients' cultural upbringing may affect their expectations of, and behaviour in the counselling relationship.

What also has to be faced here is the (false) expectation that if we come to know something then that will automatically inform or help us modify our behaviour. Even if I know that your pattern of eye contact is culturally determined and does not signify what I interpret it to mean, I will still find it hard, if not impossible, to suspend my judgements about it and allow for it, or modify my own behaviour to respond to it. Knowing and behaving are not necessarily easily linked.

If we return to Valentine's quote now, she asserts that the learning has to occur in order for us to behave in ways that are 'recognizable, predictable and understandable to others'. Certainly, when people share cultural origins and understandings, they share, often without any awareness, sufficient 'recipes' for understanding each other's present behaviour and predicting their future behaviour.

Reversing Valentine's statement somewhat, could we engage in a process of learning about our own cultural selves sufficiently to understand, recognize and predict our own behaviours? This realm of self-understanding might also then give us insights into others' cultural positions through our empathy and through our imagination. Even here, in this venture, we are likely to be considerably challenged. Viewed from an outside perspective, Scheutz (1944) suggests that 'all cultural knowledge and practices are incoherent, only partially clear and not at all free from contradictions'. This statement has two implications. First, when we view others' cultures we may have the (perhaps uncomfortable) experience of trying to understand phenomena that are not at all clear or straightforward. Second, when we examine our own, we may not even appreciate the incoherences and contradictions that do exist unless we are assisted by cultural outsiders.

In summation, this last section of the chapter has explored the immense realms of difficulty likely to be experienced in trying to move towards a greater cultural understanding of ourselves and of others. A range of methods for attaining this knowledge have been suggested, though, individually, no single method will be satisfactory in generating the range, depth and subtlety of understanding that we believe is required to be successful in any counselling ventures with culturally different clients.

## Note

1    Culturegrams are produced by the David M. Kennedy Center for International Studies, Brigham Young University, 280, Harald. R. Clark Building, Pravo, UTAH 84602, USA.

# 4 Cultural barriers to communication

> People carry culture with them. When they leave one group setting for another they do not shed its cultural premises.
>
> (Becker and Gear 1960)

> We are all culturally conditioned. We see the world in the way we have learned to see it. Only to a limited extent can we, in our thinking, step out of the boundaries imposed by our cultural conditioning.
>
> (Hofstede 1980b)

## Introduction

Having discussed the complexity of culture in the previous chapter, the intention here is to offer ideas on the huge range of factors of cultural difference that can be present when two culturally different persons meet.

The process of counselling is quintessentially based upon sensitive, understanding and accurate communication between counsellor and client. The point was made in Chapter 1 that counselling research had led the way in highlighting specific skills and styles of being that can lead to optimal outcomes for clients.

While communication constitutes part of the visible and audible aspects of people's behaviour, the inner origins of such messages come from the complex inner workings of our minds, our emotions, our memories, our relationships and so on. Within the context of this book, counsellors are being encouraged to understand more fully their inner complexities, and specifically their own cultural barriers to communication.

This chapter moves from an account of a training exercise, providing a range of ideas generated by many participants on courses, to offering three different perspectives of differences between cultures: first, the work of E.T. Hall, second, the work of G. Hofstede and third, the Iceberg Conception of Culture. Inevitably, not all theoretical perspectives or indeed cultural differences are listed here. However, the data that is offered provides a resounding range of ideas and phenomena, sufficient to make us dwell deeply on the following questions: with so many potential and actual differences between us will we ever be able to communicate satisfactorily? Has transcultural counselling any chance whatsoever?

## A training exercise

The authors have often used the following training exercise as a way of helping groups into thinking more about what such cultural barriers to communication might be. Having drawn two stick figures on the board, the group is invited to brainstorm as many cultural barriers to communication that they think may exist between any two people who come from differing cultures. In quite a short time, an amazing array of ideas can be presented. Initially, the exercise is introduced in terms of the general barriers to communication any two people would experience.

A further development is to consider that the two figures, described as being culturally and racially different to each other, are a counsellor/client dyad. This secondary brainstorm can then produce further specialized ideas relating to cultural barriers affecting the counselling process.

Figure 4.1 very quickly provides us with a huge range of issues that are potentially present in any meeting between two people who are culturally and racially different. The complexity of this situation is further realized when one takes into account that Person A, already having all these aspects, attitudes and attributes, is trying to communicate with Person B, also possessing these aspects, though differently constituted and behaved. Each is different to the other. Each also then proceeds to see, perceive, attribute and project onto the other from her own understanding of the world.

Let us illuminate this with an example.

Person 'A' is tall. She comes from a society of tall people and is thus used to conversations with contemporaries of a similar height. However, when confronted with Person 'B', a shorter person, she has to significantly change her posture to communicate. The change in posture thus affects her attitude towards the other person as it reminds her of sayings she had heard in her childhood about never trusting shorter people.

Thus Person A, within her own culture, is fine. In meeting Person B, she develops a set of reactions based upon her own culturally determined system of interpretation. Likewise Person B, from her perspective, perceives the tallness of Person A as potentially threatening and becomes fearful of her potential power. This leads B into being somewhat timid and withdrawn in A's company.

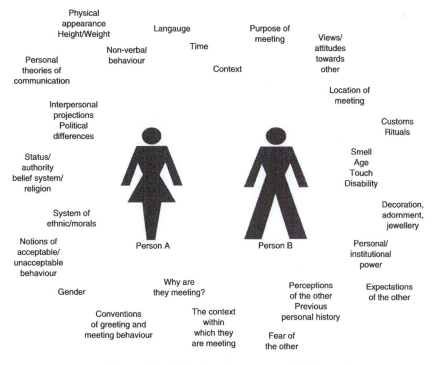

**Figure 4.1** Cultural barriers to communication.

A perceives B
A judges B on A's system of categorizing people
A's behaviour and communication is thus likely to be affected.

B perceives A
B judges A on B's system of categorizing people
B's behaviour and communication is thus likely to be affected.

This apparently very simple example of just one difference, of relative tallness, offers an insight into the potential complexity of the impact of difference upon communication. If the two persons were to be meeting for counselling, the scenario presented above indicates that, whoever was counsellor, their capacity to be accepting of and non-judgemental towards the other, as client, is already limited. This demonstrates that the counsellor may have considerable difficulty in fully offering one of the core therapeutic conditions, as defined by Rogers ([1951] 1987), for successful therapy to occur – that of acceptance or non-judgementalism.

## Culture: the work of E. T. Hall

Edward Hall has written a series of books which are featured in the Bibliography. As an author he has been concerned to stimulate the view that in addition to learning others' languages we must also grasp the need for what he calls cultural literacy. Broadly speaking, this is the ability to be sensitive to, and understanding of, the ways of being that are determined by different cultures.

For example, Triandis (1975) relates how an American visitor asked his Greek acquaintance what time they should come to his house for dinner. The Greek villager replied 'anytime'. Now, in American usage, apparently, the expression 'anytime' is a non-invitation that people give to appear polite but which they hope will not lead to anything. The Greek, however, actually meant that the Americans would be welcome any time because, in Greek culture, putting limits on when a guest can come is deemed insulting (from Furnham and Bochner 1986: 206). The consequences of such misunderstandings can lead to the attribution of negative values upon the other person and inevitably contribute towards a deterioration of the relationship. Edward Hall's books are full of anecdotal accounts from all over the world of such breakdowns in communication. Based on this wide experience and knowledge of differences between cultures, he has attempted to construct a set of hypotheses on how cultures differ (Hall, 1959, 1966, 1976a, 1976b and 1983).

He proposes five major categories of difference between cultures. These propositions are supported by considerable research literature. They are: space, time, verbal behaviour, non-verbal behaviour and context. These are detailed below.

### Space (Proxemics)

> People's feelings about being properly oriented in space runs deep . . . such knowledge is ultimately linked to survival and sanity. To be disoriented in space is to be psychotic.
>
> (Hall 1966)

Edward Hall subdivides this section on space into five sub-sections. They are:

1   *Interpersonal space*. Cultures have different conventions about the space between individuals in social situations. For example, people from certain cultures stand and converse at much closer distances than that observed by the majority culture within the UK. Feelings of discomfort can soon be generated in such circumstances by the person who feels his space is being 'invaded'. However, he is often not fully aware of why he is experiencing such discomfort!

2    *Olfactory space*. Cultures have different ways of using the sense of smell. In the Middle Eastern countries it can be a way of sensing the other person, whereas in Britain, perfumes and talcum powders are used to screen out natural smells.

3    *Thermal space*. The experience of space can be sensed through thermal sensations, e.g. 'feeling hot under the collar' or blushing.

4    *Visual space*. We use space visually to gather and convey information.

5    *Sociofugal and sociopetal space*. These terms relate to the different ways in which cultures use furniture arrangements and room designs, for example, that either enhance or inhibit interactions between people.

**Time**

Hall divides time into two broad categories, monochronic and polychronic.

1    *Monochronic time* refers, in general terms, to the increasingly dominant world view of the 24-hour day in which only that time system for measurement exists. For example, 'The train leaves at 9.35 am; 'Come to dinner at 8.00 pm'.

2    *Polychronic time*. This is a much less well known view of time but is practised by certain cultures. Hall cites the example of the Hopi Indians in the United States who have a belief in each thing, each person, as having its own time. This concept is therefore very rooted in individuals' own experiencing.

Beyond those broad divisions, we are also informed of subdivisions of monochronic time that could have enormous implications for the relationships between counsellors and culturally different clients.

•    *Appointment times*. If the counsellor sets the appointment for 7.00 pm, does the client turn up ten minutes before, or 'on the dot', or an hour later? Different cultures have different expectations and practices. 7.00 pm does not necessarily mean 7.00 pm exactly as determined by monochronic time. Cultural time modifies the precise time indicated, adding or subtracting so much time as is culturally understood and agreed.

•    *Acquaintance time*. The time considered polite in which to establish acquaintanceship before moving on to the matter that is the purpose of the meeting. This convention might have considerable implications for counsellors in terms of their behaviour in the early part of an interview.

•    *Discussion time*. In 'business' meetings who is involved, who takes the decisions, how can decisions be taken and when? If we transpose

Hall's conception of business meetings into counselling sessions, there are implications as to who makes decisions, the counsellor or the client, and who else is or should be involved in the process (e.g. family and friends).

- *Visiting time*. How long meetings or social gatherings last is also determined culturally. Counsellors, within their interview rooms, might offer 50-minute sessions. If they were to visit a client in his own accommodation it might be considered more appropriate for the client to determine (culturally) how long they should meet. This aspect has a potential clash of interests now embedded in it.
- *Time schedules*. The creation of time schedules, also, is an area full of difficulty if the persons involved have different cultural origins and therefore have different notions of how long things should take.

The term 'chronemics' has been applied to the timing of verbal exchange during conversations. British people normally expect people with whom they are having conversations to respond fairly quickly to their statements. In some other cultures, people time their exchanges to leave silences between each statement. For people within the majority group within the UK, this can be unnerving and may lead them to judge the other as shy or inattentive, or bored. As a way of coping with this discomfort British people can end up repeating themselves, paraphrasing, talking more loudly and using other strategies to cope with the apparent silences of the other (silences, incidentally, that are absolutely appropriate and conventional from the other person's own cultural domain).

### Verbal behaviour

This is a much more obvious division between cultures, especially where languages differ. However, even where both participants are using the same language, the use of similar words may have different meanings, there will be different conventions for expressing opinion and so on, and the capacity to which empathy may be extended to culturally different others may be quite limited.

Also, not only what is said but how things are said (paralinguistics) have significantly different meanings for different cultures. Ums, ahs, signs, grunts, accent, intonation, stress, pitch are all culturally determined. Similarly, how the information is structured, who manages the conversation and who says what and when falls within culturally determined conventions.

### Non-verbal behaviour

Cultural differences in non-verbal behaviour can be categorized as follows:

*Kinesics*: movements of the body (head, arms, legs and so on). Gestures in one country may well be quite inappropriate in another country.

*Oculesics*: the use or avoidance of eye-to-eye contact. The British use eye contact as a sign of listening behaviour. Research in the United States demonstrated that many American black people listened with their ears and looked elsewhere which proved disconcerting for white speakers who considered they had not been heard! The white Americans were not aware that they listened with their eyes as much as their ears. In many countries there are elaborate patterns of eye avoidance which are often linked to considerations of deferential respect for elders, those in authority and so on.

*Haptics* (touch): where, how and how often people can touch each other while conversing are culturally determined patterns of behaviour.

The differences of role, class and status are also arenas for considerable confusion between cultures as the various signals and cues to infer these positions are often quite invisible to 'outsiders'.

### Context

Hall draws broad definitions between what he terms high-context and low-context cultures. Examples of high-context cultures are the Chinese, the Japanese and some Middle Eastern countries. Low-context cultures tend to be in the west. In low-context cultures words are presumed to carry all meaning. In some cultures, words and meaning do not have such a direct connection. Notions of truth, consequently, are relative and culturally based. In low-context cultures, there is also a tendency towards fragmentation of experience evidenced by the development of all sorts of experts and a proliferation of legalistic documents and contract. By contrast, high-context cultures tend towards conservative, rigid class structures where individual needs are sacrificed to groups goals. However, these are cultures in which 'a person's word is their bond'. The context of a meeting carries the meaning, not simply the words used.

## The iceberg conception of culture

Figure 4.2, known as the iceberg conception of culture, has been used as a teaching aid in the field of international business relations. It is particularly useful in that it offers a list of interpersonal styles and expectations that pertain to the professional arena, and can consequently be modified and applied to the counselling task.

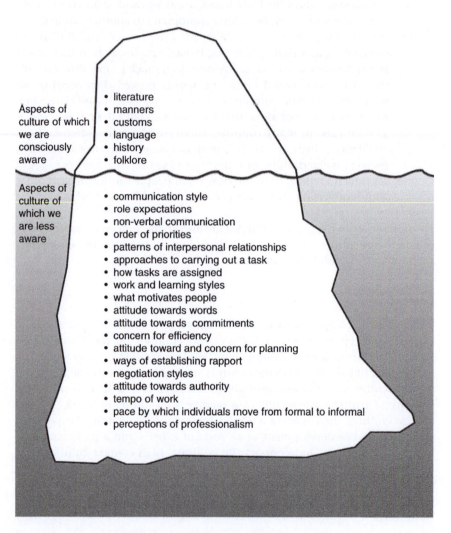

Aspects of
culture of which
we are
consciously
aware

- literature
- manners
- customs
- language
- history
- folklore

Aspects of
culture of
which we
are less
aware

- communication style
- role expectations
- non-verbal communication
- order of priorities
- patterns of interpersonal relationships
- approaches to carrying out a task
- how tasks are assigned
- work and learning styles
- what motivates people
- attitude towards words
- attitude towards commitments
- concern for efficiency
- attitude toward and concern for planning
- ways of establishing rapport
- negotiation styles
- attitude towards authority
- tempo of work
- pace by which individuals move from formal to informal
- perceptions of professionalism

**Figure 4.2**   The iceberg conception of culture.
*Source*: American Field Services (nd).

## The work of Geert Hofstede

The following data represent the outcome of research carried out by Hofstede among employees of subsidiaries of one large US-based multinational corporation in 40 countries around the globe. Some 116,000 questionnaires were sent to a range of employees, from unskilled workers to top managers. Twenty language versions of the questionnaire were used. This research (1967–73) was cross-referenced with other cross-cultural research studies and statistically significant similarities were achieved.

We have already stated that Hofstede (1980a,1980b) defines culture as the collective mental programming of a people in an environment. Culture is thus not a characteristic of individuals; it encompasses a number of people who were conditioned by the same education and life experience.

Hofstede also notes that

> culture, in this sense of collective mental programming, is often difficult to change; if it changes at all, it does so slowly. This is so not only because it exists in the minds of the people, but because it has become crystallized in the institutions these people have built together: their family structures, educational structures, religious organizations, associations, forms of government, work organizations, law, literature, settlement patterns, buildings and even scientific theories.
>
> (Hofstede 1980a)

For a set of 40 independent nations Hofstede tried to determine empirically the main criteria by which their national cultures differed. He found four such criteria, which he labelled dimensions; these were power-distance, uncertainty-avoidance, individualism–collectivism and masculinity–femininity. They are described more fully below.

### Power-distance

The first dimension of cultural difference Hofstede called power-distance. It indicates the extent to which a society accepts the fact that power in institutions and organizations is distributed unequally. It is reflected in the values of the less powerful members of society as well as in those of the more powerful ones. A partial picture of these different 'value' assumptions is shown in Table 4.1 (many more examples are offered by Hofstede in his work, 1980b).

### Uncertainty-avoidance

The second dimension, uncertainty-avoidance, indicates the extent to which a society feels threatened by uncertain and ambiguous situations and tries to avoid these situations by providing greater career stability, establishing more formal rules, not tolerating deviant ideas and behaviours, and believing in absolute truths and the attainment of expertise. Nevertheless, societies in which uncertainty-avoidance is strong are also characterized by a higher level

**Table 4.1**   The power-distance dimension

| Small power-distance | Large power-distance |
| --- | --- |
| Inequality in society should be minimized. | There should be an order of inequality in this world in which everybody has a rightful place; high and low are protected by this order. |
| Hierarchy means an inequality of roles, established for convenience. | Hierarchy means existential inequality. |
| The use of power should be legitimate and is subject to the judgement as to whether it is good or evil. | Power is a basic fact of society that antedates good or evil. Its legitimacy is irrelevant. |
| All should have equal rights. The way to change a social system is to redistribute power. | Power holders are entitledto privileges. The way to change a social system is to dethrone those in power. |
| People at various power levels feel less threatened and more prepared to trust people. | Other people are a potential threat to one's power and can rarely be trusted. |

**Table 4.2**   The uncertainty-avoidance dimension

| Weak uncertainty-avoidance | Strong uncertainty-avoidance |
| --- | --- |
| The uncertainty inherent in life is more easily accepted and each day is taken as it comes. | The uncertainty inherent in in life is felt as a continuous threat that must be fought. |
| Ease and lower stress are experienced. Aggressive behaviour is frowned upon. | Higher anxiety and stress are experienced. Aggressive behaviour of self and others is accepted. |
| Less showing of emotions is preferred. | More showing of emotions is preferred. |
| There is more willingness to take risks in life. The accent is on relativism, empiricism. | There is great concern with security in life. The search is for ultimate, absolute truths and values. |
| If rules cannot be kept, we should change them. | If rules cannot be kept, we are sinners and should repent. |

of anxiety and aggressiveness that creates, amongst other things, a stronger inner urge in people to work hard (see Table 4.2).

### Individualism–collectivism

The third dimension encompasses individualism and its opposite, collectivism. Individualism implies a loosely knit social framework in which people

**Table 4.3** The individualism–collectivism dimension

| Collectivist | Individualist |
| --- | --- |
| In society, people are born into extended families or clans who protect them in exchange for loyalty. | In society, everybody is supposed to take care of him/herself and his/her immediate family. |
| 'We' consciousness holds sway. | 'I' consciousness holds sway. |
| Identity is based in the social system. | Identity is based in the individual. |
| There is emotional dependence of individuals on organizations and institutions. | There is emotional independence of the individual from organizations and institutions. |
| Belief is placed in group decisions. | Belief is placed in individual decisions. |
| Value standards differ for in-groups and out-groups (particularism). | Value standards should apply to all (universalism). |

**Table 4.4** The masculinity–femininity dimension

| Feminine | Masculine |
| --- | --- |
| Men needn't be assertive, but can also assume nurturing roles. | Men should be assertive. Women should be nurturing. |
| Sex roles in society are more fluid. | Sex roles in society are clearly differentiated. |
| Quality of life is important. | Performance is what counts. |
| You work in order to live. | You live in order to work. |
| People and environment are important. | Money and things are important. |
| Interdependence is the ideal. | Independence is the ideal. |

are supposed to take care of themselves and their immediate families only, while collectivism is characterized by a tight social framework in which people distinguish between in-groups and out-groups; they expect their in-group (relatives, clan, organizations) to look after them, and in exchange for that they feel they owe absolute loyalty to it. A fuller picture of this dimension is presented in Table 4.3.

**Masculinity–femininity**

Measurements in terms of this dimension express the extent to which the dominant values in society are 'masculine' – that is, assertiveness, the acquisition of money and things, in contrast to caring for others, the quality of life or people – feminine. These values were labelled 'masculine' because, within nearly all societies, men scored higher in terms of the values' positive sense (in terms of assertiveness, for example, rather than its lack) – even though the society as a whole might veer towards the 'feminine' pole. Interestingly, the more an entire society scored to the masculine side, the wider the gap between its men's and women's values (see Table 4.4).

An example is given in Figure 4.3 of one of the graphs developed by Hofstede, from his findings, charting the relative location of different cultures one to another along the dimensions of 'power-distance' and 'uncertainty-avoidance'

## Summing up

> On the one hand we believe strongly that all forms of counselling are cross-cultural, that cultural issues need to be seen as central to cross-cultural counselling (not ancillary) and that by focussing just on ethnic minority issues, we may be 'ghettoizing' the problem. Yet, we believe that multicultural counselling is a speciality area as well. Although all of us are racial, ethnic and cultural beings, belonging to a particular group does not endow a person with the competencies and skills necessary to be a culturally skilled counsellor.
>
> (Sue *et al.* 1992: 477)

This chapter has offered a very wide range of ideas concerning cultural differences in behaviour. This considerable range of information has deliberately been included to demonstrate the enormous extent of the potential behavioural differences that could occur between counsellors and their culturally different clients.

The reader's attention is drawn to statements made earlier in the book in relation to the potential clientele counsellors might see within the UK. For example, those counsellors who work with recently arrived nationals from other countries (refugees, international students, victims of torture, asylum seekers, international business persons etc.) might find these chapters useful and applicable.

Where counsellors are meeting clients who have lived in Britain for a significant proportion of their lives (or indeed all of their lives), yet have culturally different origins, then the subtleties of cultural identity and behaviour might become more obscure. Indeed, such clients may be biculturally competent and feel very comfortable operating out of both sets of cultural assumptions (those of the dominant culture and those of their own root culture). On the other hand, phenomena might occur in the interview that are confusing and misleading to both parties, and the counsellor might profit-

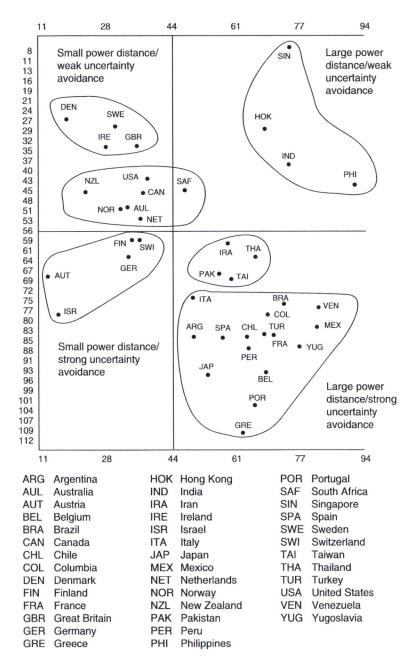

| | | |
|---|---|---|
| ARG | Argentina | HOK | Hong Kong | POR | Portugal |
| AUL | Australia | IND | India | SAF | South Africa |
| AUT | Austria | IRA | Iran | SIN | Singapore |
| BEL | Belgium | IRE | Ireland | SPA | Spain |
| BRA | Brazil | ISR | Israel | SWE | Sweden |
| CAN | Canada | ITA | Italy | SWI | Switzerland |
| CHL | Chile | JAP | Japan | TAI | Taiwan |
| COL | Columbia | MEX | Mexico | THA | Thailand |
| DEN | Denmark | NET | Netherlands | TUR | Turkey |
| FIN | Finland | NOR | Norway | USA | United States |
| FRA | France | NZL | New Zealand | VEN | Venezuela |
| GBR | Great Britain | PAK | Pakistan | YUG | Yugoslavia |
| GER | Germany | PER | Peru | | |
| GRE | Greece | PHI | Philippines | | |

**Figure 4.3** The position of 40 countries on the power-distance and uncertainty-avoidance scales.

ably gain from trying to understand these as cultural phenomena in action, rather than judging such behaviours negatively – a more frequent response in everyday interactions.

An awareness of cultural differences can enhance the processes of dialogue in cross-cultural dyads. Counsellors need to ensure, however, that their attribution of 'cultural difference' does not serve as a defence against their own prejudice and racist tendencies. The second chapter, which discusses issues of race and power, has to be held in symmetry with these last two chapters, in order to achieve a more balanced understanding of the overall dynamics in the counsellor/client relationship.

# 5 Communication, language, gesture and interpretation

Thinking follows a network of tracks laid down in the given language, an organization which may concentrate systematically upon certain aspects of intelligence and may systematically discard others featured by other languages. The individual is utterly unaware of this organization and is constrained completely within its unbreakable bonds.

(Whorf 1956)

Promoting bilingualism rather than monolingualism should be a major goal to the provision of mental health services: it is an expression of personal freedom and pluralism.

(Sue *et al.* 1992)

## Introduction

All models of counselling/psychotherapy rely substantially on the process of talking and listening. Communication comprises both the form and the content of the counselling interview. The early sections of this chapter refer to the use of spoken language. Aspects of non-verbal communication are discussed later.

Whorf's statement above alerts us to a likely major predicament in the therapeutic process. Within the British situation, for example, there are likely to be (potentially) many combinations of counsellor and client having different linguistic origins. Some of these hypothesized combinations are given below.

1   Counsellor and client have totally different languages (e.g. English and Gujerati).
2   Counsellor and client use English in the interview though, for one of them, English is their second language.

3   Both counsellor and client have apparently similar language origins but have grown up in different countries, e.g. an English counsellor with an American client.
4   Both counsellor and client have similar country and language origins but hail from different class positions from within that country.

The predicament that any combinations of the above participants in counselling find themselves in is that of potentially misunderstanding the other. Language has no existence apart from the social reality of its users, argues Suzanne Romaine in her book *Language in Society* (1994). One wonders about the nature of that social reality of the client/counsellor relationship, if both parties have different language, as in 1 above, or indeed differences in fluency, accent and dialect as depicted by examples 2, 3 and 4. All the scenarios suggest the creation of a social reality in the counsellor's room full of potential strain, exasperation and alienation. Being misunderstood begets anger, frustration, even hatred. By contrast, to be understood evokes trust, gratitude, exploration, love and aspiration. The use of language is absolutely central to the communication process and, however much good intent there is, on both sides of a conversation, if misunderstandings persist then the potential for therapy diminishes substantially, or even ceases altogether.

## Language, thought and experience

As Whorf above and Beattie (1964) remind us, people's categories of thought and the forms of their language are inextricably bound together. Whorf and Sapir were two of the earliest descriptive linguists to hint at the close relationship between language and thought (Mandelbaum 1940). According to Hall (1976a), Whorf's greatest contribution to western thinking lay in his meticulous description of the relationship of language to events in a cross-cultural context. He demonstrated that cultures have unique ways of relating language to reality. This can be one of our principal sources of information concerning cultural differences. Nothing happens in the world of humans that is not deeply influenced by linguistic form.

If both language and thought are closely related, then so too is the connection between language and experience. Sapir has suggested that

> The relation between language and experience is often misunderstood . . . (it) actually defines experience for us by reason of its formal completeness and because of our unconscious projection of its implicit expectations into the field of experience . . .
>
> Language is much like a mathematical system which . . . becomes elaborated into a self-contained conceptual system which previsages

all possible experience in accordance with certain accepted formal limitations . . . Categories such as number, gender, case, tense, mode, voice, 'aspect' and a host of others . . . are not so much discovered in experience as imposed upon it . . .

(Sapir 1931: 578)

Language, then, potentially limits experience. A problematic question is now posed as to whether a particular experience is available to someone who does not have the words to define it. Bram (1956) points out that a range of experience may be differentiated in the lexicon of one language and undifferentiated in another. Thus, taking the perception of colours in different cultures, Leff (1973) reports that Pacific Island languages fail to distinguish between blue and green and the Navaho only have one word for grey and brown. Bram's point is that though the full range of colour perceiving apparatus is present in Pacific Islanders and Navaho Indians, linguistically and practically they do not make as much use of its differentiating ability as some other peoples. By contrast, a classic example of high differentiation in linguistic category and practical usage is the considerable range of words for types of snow possessed by Laplanders.

## Language, emotion and meaning

The links between language, experience, emotion and meaning can become rather more tenuous in abstract subjects. For example, if another person states 'I see a car', and there is a car in our shared visual field, then both of us assume we are sharing a common perceptual experience. However, where there is no external, concrete referent, as in the statement 'I feel sad', the assumption of a common experience rests on more delicate grounds. Counselling and psychotherapy rely on the process of communication. Much of the substance of counselling is communication about communicating (the counsellor is told about the client's communication with other people). Further, the client's emotional state is often mentioned and focused upon. Thus statements such as the one quoted above, 'I feel sad', is potentially hazardous to the whole process of mutual understanding, especially in transcultural settings.

This implementation of the concept of empathy often demands that counsellors attempt to 'imagine' what clients are experiencing in their situation, perhaps through a comparison of a 'similar' experience of their own. Quite clearly, in a cross-cultural situation, this urge towards understanding enters the realm of possibly inadequate approximations or, at worst, 'hit or miss' hypotheses. As indicated above, there are no reliable external referents. In addition, for emotions, there are no scientific measures available to help us. Leff (1973) examined the attempts that have been made to differentiate the measurement of physiological arousal in various emotional states. Emotional states can be measured via physiological manifestations but these measurements could not differentiate between the differing emotional states – specifically different emotional states manifest similar physical symptoms.

Hall (1976a) has used a notion called 'extension transference' which, when applied to language and experience, becomes a useful theoretical concept. Thus, spoken language is a symbolization of something that happened, is happening or will happen. Written language as an extension of the spoken form is therefore a symbolization of symbolization! This intellectual manoeuvre Hall terms extension transference. The extension can become confused with or take the place of the process described.

This process of extension transference would seem to fit with Leff's hypothesis of a scheme for the historical development of words denoting emotional states (1973). Where previously one word may have existed to denote a pattern of physiological response, it is likely that that word came to denote an emotional state or experience as well as the somatic condition. The focus of meaning subsequently shifted to the experiencing of emotion and the somatic meaning faded into the background. Thus an extension transference has taken place. Finally, in the historic development of the word, it is likely that it split up into phonetically related variants, as the global state was differentiated into several smaller categories.

The possibility of accurate translation and conveyance of meaning appears to become even less possible! Maw has reported initial difficulties in responding to African students within a British student health service, where presenting complaints have been of itching sensations in the head or of stomach ache (1980). Despite closer physical inspection and treatment, the symptoms persisted. Consultations with African medical colleagues, however, revealed the possibility that the students were suffering anxiety or depression. The direct translation of their language into English revealed its use of the somatic interpretations of the experience rather than the emotional one.

Other research comparing use of language across classes (lower, middle, upper) and groups of different economic levels has revealed similar tendencies to express emotional distress in quite different ways, from the concrete somatic to much more abstract and abstruse descriptions (Crandel and Dohrenwend 1967; Bernstein 1973).

'I love her', 'I have a pain in my gut', 'My soul is injured by this' are all statements that have a myriad of meanings. Assumptions of readily understanding every client statement are fraught with danger for counsellors and psychotherapists.

There is a temptation, also, to judge others' language forms pejoratively as deficient. Similar to the concept of culture, others' language forms are different, not deficient. Pinker's study of humans' capacity for language points to the variety of mechanisms all languages and dialects employ (1994).

The counsellor needs to fully appreciate and respect the sophistication of all communication forms used by clients.

The process of the development of any language has inevitably incurred the selective development of a specific number of sounds for the purposes of that spoken language or dialect. Differentiation has thus occurred in this selection, for as Benedict (1968) points out, the number of sounds that can be produced by our vocal cords and our oral and nasal cavities are practically unlimited. Power (1981) has recently stated that in linguistic terms there seems to be no reason why people should not learn new languages and be able to speak them without a trace of accent from their first languages. However, one of the hurdles to this development is the previous exposure to the selection of sounds available in the first language which serves to blunt the listening sensitivity to a new combination of sounds.

The process of differentiation, as pointed out several paragraphs earlier, is one determined by cultural demands. Le Page (1968) has stated:

> Each individual creates the systems for their verbal behaviour so that they shall resemble those of the group or groups with which, from time to time, they may wish to be identified, to the extent that:
> 1 he/she can identify the groups;
> 2 he/she has both opportunity and ability;
> 3 his/her motivation is sufficiently strong to impel him/her to choose and to adapt his/her behaviour accordingly; and
> 4 he/she is still able to adapt his/her behaviour.

A rather simplistic extension of this section is the example of therapists who will inappropriately attempt to use slang, which they believe to be representative of the client's dialect in a mistaken attempt to join with the client. This, of course, can often be viewed as condescending (Hunt 1987) and will certainly work against the success of the counselling process.

## The limits of language

The relationship examined above between language thought and experience is one of great complexity, with the implication being that both thought and experience are dominated and limited by language. Within a situation of learning about another culture the limitations of language are shown up. Hall (1976a) describes it as '. . . by nature poorly adapted to this difficult task . . . it is too linear, not comprehensive enough, too slow, too limited, too constrained, too unnatural, too much a product of its own evolution . . .'.

Becker (1972) reports that Harry Stack Sullivan hypothesized that words are basic to the formation of a child's self-concept and are the only way in which that child can control his or her environment. Becker takes this hypothesis and develops it considerably in the sense that he suggests that what we term 'personality' is largely a locus of word possibilities: 'When we expose our self-esteem to possible undermining by others in a social situation, we are exposing a linguistic identity to other loci of linguistic causality.'

In support of this somewhat mechanistic and most certainly reductionist notion of language, he also quotes Dale Carnegie: 'It matters not what you mean, you and those around you become according to what you say.'

Thus, extracting the essence from the above range of views, language is seen not only to limit thought and experience but also, from another's perceptual field, tends to limit the other person's concept of you through your language. The implications of such a reductionist view of language are really considerable and somewhat pessimistic. The enormous attention paid to this subject by many of Britain's philosophers and sociologists in the earlier decades of this century has tended not only to 'abolish the "subject", but turn language into an autonomous and dominating entity' (Sharrock and Anderson 1981).

It is our view, however, that transcultural issues must not be reduced to the limiting interpretations of the function of language and language differences. Despite the fact that both Whorf and Sapir were considerably ahead of their time in their hypotheses, Hall (1976b) notes that they fall into the 'extension transference' trap, i.e. they believed that language was thought. This counter-assertion is most important to the subject under consideration. Language, clearly, is not thought.

> As for the idea that language limits thought . . . there are some meaty problems posed by Chomsky's arguments. If language is an infinitely productive resource, how are we to determine what cannot be said or thought in it; how are we to survey the possibilities available to it?
>
> (Sharrock and Anderson 1981)

Considered from this perspective, language has potential for infinite creativity and is subject to the speaker's capacity for ingenuity, invention and figurative, idiomatic and allusive expression. Taken from this philosophic stance, language always has the potential to express thought and to acknowledge experience. As counselling philosophy implicitly recognizes the potential for growth in people, it would seem an important component to view the nature of language within the counselling process as one that always has the potential of achieving its task of articulating the client's 'agenda'. In addition, a reciprocal task lies in the counsellor's domain – that of developing this sensitivity to, knowledge of and skill in clients' communication forms.

## Language and power

> The proper word or phrase, properly delivered, is the highest attainment of human interpersonal power.
>
> (Becker 1972)

Both Sarup (1978) and Freire (1972) have recognized the need for minority groups (political, ethnic, economic) to be helped towards recognizing and possessing their 'word', the 'Logos'. For, once recognized, the 'word' cannot be minimized or deleted and at best should enable people towards greater self-confidence, more effective communication and greater understanding of their predicament.

The process of counselling, with its accent on acceptance, listening and dialogue, has the potential to provide persons from minority groups or low-esteem positions with the opportunity to speak, practise, experiment with and thus create and develop their 'word', their symbols of meaning. Counselling, in this sense, has a very political outcome. It can help equip clients with a language and a confidence derived from their own explorations of their situation.

A counter to this radical and hopeful view is provided by Romaine (1994), who argues that questions of language are also questions of power. Certain ways of speaking are perceived as superior largely because they are used by the powerful. If the counsellor is (or is perceived to be) part of a powerful elite in society (e.g. in the UK the majority of counsellors/psychotherapists are white, middle-class and often very articulate) then their very way of speaking and being may be perceived as so superior that the client is driven further into silence and self-doubt. The effect of the client's perception of and projections onto the counsellor can be so determining here that little successful work may ensue between them.

This phenomenon also demands that counsellors become fully aware of the potential impact of their accent, dialect and vocabulary upon others. Of particular concern here is counsellors' own understanding of their political position in relation to the issues of racism and their own discourse. The scholarly work of Van Dijk points to those groups

> who define the moderate mainstream . . . all those who thus manage public opinion, dominant ideologies and consensual everyday practices. It is our claim that white group dominance in general, and racism in particular, . . . pre-suppose a creative process in which these moderate elites play a crucial role.
>
> (Van Dijk 1993: 9)

He proceeds thus:

> For most members of elite groups, this thesis is hard to swallow, being
> fundamentally inconsistent with their normative self-concept. After
> all, elites often see themselves as moral leaders and will therefore gen-
> erally dissociate themselves from anything that has to do with racism
> as they define it. As a consequence ... conclusions of research on
> racism and accusations of minority groups are often denied, margin-
> alized, or even violently attacked by elites, who thereby precisely
> confirm the plausibility of the thesis.

Many counsellors will, as a matter of course, deny their part as being
members of elite groups and quite obviously they are not politicians, journal-
ists, media persons who shape views and attitudes through language. However,
they are, in many cases, related to the elite groups in society by virtue of their
class, their education, their profession and so on.

Counsellor discourse, with their clients, with their colleagues and friends,
has to be examined by itself in order to understand further the implications of
its effect upon minority group clients. Van Dijk notes later (p. 80) that 'We are
reasonable and rational' is of course a standard ideological proposition of
Eurocentrism. Denials of racism are also the stock in trade of racist discourse
(p. 81).

This section demonstrates the complex relationship between language
and power. If clients, through psychotherapy, develop their language, a confidence in their view of the world, much has been achieved. On the other
hand, therapists must pay attention to their use of language and its potential
negative effects upon clients.

## Linguistic differences, interpreters and translation

> Culturally skilled counsellors take responsibility for interacting in
> the language requested by the client: this may mean appropriate
> referral to outside sources. A serious problem arises when the lin-
> guistic skills of the counsellor do not match the language of the client.
> This being the case, counsellors should (a) seek a translator with
> cultural knowledge and appropriate professional background or (b)
> refer to a knowledgeable and competent bilingual counsellor.
>
> (Sue *et al* 1992)

> When therapists first begin working with interpreters they tend to
> project their own critical superego onto the interpreter. Here is
> someone from the same country and perhaps the same (refugee)

community as the client. He or she will naturally understand the politics, culture and probably the personal experiences of the client better than the therapist can hope to do. Moreover, the interpreter may have interpreted in hundreds of counselling sessions with (refugees) and have seen many different counsellors and psychotherapists at work. He or she therefore has a great deal of experience and knowledge against which to assess the therapist's performance.

(Blackwell 2005: 85)

The first quote above is taken from a key article in the development of multicultural counselling in the United States. The article proposes 31 multicultural counselling competences that were, at that time, to be adopted by the American counselling profession as part of their accreditation criteria. A more extended exposition may be found in Chapter 11.

The above proposition certainly throws down the challenge to many counselling practitioners in the UK today. Parallel trends have been noted in both the USA and the UK where, for large numbers of English language speakers there is a huge reluctance to learn and acquire other languages. A certain cultural over-reliance seems to exist on the fact that English is one of the international languages and as such it is widely spoken. Therefore, the attitude proceeds along the lines of 'why bother?' This simplistic sketch doesn't do full justice, of course, to thousands of school children, college and university students studying other languages formally or to many adults who pursue language courses in their leisure time. Nevertheless, within the counselling profession the author knows of few cases where counsellors have set out to develop their knowledge of specific languages because of the client groups they are working with. It has always been easier for English-speaking counsellors to assume that clients will need to converse in English.

The proposition contains the phrase that 'counsellors take responsibility for interacting in the language requested by the client'. There will be many circumstances in which the client, for a variety of reasons, would not make such a request. For that reason we would move towards a recommendation that incorporates the following sentiments: 'That counsellors take the responsibility for ensuring that the client's preference for language within the counselling interview is respected.' This implies that counsellors would have to seek the views and wishes of clients as to the language used in the interviews. If, in doing so, they ascertained that a language other than English was required, it is likely that a crisis would ensue, the crisis being how to continue.

The proposition incorporates the possibilities of using either an interpreter or referral to a bilingual counsellor. The interpreter should be someone 'with cultural knowledge and appropriate professional background'. These criteria are both relatively specific yet may be viewed with some elasticity and discretion.

Clearly there are many advantages to the use of interpreters:

- their use infers a deep respect for the client's preferred language;
- it signals to the client the counsellor's wish to fully understand him and his predicament;
- it acknowledges that the client will be able to describe her situation as fluently as possible in her own language.

However, the use of interpreters is not without difficulty and challenge, as indicated in the second introductory quotation to this chapter. Counsellors need to be fully aware of the challenges that both the act of translation and the use of interpreters might impose. The use of interpreters immediately reduces the possibility of direct communication (see Figure 5.1) between client and counsellor, and substitutes a more indirect model (Figure 5.2). The counsellor may hope and assume that the interpreter provides a clear technical function (see Figure 5.3). (It is recognized that direct communication was already probably not possible. For a further explanation of this point please refer to the chapter on supervision and the concept of the 'proxy self'.)

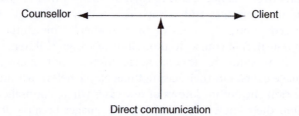

**Figure 5.1**  Direct communication between counsellor and client.

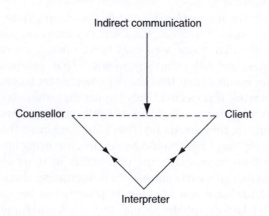

**Figure 5.2**  Indirect communication between counsellor and client through an interpreter.

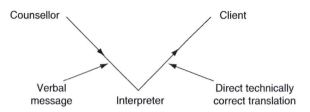

**Figure 5.3** Direct, technically correct translation of counsellor message to client.

However, the persona of the interpreter has to be taken into account. Thus, the communication process becomes even more complex.

Messages relayed from the counsellor and clients have to pass through (the technical and the personal aspects of) the interpreter. The interpreter, as a human being, is subject to the same communication and processing difficulties that a counsellor is in terms of attitudes, assumptions, cultural origins and so on. The counsellor may make statements which the interpreter considers cannot be interpreted directly, e.g. such statements may be culturally insensitive or impolite or the interpreter may be so embarrassed themselves by the question that they change the meaning of it, or they may consider that to give the counsellor certain cultural information would be to let the culture down in the face of outsiders.

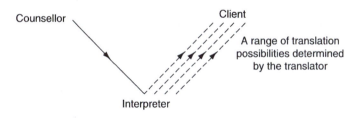

**Figure 5.4** Indirect, personalized translation of counsellor message to client.

In short, the messages that leave both the counsellor and client have the potential to be modified, changed and even contradicted through the interpreter.

The impact of the move from two persons to three in the counselling interaction has to be accommodated by the counsellor's skill and capacity to work with the increased interpersonal dynamics.

The counsellor will have to establish a credible working alliance with the interpreter for the potential success of the counselling process. The therapeutic alliance with the client is therefore 'bent' (in terms of the verbal communication) through the interpreter. At the same time a natural cultural alliance may form between the client and the interpreter. Both this and the earlier scenario

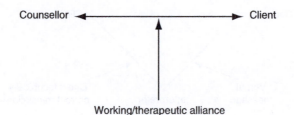

**Figure 5.5**   Therapeutic alliance between counsellor and client.

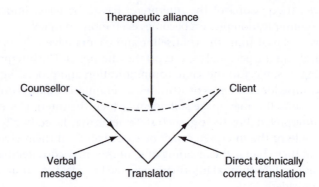

**Figure 5.6**   Different alliances between counsellor, interpreter and client.

demonstrates how the interpreter quickly moves from being a technical add-ition to the interview to enhance its effectiveness to becoming a significantly more complex component in the process.

The extent to which each of the protagonists in this three-way relation-ship are able fully to trust the other two persons may determine the capacity to which the client is helped. Figure 5.7 may make this part clearer.

- To what extent can the client dare to reveal or be more of their 'real selves', to trust the counsellor and interpreter more?
- To what extent can the interpreter understand the work of the counsellor and become an ally in the therapeutic process?
- To what extent can the counsellor skilfully incorporate all these additional facets within the counselling encounter without becoming sabotaged by the demands of this situation?

The above points serve to illustrate how working with an interpreter can complicate the counselling process. These challenges do not deny, however, the critical importance of having translation facilities available in certain cir-cumstances. Counsellors do need to consider very carefully how to manage such three-way situations in order that they can fully involve interpreters and prepare clients for the impact of this new working situation.

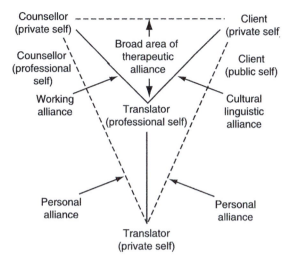

**Figure 5.7**  The personal and professional dimensions of the various working alliances.

A distillation of good practice derived from several sources suggests the following.

- Establish a good working relationship with the interpreter (Monach 2004).
- Explain how you, as the therapist, want the interpreter to work. (Blackwell 2005: 86). Where possible, offer the interpreter some clear guidelines for working together (p. 87).
- Recognize that the interpreter may have his own concerns and anxieties.
- The therapist needs to maintain the senior role (p. 86).
- Draw upon the interpreter's knowledge and experience as a resource, but do not use it uncritically or unquestioningly (p. 86).
- Spend time with the interpreter after the session to discuss what happened and to help the interpreter understand the work. Such an opportunity affords the possibility for the interpreter to contribute ideas and insights of her own (p. 87).

In groupwork it is recognized that harmony (and disharmony) within the facilitating team can become played out within the dynamics of the group being worked with. This phenomenon is useful to bear in mind, as a metaphor for the potential consequences of the therapist–interpreter alliance. Sadly, agencies and therapists may not recognize the value of dedicating additional time to the establishment of a 'good-enough' working alliance between the two professionals. However, such time together (beforehand) is likely to be reflected in the quality of the therapeutic endeavour on the client's behalf.

Again, after the interview/s, time spent together is likely to prove of great benefit. There may also be occasions where the interpreters may require additional support as a consequence of their vicarious exposure (through the client) to troubling and traumatic material. To what extent the therapist or the agency should take on this 'supervisory' responsibility is a question that each service may have to determine. Some counselling agencies offer group supervision and support to their team's interpreters.

Seeking the balance of authority, cooperation, support and professional respect with interpreters can prove a challenging scenario in itself. At worst, the various complex dynamics (e.g. of 'oppression', projection, fear, identification, etc.) that might get played out within the therapist–client dyad might also become apparent within the therapist–interpreter dyad and the interpreter–client dyad. Appropriate and due care and recognition, by both therapists and the agencies they work within, is required to fully optimize the value of interpreters within the therapeutic relationship.

## Paralinguistics

> The learning of another's language is not enough ... unless you understand the subtle cues implicit in language, tone, gesture and expression . . . you will not only consistently misinterpret what is said to you, but you may offend irretrievably without knowing how or why.
>
> (Hall 1976b)

Paralinguistics is the name give to the manner in which language is voiced. It comprises aspects of language which include accent, tone, volume, pitch, sighs, ums and ahs, grunts and silences.

Gumperz *et al.* (1981) also use the term 'prosody' which incorporates intonation, pitch and rhythm, pronoun preferences and the way information is structured in discourse. Clearly, all these have an effect on the interpretation of meaning and intent.

Confirming the quote by Hall above, Gumperz and his colleagues acknowledge the subconscious control of these features in speech. Additionally, speakers cannot use, interpret or often even recognize any alternative system to their own. 'Prosodic' conventions, therefore, when not shared (e.g. in a counselling encounter where both persons have different linguistic origins), can cause considerable misunderstandings.

The systematic and long-term research by Gumperz *et al.* has been most important in identifying various processes of paralinguistic convention that serve to irritate and miscommunicate between persons of differing cultural backgrounds. A BBC television programme made in the early 1980s provided a demonstration of a particular form of indirect racial discrimination that can occur as a result of 'prosodic' features in speech. Various scenes are depicted in the programme in which the ebb and flow of interpersonal communication between two people of differing cultural backgrounds is monitored. Each conversation that is shown (a transaction in a bank, a social security interview and a job interview) demonstrates the adverse effects of culturally different patterns of intonation in sentences and how speeches are structured.

As a result of implicit judgements, irritations and miscommunications felt and made by the interviewer (most often, in the UK situation, a person from the majority white culture), the culturally different client is likely to suffer indirect discrimination as a consequence of being misunderstood.

Recent research in sociolinguistics shows that a major contributory factor in this type of indirect discrimination can be the result of subconscious processes of evaluation during conversation on the part of majority and minority users of English. In this process, both parties tend to judge the other's behaviour in terms of criteria that they do not share and do not verbalize. These criteria have to do with the way we assess the quality and adequacy of what is said (Gumperz *et al.* 1981).

These findings reveal that the learning of another's language is often not enough to enable us to communicate successfully. One also needs to understand the subtle cues implicit in language, tone, gestures and expression, if consistent misinterpretation and irretrievable offence is to be avoided.

A simple example of the adverse effects of paralinguistics is quoted in Hall concerning the loudness with which one speaks (1976a). In Saudi Arabian cultures, in discussions among equals, the men attain a decibel level that would be considered aggressive, objectionable and obnoxious in the United States. Loudness connotes strength and sincerity amongst Arabs; a soft tone implies weakness and deviousness. Personal status also modulates voice tone. Lower classes lower their voices. Thus, if a Saudi Arab shows respect to an American he lowers his voice. Americans 'ask' people to talk more loudly by raising their own voices. The Arab then has his status confirmed and thus talks even more quietly. Both are misreading the cues!

## Non-verbal communication

> For in the final analysis every important cultural gesture comes down to a morality, a model for human behaviour concentrated into a gesture.
>
> (Hesse 1979: 44)

As with the earlier two sections of this chapter, non-verbal behaviour, as a communication system, can often cause miscommunication across cultures.

Aspects of non-verbal behaviour have already been covered in Chapter 4, namely the uses of space and the concepts of time. Other significant areas still require articulation. Amongst these are included patterns of eye contact, styles of dress, bodily signals, emotional displays, greetings behaviours, other forms of self-presentation (e.g. gift giving and visiting cards), rituals and facial expressions.

Argyle (1975) focused some attention on the problematic dichotomy between the biological and cultural origins of non-verbal communication. He asserts that there is good evidence that some bodily signals are biological. These signals apply to the main facial expressions and to laughing and crying (p. 74). He also quotes Eibl-Eibesfeldt (1972) who has found similar evidence of the universality of the 'eyebrow flash', in which eyebrows are raised to a max-imum extent for about one-sixth of a second, in greeting and flirting. However, there is some cultural variation even in these bodily signals. One dimension in which cultures vary, therefore, is in the extent to which facial expressions are restrained or shown freely.

Gestural signals present a rather different picture and often reflect and emphasize the cultural component of communication. Thus La Barre (1964) has listed the different hand movements with special meanings used in differ-ent cultures; a gesture from one culture would be meaningless in most other cultures. An important component to notice here is that though various cultures practise similar bodily movements, the meanings of such movements are very specific to each culture.

Vaughan (1977) has cited several examples of non-verbal communication from a dominant cultural perspective in the UK (p. 39):

> . . . In Ghana, our thumbs-up sign meaning OK, that's alright, fine, great etc. is a grave insult which will attract severely disapproving glances, perhaps even a spell in prison. Our nod of the head for 'yes' and shake for 'no' have exactly the opposite meaning in Japan. To accept something with one hand, especially the left is greatly dis-respectful in many, if not all African countries where children are taught very early to give and accept with both hands. Also in some countries you only eat with your right hand as the left hand is used for toilet purposes. Our ways of attracting attention may also appear rude to someone who uses their hands differently.

## 'Syncing'

Hall (1976a) cites studies of the use of movements in conversations between people. He uses the term 'syncing' from the observation that when two people talk to each other their movements often become synchronized. Hall suggests that in viewing films in slow motion, looking for synchrony, one realizes that what we know as dance is really a slowed down stylized version of what human beings do whenever they interact. These studies suggest that 'syncing' is panhuman. From this it appears that syncing is perhaps the most basic element of communication and the foundation upon which all subsequent speech behaviour rests.

Other aspects of this research revealed that very young English children 'synced' with Chinese children just as well as they did with English. As people grow older, however, there are indications that people 'sync' within, and are tied to each other by, hierarchies of rhythms that are culture-specific and expressed through language and body movement. Thus kinesics (body movements) are culturally determined and must be viewed against a cultural backdrop. Hall suggests that 'syncing' as a process of natural rhythm or 'dance' can affect people in their everyday situations; thus, for workers, when the talk slows, the work slows; it is also well known that sea shanties and work songs established rhythms of work. Hall also analysed slow motion films of children in school playgrounds and noticed that 'pan-playground syncing' can occur (despite a lot of children playing various games) and also that when syncing was absent or disturbed, socially disastrous effects were the result.

Given the possibility of 'syncing' in such a macro-situation, Hall provides us with another theoretical understanding of the occurrence of 'atmosphere' in concerts and dances that are a success. He recognizes that music and dance operate as extension transference of syncing. If audience and artist are syncing successfully, they are part of the same process, a socially rewarding experience.

Though interesting, the above section may appear of only peripheral interest to us. However, the notion of 'syncing' within a counselling situation clearly has enormous implications to the quality of communication that occurs. The counsellor's task in a transcultural situation may be somewhat more difficult, however, owing to the culturally limited patterns that dictate the synchronous rhythms. Nevertheless, the degree to which a sense of synchronization is achieved in the ebb and flow of a counselling interview between client and counsellor may be an important indicator as to the effectiveness of what is happening therapeutically.

# 6 Western theories of counselling and psychotherapy: intentions and limitations

My patients and their problems are not entirely separable from the outside environment they have created and in which they function. With a good conscience, I, as the psychotherapist, cannot divorce my patients from their social and cultural background; they are, after all, a specific group of people who have reacted in a specific way to their problems . . . a human being does not live in a sterilized plastic bubble . . .

(Cooper 1984: 314)

## Introduction

Therapists in Britain are profoundly and inevitably influenced in their counselling practice by therapeutic theory. The theories by which they operate are often acquired through the therapists' original training programme and then reinforced or modified by their working environments. Thus, counsellors are significantly influenced in the ways they approach, reflect upon and predict the outcome of their work by the tutorial and theoretical influences they were exposed to whilst in training or in post. These influences may be described in terms of cultural imposition and acquisition. That is, the theories have been handed down by senior representatives of the culture (counselling lecturers) to the trainees or initiates who are then schooled in, and assessed according to their successful acquisition of such principles.

Many of the current theories of therapy are rooted, historically, in central European and more latterly North American culture. As such, these theories are culturally and historically bound and as a consequence also have limitations as to their applicability to all situations and persons in a multicultural/multiracial society.

The various therapeutic theories have been numbered as in excess of 400 distinct models (Karasu *et al.* 1984), though it is widely recognized that there are three or four broad categories or approaches into which the large number cited above can be fitted. Often described as the first, second and third forces in psychology/counselling, they represent psychoanalytic, behavioural and humanistic ways of viewing human beings and their problems (Mahrer 1989).

A fourth force was historically ascribed to theories involving trans-personal/metaphysical dimensions though, interestingly, in the United States, 'multiculturalism' has begun to be hailed by the same name, the fourth force (Pedersen 1991). This theme is revisited in later chapters. Given that the activity of 'transcultural counselling' will occur within each of the original four major theoretical styles (psychoanalytic, humanistic, behavioural and transpersonal), it seems wise to assert that a transcultural approach should underpin and inform each mode of therapeutic working.

Another analysis of therapeutic intentions is offered by Frey and Heslett (1975). They posit that the four goals – of facilitating insight, encouraging new action, appreciating affect and stimulating new thinking – can be placed in a matrix and the various models of therapy can be located between these axes. Again, transcultural therapeutic practice will constitute the arena in which the above therapeutic aims are pursued.

Though there clearly are limitations as to the unthinking applicability of these theories to the field of transcultural therapy, we do know that counselling approaches are generally seen as valid, relevant and effective in this culture at this time (McLeod 1993). Indeed, Wood (1990) has elaborated further on this theme of 'fit' between therapy and culture, recognizing the importance of cultural acceptability of the healing form. Describing counselling as a 'subtle but powerful ritual', he recognizes that the ritual may be on the cutting edge of cultural change. The relationship therefore between a culture and its healing rituals is an interesting and complex one. Society permits certain degrees of experimentation; indeed, some rituals may run counter to other important cultural values. Nonetheless the commanding principles of the ritual, the counselling process, are probably developed in response to emerging needs of the culture and may lose effectiveness over time. One example of this loss of effectiveness could well be part of the original raison d'être of this book and others on the same theme. That is, the current forms and modes of counselling and psychotherapy are not proving to be adequate in response to the changing and contemporary needs of a multicultural, multiethnic and multiracial society.

## The historic and cultural origins of counselling and psychotherapy

The historic and cultural origins of counselling are well presented by McLeod (1993: 8–16). Citing a range of sources, he asserts that the origins of counselling and psychotherapy as we know them today can be traced back to the beginning of the eighteenth century, which represents a turning point in the social construction of 'madness'. A shift occurred at this time, from dealing with problems encountered in living through religious perspectives implemented at community level towards the 'medicalization' and individualization of human difficulties.

This historic period incorporates the major changes involved in society moving from a predominantly rural/agricultural base to an industrial one. Through the industrial revolution, capitalism began to dominate economic and political life and the values of science began to replace those of religion. In addition, Albee (1977) has argued that this emerging capitalism required the development of a high level of rationality accompanied by repression and control of pleasure seeking. This required the development of a work ethic, an increase in personal autonomy and independence. The accompanying psychological shift that occurred was from a 'tradition-centred' society to one in which inner direction was emphasized. The philosopher Descartes had already laid a basis for this shift to secular individualism in the seventeenth century (Flew 1972). Through recognizing the movement from small rural communities where everyone knew everyone else and behaviour was monitored and controlled by others, to urban industrial societies where life was much more anonymous and internally focused, one may understand some of the underlying historic conditions that have led to contemporary forms of interpersonal help, which focus on the individual, inner life of the person.

Prior to the eighteenth century, people who suffered mental ill health would have been nursed by their extended families and local communities. The advent of larger urban areas, factory conditions, fragmentation of communities and greater anonymity between people eventually led to the establishment of workhouses and asylums, society-based responses. People who were deemed mad or insane were certainly not productive and in many cases were disruptive. It is not appropriate here to provide a wealth of detail of this period, interesting though it is, but it is crucial to understand that through this historical period the medical profession came to assume control over asylums (Scull 1975). The defeat of moral treatment can be seen as a key moment in the history of psychotherapy: science replaced religion as the dominant ideology underlying the treatment of the insane (McLeod 1993).

New medical–biological explanations for insanity were formulated and many different types of physical treatment were experimented with (Scull 1979). By the end of the nineteenth century psychiatry had achieved a dominant position in the care of the insane. According to Ellenberger (1970), the earliest physicians to call themselves psychotherapists were Van Renterghem and Van Eeden who opened a clinic of Suggestive Psychotherapy in Amsterdam in 1887.

## Altered states of consciousness and hypnosis

Through applying the theoretical constructs of ritual to the counselling process, Wood (1990) notes that the healing process provides the means for clients to enter an altered state of consciousness and offers a structure within which their personal experience may be constructively reorganized. There are a considerable number of references to altered states of consciousness in the next chapter, which deals with indigenous forms of healing, and McLeod (1993) also cites several sources that have observed this important use of trance states and altered states of consciousness in the healing rituals of traditional societies. Indeed, he asserts that the appearance of Mesmerism and hypnosis through the eighteenth and nineteenth centuries in Europe and their transformation into psychotherapy can be viewed as representing the assimilation of a traditional cultural form into modern scientific medicine. Instrumental in this process were the extraordinary contributions of the work of Sigmund Freud.

## Sigmund Freud and psychoanalysis

> Such is the influence of Freud's work on European and American thought and culture, even in the popular mind, that it is difficult to imagine that time when his ideas were so innovative and, indeed, shocking.
>
> (Jacobs 1984)

Sigmund Freud (1856–1939) was born in Freiberg, Czechoslovakia, to Jewish parents where he was one of a family of two boys and five girls. He apparently excelled at school and though his interests were 'directed more towards human concerns than natural objects', medicine itself, though he chose to pursue it as a career, had not been a natural choice.

He trained initially as a neurologist conducting research into the histology of nerve cells as part of his medical training (Nelson-Jones 1988). In the General Hospital of Vienna, as a physician, he gained experience in several departments and became an active researcher in the Institute of Cerebral Anatomy during which time he began to study nervous diseases. On the award of a travelling scholarship Freud went to Paris in 1885 to study under Charcot, whose research work was concerned with hysteria and who employed hypnotherapy as a major helping mechanism.

McLeod (1993) points out that whilst not 'denying the genius and creativity of Freud, it is valuable to reflect on some of the ways in which his approach reflected the intellectual fashions and social practices of his time'. For example:

1   Individual sessions with an analyst were an extension of normal practice of one-to-one doctor–patient consultations prevalent at that time.
2   Freud's idea of a unitary life-force (libido) was derived from nineteenth-century biological theories.
3   The idea that emotional problems had a sexual cause was widely accepted in the nineteenth century.
4   The idea of the unconscious had already been employed not only by the hypnotists but also by other nineteenth-century writers and philosophers.

(McLeod 1993: 12)

'Freud's distinctive contribution', McLeod continues, 'can probably be regarded as his capacity to assimilate all of these ideas into a coherent theoretical model which has proved of great value in many fields of work.' Indeed, he has been described as 'striding like a colossus over the twentieth century'. His work has influenced many fields including psychology, philosophy, literature, literary and art criticism, psychiatry and social work practice. Words and phrases such as 'Freudian slip', the death instinct, the pleasure principle, defence mechanism and many more derive from his original works.

Predating both the humanists and the behaviourists and thus perhaps laying a basis or form conceptualizing psychotherapy, Freud developed his theoretical and clinical work in two major areas: first, in the art, technique and practice of psychotherapy and second, in the theoretical development of ideas and concepts on the formation and nature of personality.

Nelson-Jones (1988) lists some of the major concepts and ideas developed by Freud. These include: the pleasure principle, the instincts, the unconscious and consciousness, the structure of mental apparatus (id, ego, super-ego), anxiety, psychical energy and bisexuality. In relation to the development of personality he wrote about infantile sexuality and amnesia, sexual development, identification, defence mechanisms (repression, sublimation, reaction-formation, denial, fixation, regression projection) and the development and perpetuation of neuroses. In developing psychoanalysis he used different techniques including hypnosis, free association, resistance, interpretation, interpretation of dreams, and wrote extensively on the therapeutic relationship between patient and therapist (technically named as transference and counter-transference).

Jacobs (1984) reminds us that Freudian theory arose from psychotherapy and not from formal research, adding the rider by Winnicott (1965: 26): 'It is more difficult for an analyst to be truly original than for anyone else, because everything we say, truly has been taught us yesterday, i.e. by patients!'

The extraordinary range of hypotheses developed by Freud and listed above dramatically extended the understanding of psychological complexity into the 'darker recesses of the soul'. During the same period new scientific discoveries which radically changed our view of the world were also being made. These included radioactivity, the nuclear atom, quantum theory, the rediscovery of Mendel's law of inheritance and the science of genetics. There is no doubt that Freud was therefore in the vanguard of scientific development, contributing to the major paradigm shifts that occurred in scientific development in the early decades of this century (Clark 1980).

One of the key developments in the move from psychoanalysis, which by and large was only accessible to the middle and upper classes, to counselling and psychotherapy as we know it today was the emigration of psychoanalysis to the United States (McLeod 1993).

> The rise of fascism in Europe led to several prominent analysts . . . moving to New York and Boston where they found a willing clientele. Compared to Europe, American society demonstrated a much greater degree of social mobility, with people being very likely to live, work and marry outside their original neighbourhood, town, social class or ethnic group. There were therefore many individuals who had problems in forming satisfactory relationships or having a secure sense of personal identity. Moreover the 'American Dream' insisted that everyone could better themselves and emphasized the pursuit of happiness of the individual as a legitimate aim in life. Psychotherapy offered a fundamental, radical method of self-improvement.
>
> (McLeod 1993: 13)

## Behaviourism and the development of cognitive-behavioural therapy

American academic psychologists had become very interested in and influenced by behaviourism at the end of the First World War and were consequently somewhat resistant to the invasion of psychoanalytic thought and practice mentioned above (as indeed they were to the development of the humanistic theories featured in the next section).

Based upon the work of the Russian psychologist Pavlov (1849–1936), who developed theories of behaviour through conditioning in his animal research using dogs, theorists such as John Watson and Frederick Skinner applied their attention to human psychology.

Nelson-Jones suggests that:

> as an overall theory the distinctive emphasis is on the overwhelming role of environmental contingencies in influencing the acquisition and perpetuation of behaviour. In its most radical form the

behavioural model sees human actions as derived solely from two sources: biological deprivations, such as hunger and sexual tension, and the individual's learning history.

(Nelson-Jones 1988: 108)

In contrast to other forms of psychological treatment which emerged largely from clinical practice, behaviour therapy was regarded by its founders as the applied branch of a basic science. Since it had proved possible to create phobias experimentally through classical conditioning (Watson and Rayner 1920), it was argued that all neurotic disorders could be seen as inappropriate learned responses which could be 'unlearned' through the application of procedures derived from the work of Pavlov and Skinner. Thus Wolpe (1958) defined this approach as the use of experimentally established principles of learning for the purpose of changing unadaptive behaviour (Mackay 1984).

According to the original tenets of behaviourism, only actions that are observable and measurable can be studied scientifically. Hence only client problems which are specific and externally observable can be treated. Broadly speaking, behaviour therapists have denied the importance or verifiability of intrapsychic processes (Feltham and Dryden 1993). A variety of treatment techniques have been developed including systematic desensitization, implosion and operant conditioning, and it has been noticed that behaviour therapy appears to be more successful in treating conditions such as obsessive-compulsive disorders, phobias and panic attacks.

Later work in the United States by Bandura (1969) and Kanfer and Phillips (1970) led to the development of cognitive change methods being used in conjunction with standard behavioural techniques. Feltham and Dryden (1993: 31) define cognitive-behavioural therapy as

an umbrella term for those approaches based as, related to or developing from behaviour therapy and cognitive therapy . . . the core concept of cognitive-behavioural therapy is that beliefs about events in our lives are open to examination and change, and that changing beliefs results in greater control of our lives and reduction in dysfunctional behaviour. A hallmark of all these approaches is their clinical insistence on changing behaviour through the interrelationship of cognition and behaviour.

The technology of early forms of behaviour therapy has now given way to the development of effective coping strategies: 'Technology has been replaced, to a large extent, by talking treatments' (Mackay 1984).

A model of human beings, as depicted by the cognitive behavioural construct, is someone who is concerned to see themselves as being in control of their environment, both in their internal and external worlds. They are happiest when they have evolved a clear plan for living, when their body behaves as they want it to and when they have the skills and aptitudes necessary to achieve the goals they set themselves (Mackay 1984). This 'success and control-focused' model is certainly consistent with a view of western individuals held by Palmer (1991) who also extends this concept to a western belief that nature itself exists to serve individuals.

## Humanistic psychology

> That school of psychology which, in contrast to psychoanalytic and behavioural psychology, emphasizes human goodness, potentiality and wholeness. Sometimes called 'third force psychology', humanistic psychology is made up of the approaches of Rogers, Perls, Reich, Moreno, Schutz, Assagioli and others. Humanistic psychology has been called abundance-orientated (positive and forward-looking) rather than deficiency-orientated (preoccupied with pathology). It is inclined towards experiment, co-operation and the stretching of boundaries. It spans therapeutic work from the intrauterine to the spiritual . . .
>
> Feltham and Dryden (1993)

Similar to the previous sections on psychoanalytic and behavioural thought, and as indicated in the above quote, there now exists a vast range of theories that can be described as humanistic approaches. A few of these humanistic theories of psychotherapy are summarized below.

### Transactional analysis

Eric Berne (1910–70), despite many years of psychoanalytic training following a medical training, was apparently spurred on to develop TA after experiencing very long delays in the assessment of his suitability to become an analyst (Collinson 1984). Berne's image of the person was in a sense contradictory. He saw each person as capable of being in charge of her own destiny, of almost instinctively wanting to attain autonomy (or rather reattain autonomy), for autonomy is the province of the uncorrupted child before its life is invaded by the 'trash' of negative parental influences. Autonomy, according to Berne (1968), is manifested by the release or recovery of three capacities: awareness, spontaneity and intimacy.

### Rational emotive therapy

Albert Ellis, the founder of RET, developed his approach to therapy through reflection upon and then application of theories of philosophy. Having trained originally within the analytic tradition he is reputed to have been disappointed by the long-term results of his patients (Dryden 1984).

RET holds that humans are essentially hedonistic; their major goals are to stay alive and to pursue happiness efficiently and, enlightened by the fact that they live in a social world, they have the capacity to be rational (which helps them achieve their goals), though they have a tendency toward irrationality. Ellis acknowledges that humans are enormously complex organisms and constantly in flux. Humans can best achieve by pursuing their goals actively.

### Personal construct therapy

This particular, and indeed very scientific, approach to psychotherapy was developed by George Kelly who, it is argued by Fransella, was never convinced of the dominant doctrine of behaviourism he first learnt as a student. Interestingly, he took a first degree in physics and mathematics before going on to gain a masters degree in educational sociology, a bachelors degree in education and finally a PhD in psychology (Fransella 1984).

His model of the person is thus couched in the language of science, as is his whole theory. His theory, however, is based on the philosophy of constructive alternativism and acknowledges the constant state of motion of both humans and reality.

His model of human beings posits that:

- we are active beings;
- we approach the world not as it is but as it appears to be;
- we approach the world as if we are scientists;
- we have theories about how and why things happen, we erect hypotheses derived from these theories and we put them to the test and check their validity;
- we can come to understand ourselves and others in psychological terms through studying the psychological constructs we have evolved in order to help us predict events in our personal worlds.

Fransella (1984) believes that Kelly's work bears a close resemblance to existentialist thinking but notes interestingly that there is no evidence that translations of Sartre or other existentialist writers were available during the period in which he was developing his theories in the United States.

### Existential therapy

Existential therapy is still considered by Van Deurzen-Smith (1984) to be in its 'early formative stages', having its origins in existential and phenomenological philosophy. Significant thinkers inspiring these philosophies include

Kierkegaard, Neitzsche, Husserl, Heidegger, Sartre, Merleau-Ponty and Camus. Early applications of existential theory to psychotherapy were made by Binswanger in Switzerland, Minkowski in France and more recently by Boss (van Duerzen-Smith 1984: 153–4). Indeed, she argues that in the United States Rollo May, Irving Yalom, Carl Rogers, Fritz Perls and Albert Ellis developed certain existential and phenomological ideas within their therapeutic models.

The tenets of existential therapy can thus be summarized as follows: humans define themselves not by essence but by existence; it is only in the way in which I choose my actions and my existence that I define myself as I become. The being of humans is closer to nothingness. It can only come into existence by choosing a particular way to fill the nothingness that exists both inside and outside people.

The tasks we face in life are broadly categorized into our relations with

- the Umwelt (the world around us);
- the Mitwelt (the world with others);
- the Eigenwelt (our own world);
- the Uberwelt (the world above).

However, under normal conditions society encourages the perpetuation of false self-adaptation and therefore of psychological disturbance. Our western economy is based on the craving for falsehood and illusion: machines and appliances, houses and clothes are over-produced in order to satisfy the urgency of escape from reality. Our task then, as humans, is to face the world with authenticity and relinquish the deceptions of society, to clarify our inner value systems and to come to terms with life by relying on our inner selves.

## The person-centred approach

This approach was developed by the late Dr Carl Rogers and emerged from his own clinical experiences, which in his early career had been influenced by analytic thinking as applied to diagnosis and treatment. Both Kirschenbaum (1979) and Thorne (1984) chart the development of Rogers's thinking and formative experiences that led to the significant publication *Client-centred Therapy* in 1951 (Rogers [1951] 1987).

Rogers is perhaps best known for his theory of therapy, which was developed and refined through substantial research, and perhaps less well known for his theory of personality development. A study of these two strands – the psychology of personality development and the therapeutic approach – reveals a direct connection between the two.

The single motivating factor in Rogers's theories is the notion of the actualizing tendency (Rogers 1959). All living organisms are subject to this inherent tendency to maintain and enhance their growth. Very early in life human beings develop a self-concept, which, dependent upon early experiencing, can develop at odds to the overall development of the whole organism. Thus, conflicts arise between the actualizing tendency and the self-concept, creating dissonance and disturbance for the person. Rogers's concentration upon the values of acceptance and empathy in therapy directly counters the person's earlier experiencing that has resulted in internalizing external conditions of worth.

Thus, person-centred therapists start from the assumption that both they and their clients are trustworthy, this trust emanating from the belief in the actualizing tendency and its instinctive movement in humans towards the constructive accomplishment of inherent potential. The therapist's task, then, is to provide the therapeutic conditions for psychological growth, conditions that offer the client the opportunity to review and validate his own experiencing and to move away from dependency upon his internalized beliefs of external values.

Using Pedersen's ten frequent assumptions of cultural bias in counselling (see the section entitled 'Further frequent assumptions' later in this chapter), Usher (1989) evaluated client-centred theory for its cultural relevance. She found that six assumptions underlying the theory were culturally biased. The biased assumptions were: an emphasis on both individualism and independence; a here-and-now time orientation; minimal focus on external influences; abstract concepts that are meaningless or offensive to minority clients; and a narrow theoretical foundation. Ridley (1995) notes that Usher's critique of Rogerian theory is an excellent model for examining cultural bias in other theories. The critique is particularly noteworthy in the light of Rogers's strong ideographic stance. If cultural bias can be found in his theory, he asserts, the relevance of other theories (to transcultural therapy) can certainly be questioned.

Uniquely, amongst the earlier theorists featured in this chapter, Rogers also left valuable recordings of his work. Amongst several demonstration interviews that Carl Rogers recorded (filmed interviews that have both been extensively played to trainee therapists as well as providing the basis for analyses of therapeutic work) are two interviews he conducted with an African American client. Entitled *The Right to be Desperate* and *Carl Rogers Counsels a Client on Hurt and Anger*, these two videos, originally recorded in 1977, have been critically reviewed in a new book (Moodley *et al.* 2004). Though some other contemporary theorists to Rogers also recorded demonstration tapes, these particular sessions offer a demonstration of cross-ethnic therapy from a client-centred therapist's perspective. They thus constitute an invaluable resource for historical and theoretical critique.

Rogers also recorded two further demonstration interviews with black clients, one American and one British. This later American video was a recording made on a single hand-held camera at a college meeting and thus lacks 'televisual' quality, but nevertheless offers a view of Rogers some years later than the first recordings referred to above. The video recorded in Britain was made within a training course but is not publicly available.

In short, the original recordings by Rogers and the subsequent book by Moodley *et al.* (2004) provide a unique and contemporary analysis of the challenges inherent in cross-ethnic therapy. There is no doubt, as evidenced by many of the chapter writers in the above book, that Rogers's work with these clients in effective and therapeutic. However, analyses of the first two videos (mentioned above) revealed that the therapist's non-recognition of the client's racial heritage in his responses, despite the client's own references to this aspect of his identity, would have restricted the efficacy of their work together. 'Race avoidance' by the therapist can both restrict the extent to which clients can utilize the therapeutic relationship and may speed up client withdrawal from the process (Thomson and Jenal 1994).

### Multimodal therapy

Palmer (2002), Ridley (1984, 1995) and Ponterotto (1987) recommend multimodal therapy as a flexible approach suitable for treating minority clients. The approach rests upon the assumption that unless seven discreet but interactive modalities are assessed, treatment will probably overlook significant concerns (Lazurus 1989). These modalities are defined as follows: behaviour, affective responses, sensory reactions, images, cognitions, interpersonal relationships, drugs and other biological interventions. Ponterotto added an eighth modality to this list when he proposed that the arena of 'interaction with the oppressive environment' also needs to be addressed when counselling ethnic minority clients.

The approach is extremely eclectic as it employs techniques used within many different therapies. Palmer (2002: 62–3) cites an extensive array of 57 techniques and interventions commonly used in multimodal therapy. These span from psychodrama to biofeedback, from hypnosis to yoga, from bibliotherapy to focusing and so on. In addition Palmer asserts that these interventions could also include traditional healing practices or at least referral to another therapist who is qualified to do this work.

Somewhat contrary to Rogers's person-centred approach, multimodal counsellors are expected to adopt their interpersonal style and approach to the counselling relationship. Defined by the term 'authentic chameleon' (Lazurus 1995), therapists are encouraged to develop differing styles of interaction with different clients. This therapist behavioural range includes the counsellor variously being more or less directive, warm or cool, formal or informal and so on. The idea is that counsellors, in exhibiting different parts of themselves, will meet client expectations more accurately, thus contributing to the enhancement of the working relationship.

## An overview and critique emanating from the above models of therapy

In preparing this chapter, we were struck by the cumulative impact of the cultural values embedded in this wide range of counselling theories, which are briefly described above.

The principal points or cultural beliefs emanating from them are as follows.

- Individuals are in charge of their own destiny.
- Humans are in a constant state of flux, of movement, of 'becoming'.
- There is a requirement to be active in one's life, not passive.
- The process of growth through therapy is to throw off or shed the effects of parental, family and community influences that have had perceived negative effects.
- The challenge is to live authentically in the social world, to be truly oneself.
- As human beings we have scientific/rational tendencies.
- The world is as we perceive it to be (all the theories agree on this notion).
- The sanctity of personal authority is not questioned, which implies that all parental and cultural values are open to questioning.
- The concept of personal choice is highly valued.

Several of these themes are gathered within the following quotes from Samuels who, in describing Jung's concept of individuation, states that

> The essence of individuation is the achievement of a personal blend between the collective and universal on the one hand and, on the other, the unique and individual. It is a process, not a state; save for the possibility of regarding death as an ultimate goal, individuation is never completed and remains an ideal concept.
>
> (Samuels 1985: 101)

> Individuation can also be taken to mean 'Being oneself', i.e. who one 'really is', 'achieving one's potential', etc.
>
> (p. 103)

McLeod acknowledges such culturally determined influences when he writes

> Freud had lived in a hierarchically organized, class-dominated society, and had written from a world-view immersed in classical scholarship

and biological science, informed by a pessimism arising from being a Jew at a time of violent anti-semitism. There were, therefore, themes in his writing that did not sit well with the experience of people in the USA. As a result there emerged in the 1950s a whole series of writers who reinterpreted Freud in terms of their own cultural values . . . Many of the European analysts who went to the USA . . . were also prominent in reframing psychoanalysis from a wider social and cultural perspective, thus making it more acceptable to an American clientele.

(McLeod 1993: 14)

Parallel to the range of individual therapies addressed briefly above, our contention is that the wide range of other therapies that have been developed during recent decades to service couples, families and groups similarly reflect some of the dominant cultural values embedded in American and some specific European cultures.

By contrast with older societies in which there may have been only one form of healing, contemporary society has within it many different approaches and practitioners. In part, this huge variety can be seen to be consistent with the ideals of market forces, capitalism and personal choice.

By far the greater number of counselling contacts are made at the present time through telephone counselling agencies, in situations where the client has much more control over how much he or she is known and how long the session will last (McLeod 1993: 17). This reflects the cultural values depicted above combined with one aspect of widely available modern technology – the telephone. Indeed, as society and science move on, some of the technical developments emerging, for example, within computer development and information technology will mean that newer forms of therapeutic response will have to be developed, as has already been noted through email systems and the internet (Neely 1995). Indeed, the use of technology itself will not reduce or remove the complexity of cultural components, as has been demonstrated already in the field of international telephone and television conferencing.

Whilst it can only be briefly addressed here, Thompson (1992) draws our attention to the ascription of abuse and deprivation, not onto individual clients but onto the very cultural context from which they emanate. In her opinion abuse and deprivation are a holding pattern of our society and culture and are embedded in the collective unconscious. Our culture, itself, therefore has features that are psychonoxious for both families and individuals within it.

## Further frequent assumptions of cultural bias in counselling

The above subheading is slightly transposed from the title of an article by Pedersen published in 1987 in which he lists ten frequent assumptions that most consistently emerged in the literature about multicultural counselling and development. These assumptions reflect European and American culture and are propagated by social scientists through textbooks, research findings and psychological theories. These are often presented as if they represent a world norm and certainly do not reflect the numerical reality that many more peoples in the world are in cultures enjoying non-western perspectives.

An examination of the assumptions that underlie our beliefs and practices 'must become an important part of the curriculum in the development of counsellors for a world that includes many cultures' (Pedersen 1987a). He lists them as follows.

1   Assumptions regarding normal behaviour.
2   Emphasis on individualism.
3   Fragmentation by academic discipline.
4   A dependence on abstract words and technology.
5   Overemphasis on independence.
6   Neglect of clients' support systems.
7   Dependence on linear thinking.
8   A focus on changing the individual, not the system.
9   Neglect of history.
10  Dangers of cultural encapsulation.

To a certain extent, the previous section has already addressed points 2, 5, 6 and 8 from Pedersen above. The following paragraphs, therefore, offer partial accounts of Pedersen's other points.

### Assumptions regarding normal behaviour

There is an assumption that all people share a common measure of 'normal' behaviour. 'People frequently presume', Pedersen states, 'that when I describe a person's behaviour as "normal", this judgement is meaningful and implies a particular pattern of behaviours by the normal person.' Implied within this assumption also is that the definition of normal is more or less universal across social, cultural, economic and political backgrounds. Painful experiences of inaccurate diagnosis within psychiatry are reported in Thomas and Sillen (1972).

As Kuhn (1962) pointed out, when a principle of scientific theory has become accepted by society, it functions as a selective screen for defining problems and evidence that coincidentally fit within the scientific principle. Evidence that does not fit the pattern is rejected as irrelevant or too chaotic to consider. Society is thus protected from reality by the fixed form of abstract principles. Research data itself becomes something used to defend abstractions that posit stereotypes and inaccurate generalizations about normality. Quite obviously, what is considered normal behaviour will change according to culture, context, situation, who is judging and why, and so on.

### Fragmentation by academic discipline

Pedersen is referring here to the complexity and variety of theoretical frameworks that exist for different professionals – doctors, theologians, sociologists, counsellors and so on. Such frameworks not only differentially define clients' difficulties but are held within each discipline. Seldom do helpers exchange insights, information or questions between the disciplines as they should. Further, the clients with their problems do not necessarily fit into these artificial constructs and indeed they may actually confront directly the professional's beliefs about them and the helping method.

### Dependence on abstract words

Quoting Hall (1976a), Pedersen introduces the concept of high- and low-context cultures. In a high-context culture, people search for and expect meaning to be embedded in the context of different situations. Low-context cultures, on the other hand, relate concepts of meaning to words and phrases. Western cultures, within Hall's theoretical framework, are low-context and as such there has been a considerable development of abstract words and concepts within many disciplines. Such abstractions are often difficult if not impossible to comprehend if one has originated from outside this culture.

### Dependence on linear thinking

Linear thinking is described as the process whereby each cause has an effect and each effect is tied to a cause. The assumption is that everyone depends on this causative relationship. 'How then can counsellors adapt counselling to a cultural context', Pedersen asks, 'where the cause and the effect are seen as two aspects of the same undifferentiated reality (as in the concept of yin and yang) with neither cause nor effect being separate from the other?' In some cultures events can be described independently of their relationship to surrounding, preceding or consequent events.

### Neglect of history

History has an appropriate relevance for a proper understanding of contemporary events. Many counselling approaches focus on the present even when some of the client data is based upon their own past. Counsellors are much less likely to attend to clients who share the history of their people, for example. In many cultures the connection between past and present history makes it necessary for counsellors to clearly understand the client's historical context in order to understand their present behaviour.

Pedersen, of course, is writing from an American background, acknowledging that counselling is a young profession in a young country. He suggests that counsellors therefore are less conscious of history than those who belong to nations with longer traditions. In the UK there is a slightly different combination of these two factors: counselling is a much younger profession than in the USA and yet Britain has a long and complex history. This combination would be interesting to research in terms of its effects within therapy.

Pedersen believes that not only do counsellors lack a sufficient awareness of the ways in which people solved their problems in the previous thousands of years; they also lack the patience for a longer perspective in which the current situation may be transitional. Lacking respect for tried and tested ways in which a particular culture has dealt with personal problems, the preference or tendency will be towards trying out the latest trend or fad in counselling methods.

### Dangers of cultural encapsulation

The final assumption that Pedersen offers is that counsellors already know of their assumptions! Within a multicultural/multiracial society and as a consequence the counselling setting, counsellors need to recognize the danger of any closed, biased and culturally encapsulating system that promotes domination by an elitist group. If counsellors are unwilling to challenge their own assumptions they will be less likely to communicate effectively with persons of different cultural backgrounds.

## Suggested principles and steps for counsellors towards 'multicultural competency'

Charles Ridley (1995) suggests the following five principles and twelve steps as guides to successful multicultural practice. Under the guiding rubric of 'counsel idiographically', we are reminded that every client is unique, even when they apparently hail from similar origins, culturally, racially and ethnically.

Ridley's five principles are:

- Every client should be understood from his/her unique frame of reference (Rogers 1961).
- Nomothetic, normative information does not always fit a particular client.
- People are a dynamic blend of multiple roles and identities.
- The ideographic perspective is compatible with the bio-psychosocial model of mental health.
- The ideographic perspective is transtheoretical.

These are followed by Ridley's twelve steps for recommended counsellor behaviour:

- Develop cultural awareness.
- Avoid value imposition.
- Accept your naïveté as a 'multicultural counsellor'.
- Show cultural empathy.
- Incorporate cultural considerations into your counselling.
- Do not stereotype.
- Weigh and determine the relative importance of the client's primary cultural roles.
- Do not blame the victim.
- Remain flexible in your selection of intervention.
- Examine your counselling theories for bias.
- Build on the client's strengths.
- Do not protect clients from emotional pain.

These recommendations by Ridley stand well alongside other ideas for enhanced counsellor behaviour that are featured in the later chapter on training therapists to work with different client groups.

## Brief reflections on and of 'western' therapists

In a fascinating penultimate chapter of their edited book *On Becoming a Psychotherapist*, Dryden and Spurling (1989) present their analysis of the preceding ten chapters written by eminent psychotherapists from different theoretical backgrounds. The chapters offer personal and often moving accounts of some of the motivating experiences that contributed to their wishes to become psychotherapists.

A recurring theme in the writings of several of the therapists was that of the experience of being a 'stranger' or 'outsider' (p. 196). Many childhood experiences were recounted in which the combination of observing others in distress, feeling for them and a desire for intimacy featured. Often these experiences had led to a need to understand the nature of relationships. Several also discussed the experience of deeply understanding or knowing what others were going through as if their empathic qualities were already highly tuned. Some of these dimensions were construed as coming together in the practice of therapy as a form of detached intimacy.

Considerable emphasis was also placed upon the 'being' of the therapists and that this was construed to be as important as the doing, in relation to the clients. Images, perhaps, of the wounded healer abound here, as does the idea propounded by Dryden and Spurling of the self standing for the imprinting of theory. 'The language of the self is an expression of the need for theory in psychotherapy to be impure' (p. 207). The personality of the therapists and the extreme difficulties of fully explaining what happens in psychotherapy lend to this impurity.

Dryden and Spurling (1989) quote Chertok (1984) in considering the phenomenon of the relationship between client and therapist which runs through the history of psychotherapy: 'This relationship has taken many different forms and been called various things down through the ages: Mesmeric fluid, suggestion, transference, empathy, symbiosis and so on. But the fact is inescapable that, in spite of its long history, we still know very little about it.'

Many of the writers used metaphoric concepts such as process, rhythm, dance, journey in attempting to describe their work. Interestingly, it was also noted how psychotherapeutic language borrows and transposes ideas, ways of thinking, and metaphors from other traditions of thought, e.g. religion, politics and the narrative tradition. This apparent openness to other influences and systems of thought bodes well for therapists who are sincere in getting to grips with the challenge of understanding culturally different clients and their own systems of thought.

The nature of persons who become psychotherapists is extremely fascinating, as presented by this evidence, and further complicates the relationship between theory, practice and culture as embedded in the persona of the counsellor. The above brief data suggest that those who become therapists are potentially persons who have striven to understand the difficulties that have beset their lives, have had the capacity of being emotionally in tune with others, have also experienced their own distance or alienation from others and have attempted to transpose those experiences into a constructive helping mode, that of being a psychotherapist.

As a link to the next chapter it seems appropriate here to quote from Victor Turner, an anthropologist, who is describing a shaman in a traditional society (cited in Dryden and Spurling 1989). His description, perhaps, could be attributed to many psychotherapists today.

In many ways, he was typical of Nolembu doctors: capable, charismatic, authoritative, but excluded from secular office for a variety of reasons, some structural, some personal. He was the typical 'outsider' who achieves status in the ritual realm in compensation for this exclusion from authority in the political realm.

(Turner 1967: 371)

# 7 Non-western approaches to helping

A white woman kneels in the centre of a hardened cow-dung floor, surrounded by 100 or more Zulus. The Zulus wear an assortment of beads and animal skins, and they are dancing to an incessant drum beat which reverberates around the grass and mud hut. The woman is about 30 years old and is looking nervously at a white goat held upright in front of her by a couple of black youths. They spread open its legs as a razor-sharp short spear, an *assegai*, is pressed against the animal's belly. The goat lets out a terrified scream. A murmur of approval goes up from the spectators.

The *assegai* is plunged into the beast's heart, killing it swiftly. The woman bends down and puts her lips to the wound; the blood trickles down her chin. During the week this woman works as a state prosecutor. Today, in this remote 'kraal' in the rolling hills of Zululand, she has just completed her initiations as a witch doctor.

(Hobbs 1993)

## Introduction

The ways people cope, attempt to solve their problems and seek assistance are shaped by the social and cultural norms and the symbolic meanings of distress within their culture. Further, several authors have pointed out that differences do exist between cultures on what is even deemed problematic (Torrey 1972; Yui 1978; Herr 1987; Westwood 1990).

Five principles have been identified by Torrey (1972) as crucial to successful helping in any culture. These are that

- the client's problem is named;
- the personal qualities of the counsellor are extremely important;
- the client's specific expectations must be met;

- the counsellor must establish credibility through the use of symbols, skill or power; and
- the counsellor must apply certain techniques designed to bring about relief to the troubled client.

An immensely useful model of contextualizing healing activities is provided by Tseng and Hsu (1979) (already alluded to in Chapter 1), who assert that 'in all cultures at all times there have been four dominant modes of healing' (see Figure 7.1).

To recap briefly the matrix (Figure 7.1) depicts four major areas of concern and activity involved in the healing/helping process. In traditional healing practices healers have often worked in and with all four domains with their troubled 'clients'. We could imagine, then, a situation in which such a healer would listen and talk to the troubled person (socio-psychological), might prescribe medicines, lotions etc. (medicinal/physiological), recommend or instruct the client towards certain behaviours (natural bodily functioning) and pray or engage in spiritual ceremonies seeking divine blessing (supernatural intervention).

In contrast to the above very inclusive healing model, the western development of expertise (in which specialists concentrate upon more discrete areas of activity) has led to the separation of the four domains depicted above into medicine, priesthood, behaviourism and counselling/psychotherapy. From this perspective we gain an overview that indicates the relative impoverishment of the separation of any one healing form from the others as compared to traditional practices. According to this model a counsellor, a doctor, a priest

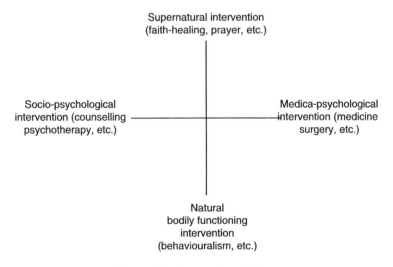

**Figure 7.1** Four healing activities.

or a behaviourist is only each addressing one quarter of the healing spectrum! A further complexity is that a multitude of theories of counselling and psychotherapy now exist (432 named theories according to Karasu *et al.* 1984). Therefore, in one quarter alone of the above healing matrix, there are over four hundred approaches!

Though a little dated, the views of Torrey (1972) still seem to obtain, in which he asserts that western-trained helping personnel (psychiatrists, social workers and trained counsellors) are socialized to see alternative forms of helping as inferior to their own. Such attitudes in the professional domain might mean that practitioners not only fail to respect other healers but also do not consult, refer to or indeed work in association with other healers on their clients' behalf. If we are truly concerned with maximizing the potential for helping culturally different clients and we know that those clients are also consulting different practitioners it seems incumbent upon us to support the belief systems and self-healing impetus of clients by being open to other healing approaches.

## Philosophic assumptions underlying world views

In an important article that asserts the importance of understanding the philosophic assumptions underlying world views (the deep structures of culture, as Jackson and Meadows (1991) term them), three sets of hypotheses are offered for understanding European, Asian and African conceptual systems of culture. These are described as follows.

The European system emphasizes a material ontology, with the highest value (axiology) placed on the acquisition of objects. External knowledge is assumed to be the basis of all knowledge (epistemology), and one knows through counting and measuring. The logic of this conceptual system is dichotomous (either–or), and the process is technology (all sets are repeatable and reproducible). The consequence of this conceptual system is an identity and self-worth that is based on external criteria (e.g. how one looks, what one owns, prestige and status symbols) (Myers 1988).

The Asian conceptual system emphasizes an ontology of cosmic unity, with the highest value (axiology) on the cohesiveness of the group. Internal and external knowledge is assumed to be the basis of all knowledge (epistemology) and is an integration of mind, body and spirit, which is considered to be three parts of the same thing (Cox 1988). The logic of this conceptual system is *nyaya* (a unity of thought and mind) and the process is cosmology (all sets are independently interrelated in the harmony of the universe). The consequence of this conceptual system is an identity and self-worth based on being and on an internal and external reality.

The African conceptual system emphasizes both a spiritual and material ontology with the highest value (axiology) on interpersonal relationships between women and men. Self-knowledge is assumed to be the basis of all knowledge (epistemology); one knows through symbolic imagery and rhythm. Therefore, the primary emphasis of the counselling pair should be building the relationship and recognizing the importance of the knowledge that the client has within himself or herself. The logic of this conceptual system is diunital (union of opposites), and the process is ntuology (all sets are interrelated through human and spiritual networks). The consequence of this conceptual system is an identity and self-worth that is intrinsic.

The above underlying systems of cultural assumptions will inevitably be embedded within the indigenous healing systems of those cultures. Let us now look rather more specifically at some different approaches.

## An overview of various treatment methods

In an attempt to review indigenous models of helping in 'non-western' countries, Lee *et al.* (1992) received completed questionnaires from mental health and related professionals in seven countries (Barbados, Korea, Nigeria, Pakistan, Singapore, Sudan and Zambia). Three categories of assumptions about the causes of psychological distress and behavioural deviance in these countries were reported: family dynamics, fate and possession by evil spirits. This study also revealed that two indigenous models of helping seemed to be pervasive. These are described as 'kinship systems' and 'spiritualism–religion'.

Within the first category of kinship systems the evidence suggested that the family plays the most significant role in the resolution of mental health problems. An underlying notion seems to be that the whole family shares the problem and suffers with the individual and it is the family that will help the disturbed individual. In many of the countries surveyed a great deal of stigma and shame was attached to mental illness and as a consequence it was only when the problem could not be contained that family members would seek other forms of help, often from within the extended family.

Beyond the family system community members also offer an abundance of support to troubled individuals. An example is given from Nigeria where large assemblies of 'clansmen' are brought together and are presented with an individual's problem. A group effort is then involved to solve the problem. Additionally, friendship was also noted as an important therapeutic tool, with friends becoming involved in the helping process.

The other dominant form of approach to helping that featured in this survey, that of 'spiritualism–religion', is also a key element in the various specific methods described later in the chapter. By contrast, western theories of counselling and psychotherapy have become secularized from religious beliefs and do not, in themselves, address this aspect of life, let alone use teachings or rituals from within a religious perspective.

In writing the previous sentence I am aware of being dangerously simplistic. There are western theories of therapy that do acknowledge the importance of spirituality (e.g. transpersonal, Jungian, psychosynthesis) but these tend to be in the minority in relation to the large number of therapies quoted previously in this chapter. Since the publication of the first edition, there does seem to have been an increasing interest and openness to the exploration of issues of spirituality in relation to therapy, as evidenced by increased publications, key conferences and supervision group dialogues (known by and reported to the author).

Great importance was placed by the respondents to the study by Lee *et al.* (1992) upon traditional healers who were identified by a variety of names such as shamans, medicine men, piris, fakirs, black magic experts, hakeem, motwaas, alfa and Sufis. Shamans tend to operate by entering an altered state of consciousness to contact and use an ordinarily hidden reality to acquire knowledge and power, and to help others (Harner 1990).

- Medicine men were reported as being popular and widespread in Brazil, Senegal, Nigeria, Zambia and Korea, prescribing herbs and other traditional medicines for both mental and physical illnesses.
- The piris and fakirs, mentioned above, are religious men of the Muslim faith (reported in Pakistan and Sudan) who use verses of the Koran in different ways to treat mental illness.
- The report revealed that black magic experts were also found in rural areas of Pakistan, claiming to have extraordinary powers that they can use to either help or harm others. Conceptualizing diagnosis in terms of evil spirits, such practitioners would often provide weekly visits and offer special magic words for individuals to wear or keep in their rooms to ward off the spells.
- The hakeem are traditional healers from Saudi Arabia who are generally found in small villages. They are called on to deal with various illnesses and their methods include dietary therapy and the use of coal on the nerves, each hakeem also being described as having a particular specialization.
- Motwaas are religious men also found in Saudi Arabia. They cite verses from the Koran and prescribe herbs to treat the mentally ill.
- Alfas are Nigerian spiritualists. There seems to be a trend in Nigeria to go to spiritual churches or religious healing houses in cases of distress. Alfas are the spiritualists in these traditional healing houses.

Recognition is made by Lee *et al.* (1992) of the tendency for these traditional systems to be more popular in rural areas in these countries than in urban communities, though even in urban areas there are reports of people being treated unsuccessfully by western adopted methods and reverting to traditional systems of belief for cure. Personally (and culturally) held systems of belief in relation to the cure of ills are obviously profoundly embedded in the individual and the collective psyche. Such belief systems cannot be easily accounted for and overcome by western technology as the parallel example of research into the surprising effectiveness of some placebo treatments in western countries powerfully indicates (Park and Covi 1965; Frank 1973).

## A study from anthropology

During a training day that I led at the University of Abertay (February 2005) on the subject of 'Cultural Dimensions of Counselling: Theory and Practice', some postgraduate students offered to enact a case originally published by Victor Turner, an anthropologist, in 1964. (This case is also discussed in Kareem and Littlewood 1992: 48–50.) Entitled An Ndembu doctor in practice', Turner (1964) describes the work of Lhembi, the Lhamba doctor with a troubled young man, Kamahasanyi. A multiplicity of reasons seem to underpin the 'client's' difficulties and physical complaints. He has recently suffered consistent bad luck in hunting successfully; he had experienced difficulty in being accepted in his mother's village of origin; he has experienced troubles in his marriage – his wife has been unfaithful, this constituting a threat to his authority in the village. He is also seen to be 'snobbish and unfriendly' by the villagers. As the obvious acting head of the village, he has lost all power of authority. The 'symptoms of his illness consisted of rapid palpitations of the heart, severe pains in the back, limbs and chest; and fatigue after short spells at work. He felt that people were always speaking things against him, finally withdrawing from village affairs and shutting himself up in his hut for long periods' (Turner 1964: 255).

Whilst the enactment of this scenario graphically illustrated (an interpretation of) a number of therapeutic themes and techniques pertinent to that part of Zambia in the 1950s, interesting parallels and questions might be drawn from this case for the application of therapeutic interventions within a 'western' setting. From the original account by Turner, acknowledgement is made of the use of 'private treatments' by those who are troubled – in this case the consultation of an herbalist (p. 231). However, what consistently emerges from this account is the simultaneous treatment response by the healer to both the troubled client and the community surrounding him, with its web of complex relationships, past hurts, gossip and grudges. This therapeutic process attends to the individual and his or her social context. Turner reports a series of seven rites that were performed by the doctor in relation to this 'client' over several months, a time duration that, to Turner, indicated the level of serious disturbance (p. 242).

Some key points of the treatment process are listed below. Where contemporary questions, parallel phenomena and other issues arise from the perspective of western theories of therapy, these are featured in italics. They are also presented with some trepidation and caution, as contrasts, inferences and comparisons are perilously easy to draw from the 'outsider's' position and may hold doubtful analogy with the original case (and its circumstances).

- The therapy takes place over a period of time. *(Medium to long-term work.)*
- 'Disease' is viewed not only as private or 'idiographic' but also within a public or social structural network. *(A considerable proportion of psychotherapeutic work is in response to clients' concerns about their relationship to significant others in their lives.)*
- 'Therapy then becomes a matter of sealing up the breaches in social relationships simultaneously with ridding the patient of his pathological symptoms' (Turner 1964: 231).
- Divination *(assessment?)* looks both backward to causation and forward to remedial measures (p. 232).
- 'Distant diviners are believed to give more reliable diagnoses than local ones' (p. 232). *(This might be a parallel to the common saying of the saviour not being recognized in his or her own land!)* However, Turner also notes that the particular healer in his account was capable and authoritative, but was excluded from secular office for a variety of reasons. 'He was the typical "outsider" who achieves status in the ritual realm in compensation for his exclusion from authority in the political realm' (p. 241). *(The parallel here with therapists in the west is strong: choosing to work within the therapeutic realm rather than in the outside world. Also, this point hints at the importance of 'boundaries'; (physical, psychological, social), a concept that is much considered in contemporary professional practice.)*
- 'The patient in any given cult ritual is a candidate for entry into that cult' (p. 232). *(Many clients are inspired to become therapists, either through their own previous suffering, e.g. the wounded healer idea or as a consequence of engagement in therapy.)*
- 'The particular "shade" (spirit) that had afflicted him in the first instance, when propitiated, becomes a tutelary who confers on him health and curative powers for that particular mode of affliction' (p. 233). *(A creative transformation is achieved through learning from the previous problem.)*
- '. . . Part of the process consists in the doctor's summoning kin of the patient . . . and inducing them to confess any grudges and hard feel-

ings they may nourish against the patient . . . The patient, too, must acknowledge his own grudges against his fellow villagers if he is to be . . . (cured)' (p. 236). *(This could be likened somewhat to the processes in social therapy, e.g. group work and family systems, though the extent to which western therapists might agree with the notion of inducing confessions might be debatable.)*

Turner concludes this account by noting that

stripped of its supernatural guise, Ndembu therapy may well offer lessons for western clinical practice. For relief might be given to many sufferers from neurotic illness if all those involved in their social networks could meet together and publicly confess their ill will toward the patient and endure in turn the recital of his grudges against them.
(1964: 263)

## Sufism

'Muslim Sufis' major role all over the world is to provide succour or relief to persons in distress and pain.' This is the opening sentence of Kemal's recent article explaining the Sufi tradition (1994) and from which the following details are taken.

There are several steps in the Sufi helping process, often carried out in Khangahs or seminaries, where the Sufis abide. The first step, after having been given food and shelter, is to see if there is something in the seminary to meet the troubled person's interest. The second step is to form a contact with the 'Master' (this title is applicable to both genders) which gives the person with the problem an opportunity to speak his mind. He can either be specific in defining his problem or he can talk at length, giving vent to his hurt and pain. This may be in one sitting or continue over a period. In this process the Master Sufi tries to 'understand the person's problems and the person within him'. Once it becomes clear to the Master what the problem basically is, the next step is to find out whether the person has the ability to see the conflict and resolve it.

There is an entire collection of Sufi literature (stories, parables, anecdotes, sayings) which can be used for the individual's help, to enable her to see the light. Through literature, the client is given enough information and facts to help her identify her own problem. As in any other form of counselling or analysis, the ability to see the truth and accept it takes time.

The next step is to give the individual a wider perspective and a broader idea of the role of human beings in the universe so that he can see his own role. What the Khangah does is to give the individual support and acceptance until the conflict or the influences of the society and the system are under-stood and she gains enough insight to face life and her role in it, with the proviso of returning to the Khangah should she so wish. Sufis also encourage the use of meditation exercises through which individuals are enabled to experience ascension of arc – in mystic terms this is also known as initiation, meditation, invocation, contemplation and actualization.

Knowledge according to the Sufis has three aspects: knowledge through communication, knowledge through observation and knowledge through experience. Sufism, as described above, offers a combination of nurture within residential settings, significant attention from a healer, the use of historical collected wisdoms and meditation exercises embedded within a religion/philosophic system that embraces a view of the world and humans within it.

## The healing processes of the !Kung hunter-gatherers

> A study of !Kung healing may suggest principles fundamental to human healing and development, shedding light on their origins and evolution.
>
> (Katz 1989b)

The following information is taken from the chapter by Richard Katz in Colleen Ward's edited book, *Altered States of Consciousness and Mental Health* (1989).

'Among the !Kung hunter gatherers of the Kalahari Desert, healing is a central community ritual with significance far beyond affecting a cure.' Katz proposes a definition of healing based on his anthropological work with this group as 'a process of transitioning towards meaning, balance, connectedness and wholeness' (p. 207). The healer serves as a vehicle to channel healing to individuals and the community, without accumulating power for personal use. As an aside, it is worth noting here that contemporary professional codes of ethics also embody this important principle.

The primary ritual among the !Kung, the all-night healing dance (which can happen as often as four times a month) epitomizes characteristics of sharing and egalitarianism, strong concepts in !Kung life. The healing power, or n/um is the most valued resource at the dance (and one of the most valued resources in all community life). As the healing dance intensifies, n/um ('energy') is activated in those who are healers, most of whom are amongst the dancers. As n/um intensifies in the healers, they experience !Kia ('a form of enhanced consciousness'), during which they heal everyone at the dance.

The intensified experience of !Kia (when the n/um has risen up and awoken the healer's heart) leads to an altered state of perception that facilitates a process of 'seeing properly', a capacity that allows the healer to locate and diagnose the sickness in a person. Sickness is then pulled out as healers bring their vibrating hands close to or in contact with a person. The healers are putting their n/um into the other person and at the same time pulling the sickness out of the other and into their own bodies. This is difficult, painful work. The sickness is then expelled from the healer.

Fiercely egalitarian, the !Kung do not allow n/um to be controlled by a few religious specialists, but wish it to be spread widely among the group. All young boys and most young girls seek to become healers. By the time they reach adulthood more than half the men and 10 per cent of the women have become healers. N/um, an unlimited energy, cannot be hoarded by any one person. A public, routine cultural event to which all have access, the healing dance establishes community, and it is the community, in its activation of n/um, that heals and is healed.

## Therapeutic use of altered states of consciousness in contemporary North American First Nations' dance ceremonials

The above title is that used by Wolfgang Jilek in his exposition of three different dance ceremonials in the edited book by Colleen Ward (1989). The following information constitutes the major elements identified in these rituals.

### Salish spirit dancing

The Winter spirit dances are the major ritual activity of the Salishan-speaking Indians of the Pacific Coast of North America. While much of Salish Indian culture crumbled, the ceremonial was performed clandestinely by older people, despite efforts by government, churches and school authorities to suppress this 'pagan' ritual in the nineteenth century. Spirit dancing was openly revived in the 1960s.

Today, in the revived ceremonial, the initiation itself is the way to acquire power for self-healing. The major purpose of the initiation process now is to cure serious psychosomatic, psychosocial behavioural disturbances of young Salish Indian people who are seen as suffering from spirit illness due to alienation from traditional 'Indian ways'. Salish ritualists consider American Indian persons suffering from depression, anxiety and somatic complaints that are unresponsive to western treatment, as well as young Amerindians with behavioural, alcohol and drug problems, as candidates for spirit dance initiation.

The death and rebirth myth is the central theme of the collective suggestions surrounding the spirit-dance initiation. According to contemporary

Salish theory, it is the spirit power that acts through the initiator on the initiates, and it is this spirit power, not the initiator, that cures the novices, burying their ailments and conflicts together with the old personality and at the same time giving them rebirth into a new life. A three-stage process of this therapeutic approach is discerned by Jilek and described as depatterning through shock treatment followed first by physical training and then by indoctrination.

The various stages of the initiation process are as follows. First, initiates are kept in a dark cubicle or 'smokehouse tent' within a longhouse for a period of usually ten days, during which time they are called and treated as 'babies'. They are bathed, fed, dressed and constantly attended by babysitters. Regression is thus imposed on the initiates, to a state of complete infantile dependency, who, within the uterine shelter of the darkened longhouse, hatch their power, prepared to grow with it into a more rewarding and healthier existence.

Through the four days of the depatterning process the initiates are blindfolded, subject to repeated and prolonged treatment of bodily seizure, immobilization of limbs, hitting, biting, and tickling, kinetic stimulation (being whirled about, lifted and dropped etc.) and intensive acoustic stimulation (loud drumming, rapid rhythms etc.). Initiates are also starved and fluid intake is restricted.

Then follows a phase of physical training which is associated with intense indoctrination and is 'supposed to make the baby strong'. Long runs, often in snow, and cold water swims constitute the main activities of this phase. Running in the longhouse is accompanied by drumming and chanting and clapping of the crowd. Released from their incubation the initiates 'feel their newly acquired power wherein the song bursts forth from them and these leaping steps of their first dance carry them through the longhouse'.

Jilek's analysis of the drumming rhythms of the Salish spirit dance reveals that the frequency cycles used are consistent with frequencies preponderant in ceremonies associated with trance behaviour, being effective in the production of trance states. Jilek concludes that this ceremony combines the following therapeutic modes:

- occupational/activity therapy;
- group therapy;
- cathartic abreaction;
- psychodrama;
- direct ego support.

### The Sioux sun dance

The sun dance originated with the plains Algonquins around 1700 and by the 1800s had become the most magnificent ceremony of this culture, involving complex group rites associated with mythological themes revolving around war and the bison hunt. Officially banned by the authorities, the dance ceremonial was changed into a therapeutic instrument dealing with health and community problems that directly or indirectly were to do with the white intrusion.

The sun dance has the characteristic features of Shamanic initiation: calling and instruction by dream visions; guidance and teaching by a shaman; ordeal experience with fasting, thirst, pain and privation; and finally questing for and receiving a personal vision in the last dance.

### The gourd dance

Modern gourd dancing has developed its own characteristic choreography. Historically embedded in the traditional societies of the plains and prairie tribes, the 1960s and 1970s saw enthusiastic adherents carrying the dance from its nuclear area in Oklahoma to plains and prairie tribes throughout the USA and Canada.

The classical Plains Indian style of gourd dance, popularized by the media, appeals to the younger generation of Amerindians from diverse reservation backgrounds who strive to move beyond a tribal identity towards a pan-Indian identity. Participants see in the gourd dance a recognized means of experiencing their American identity and a way to change their life to a more wholesome existence. The dance has considerable ego-strengthening and rehabilitation potential and the therapeutic effects account for its success as a popular movement among rural and urban Amerindian populations.

## Mediums in Brazil

This section is based on Stanley Krippner's chapter on 'Entry Patterns in Brazilian Mediumship' in Ward (1989).

In early African cultures, as in many traditional cultures today, an individual was seen as being intimately connected to nature and the social group (Katz 1989b). As an aside, this assertion is categorically opposite to the predominant values in many western countries today, particularly the UK, America and Australia, where individuals are connected more to technology and the pursuit of individualism. Connections to the social group are considered to be weakening and some writers have urged that more focus is required by therapists on small and large group work to reawaken this vital human element of relatedness (De Marre 1975; Samuels 1993; Lago 1994).

Returning, however, to these early African cultures, each individual was thought to be part of a web of kinship relations, existing only in relation to the larger family and community networks. Strained or broken social relations were the major cause of disease; anger, jealousy and envy could lead to serious illness. A harmonious relationship with one's community was necessary for health; the relationships one's ancestors had with the community were also important. At the same time an ordered relationship with the forces of nature was essential for mastering the well-being of the individual and community. Long before western medicine recognized the fact, African traditional healers had taken the position that ecology and interpersonal relations affected people's health (Raboteau 1986).

The medium, or person through whom the spirits spoke, achieved a trance state brought about by dancing, singing and drumming in order for incorporation to occur (the voluntary surrender of mind and body to the discarnate entity). Treatment for afflicted people included herbal preparations, prayers and sacrifices. It frequently included spirit incorporation. Preventative medicine consisted of using charms and rituals, as well as living within the social constraints of one's culture.

Of the Brazilian spiritistic movements, Candomble is the one most closely resembling the pure 'Yoruba' religion of Africa, retaining the original beliefs and rituals. The majority of healers are women, though in some regions there are men. Aside from learning how to sing, drum and dance, they (the novices) also learn about the herbs and special teas and potions given to troubled members of the community.

Other Brazilian spiritistic groups include:

- *Kardecismo* – a spiritistic movement (circa 1818) organized around the principles of homeopathy. Kardscist mediums alter their consciousness usually by 'turning inward' (often aided by soft music and the presence of a supportive social group) and providing an 'opening' for the incorporation of their guide.
- *Umbanda* – the name seems to have come from the Sanskrit term Aum-bandha, the 'divine principle'. Alterations of consciousness in the low 'Umbanda' sects may be facilitated by drumming, chanting, smoking cigars, drinking rum, making sacrifices of fowl and small animals and drawing cabalastic signs on the floor with chalk.

  'High' Umbanda sects do not engage in these practices but use trance-induction methods reminiscent of Kardecismo. Both groups emphasize the importance of spirit incorporation and all Umbandistas venerate Jesus Christ.

All the ceremonies of these three major groups vary, yet they share three beliefs: humans have a physical and a spiritual body; discarnate spirits are in constant contact with the physical world; humans can learn how to incorporate spirits for the purpose of healing. There are also other less popular spiritist groups (e.g. Batugur, Cabock, Quimbanda, Macumba, Xango).

The use of trance states depicted in the last five examples (the hunter-gatherers, the Native American dances and the Brazilian mediums) point us to the importance of this form of healing. As Wittkower has written:

> There can be no doubt in anybody's mind that trance and possession states in the countries in which they play a part of religious rituals have an important distress relieving, integrative, adaptive function. As far as mental illness is concerned, they may be of prophylactic value. An increase in mental illness may have to be expected when as a result of culture change they have ceased to exist.
>
> (Wittkower 1970: 160)

## Spiritual influences on healing amongst Afro-Caribbean groups

In a book entitled *Working with West Indian Families*, written from an American perspective, Gopaul-McNicol (1993) suggests that:

> One reason West Indians have not fully accepted the concept of psychotherapy is that their approach to solving problems is internally orientated. Problems are kept within the family and solved there. The only outsiders who are permitted to intrude are priests or ministers and the church's role is basically one of providing emotional support and reaffirming the family's belief that God will solve this problem in the right time. Some families in distress may consult spiritists. Such 'Obeah' practitioners are believed to be able to control evil spirits which tend to be perceived as the causes of family troubles.

She goes on to suggest that:

> If an individual or family problem is not seen as a medical one, then it is usually categorized as a spiritual one. In such cases West Indian clients first go, not to a mental health professional but to an Obeah practitioner (a spiritist or person who practices witchcraft) or a member of the clergy. The Obeah practitioner takes into account various aspects of the family situation, such as recent success and failures; puts them in the context of the cultural beliefs in spirits; and works out a plan of action according to his/her conclusions.

The healing of an individual normally takes place in a group ceremony known as a seance (although it can be done individually as well). The group is usually comprised of junior spiritual leaders, family and friends. The Obeah practitioner who serves as a medium attempts to establish contact with the spirit world in order to determine which evil spirits are creating the person's dysfunction and which good spirits can be enlisted to protect the person. An attempt is made to convince the evil spirits they should 'do good' rather than 'do evil'. The practitioner will then interpret the spirits' messages for the family and will prescribe medicinal herbs, ointments, spiritual baths, prayers and/ or massages, all with the goal of helping the individual gain spiritual strength.

## Chinese psychiatry

In an interesting chapter on Chinese psychiatry, Wen-Shing Tseng offers an account of a system of mental health practice that combines Chinese tradition with contemporary interpretations and western modes of treatment (Cox 1986). 'Chinese medicine', he writes, 'especially psychiatry, has been relatively less influenced by religious thoughts and movements throughout the course of history'. The study of medical textbooks reveals that the theoretical system of Chinese medicine as a whole is 'nature'-orientated and is based primarily on the concept of yin and yang, the theory of five elements and the idea of correspondence between microcosm and macrocosm. Such a theoretical orientation also applies to psychiatry. The cause of mental disorders is attributed to natural factors, psychological stimulation and the individual's own attributes.

The influence of emotional factors upon the occurrence of physical illness has long been recognized in Chinese medicine and the improvement of the emotional condition was emphasized as a way of encouraging recovery (Chen 1963). Chinese medicine in actual practice is very much orientated to the prescription of herbal medicines. More than 400 types of material from vegetable, animal and mineral sources are frequently used in traditional medicine. Among these, nearly 100 are used in the treatment of psychiatric disorders.

Present practices in China comprise:

- community psychiatric services – mental health delivery systems follow the government's four main principles of health:
  - primary concern for labourers, farmers and soldiers;
  - emphasis on prevention;
  - the combined use of Chinese traditional medicine and western medicine; and
  - the combining of mental health work with mass movements.
  Care in the community occurs where patients' families, neighbours and retired workers assist in the care of patients. It usually takes two or three people as a team to take care of one patient. This team observes

the patient's condition, supervises the taking of medication, provides guidance and education and assists the patient in socio-family rehabilitation.

- A combination of traditional and modern medicines:
  - – use of traditional herbal medications
  - – use of acupuncture
  - – use of western methods including ECT.
- Predominance of biological descriptive orientation (influenced by traditional approaches to medicine). Relatively scant attention is paid to sociocultural and psychological aspects of mental health and illness, not to mention the emphasis on the dynamic orientation of human behaviour, mind and psychopathology evidenced in some American textbooks. A predominance of biological descriptions of mental ill-health pervade the literature.

Given the shortages of mental health workers and the widespread diagnosis of certain forms of mental ill-health (e.g. neurasthenia – not a diagnosis often used in the west), the Chinese developed an 'accelerated–integrated therapy' for treating such patients. The emphasis of this treatment was to integrate all available modes of treatment to deal with the patients as a group and to accelerate the pace of treatment within a short period of time – usually several weeks.

The treatment programme took several forms:

- group therapy – emphasis on educating patients about their disorders;
- life pattern reforming with emphasis on physical activities and intellectual encouragement;
- adjunctive somatic treatment of various kinds including medication, acupuncture and so on.

## Summing up

In reflecting on three major studies (two in the USA, one in the UK) that explored the nature of people's religious experiences, Valla and Prince note that all three surveys indicate that some 20 to 40 per cent of the population at large report mystical or religious experiences and that such experiences (in the USA surveys) were more commonly reported by blacks than whites. Two of the studies found that frequent experiences were involved with higher social class and the remaining survey found the reverse (Ward 1989).

In summing up they note that healers around the world have shaped and developed 'spontaneous experiences' (as explored in the surveys reported above) to arrive at highly elaborated healing systems. Meditation traditions, drum- and dance-related trance-inducing systems and healing practices employing psychedelic drugs are well-known examples. Such religious experiences (within a US/British location) are posited in terms of valuable self-healing functions.

In attempting to draw conclusions from the above wide range of material presented in this chapter it is crucial to note that, at a basic level, we are not comparing like with like. Most western therapies have an individual emphasis; others described here have a community or family focus. Most western therapies are delivered in a one-to-one setting; others described here may use several healers and they work in group settings. Most western therapies do not involve friends or family members in the therapeutic process. They do not induce, deliberately, altered states of consciousness through ritual dancing or chanting. However, writers such as Rogers (1980) and Wood (1990) acknowledge that clients and therapists may experience altered forms of consciousness in the therapeutic process.

In short, the western concepts of psychotherapy, though having a broadly similar aim to many other culturally different healing forms, do focus on individual interactive processes most frequently based in dialogue. However, there are many contradictions to this assertion. There are western therapeutic methods that use behavioural approaches, use creative activities (movement, dance, sound, art), involve meditative processes (relaxation, stress reduction), respect and work with metaphysical and spiritual issues, have systems of befriending (e.g. Alcoholics Anonymous), work with families, small and medium groups and so on.

We have to recognize this breadth and complexity of the spectrum of healing approaches embedded in all societies and note that each has its validity within the cultural frameworks from which it originates. In addition, there are often similarities between the forms of activity used by different cultures, e.g. trance states, though the rituals may be differently structured.

All the healing systems described in this chapter are certainly community or communally based, i.e. they involve numbers of people. But so too does western psychiatry, where doctors and nurses and occupational therapists are all involved. However, at the other end of this western spectrum is the example of isolated people, living on their own, who consult individual private therapists on an hourly basis once a week. The therapist seldom addresses the need for others to be involved, and indeed there may be no convenient other person. The clients themselves may be very anxious about such initiatives occurring until they themselves are ready to embark on such socializing.

In short, any simplistic comparisons with other therapeutic forms are doomed to failure. Therapists are urged, however, to respect and to take very seriously their culturally different clients' wishes and views in relation to what they conceive as helpful. A preparedness to attempt to accept other healing perspectives and approaches even when not understanding them is crucial. One's task, where there are apparently competing healing systems within the client's frame of reference, seems to be to effect, as much as possible, a way of working that encourages the client in his help-seeking mode, and to explore methods of cooperation with other helpers.

# 8 Training therapists to work with different and diverse clients

A body of literature exists that documents the widespread ineffectiveness of traditional counselling approaches and techniques when applied to racial and ethnic minority populations . . . it is apparent that the major reason for therapeutic ineffectiveness lies in the training of mental health professionals.

(Sue *et al.* 1992)

## Introduction

Many basic counselling training courses within the United Kingdom spend relatively little time and attention on the preparation of counselling trainees to work with culturally and racially different clients. Given the huge amount of material to be learned in terms of knowledge acquisition and skill development in counselling and psychotherapy this situation is understandable, though it becomes less defensible within the reality of the UK as a multiracial society.

At a theoretical level there is an important debate as to when specialist training in transcultural therapy should take place. By contrast with the United States and Canada, where it is possible to do graduate and postgraduate degrees in this subject, the majority of therapist training in the UK is part-time, attracts students who are often mature and already professionally qualified (within other disciplines) and is frequently geared to a mono-theoretical view (i.e. a training in psycho-dynamic or person-centred or gestalt approaches and so on). These issues of training are clearly related to the relatively short history of the activity/ profession within Britain, the reality that many counsellors are part-time or voluntary, and to the fact that there is not an easily identifiable or coherent professional structure of careers within counselling and psychotherapy.

In the training of transcultural therapists a primary debate has to be that of considering whether this training can be effectively done at initial qualification level or on post-qualification courses. The argument of high-volume input on initial courses mentioned above has to be balanced with that of considering students who may be highly motivated to work in transcultural therapy but who cannot afford or are not traditionally qualified to pursue higher courses.

Certainly Boyd-Franklin (1989) and Lee and Richardson (1991) value the importance of ongoing professional training and development opportunities after initial training. Initial counsellor training, however, must begin to help students address some of the basic issues, thus laying in place a sensitivity to the whole subject (Boyd-Franklin 1989). Specialist courses within Britain on this subject are still few and far between and tend more towards short workshop programmes rather than being longer qualification-based academic courses. The selection of students is always a difficult task for trainers. Selection based purely on culture or race will be too simplistic, and would not recognize that shared cultural background does not guarantee a successful therapeutic relationship (D'Ardenne and Mahtani 1989; Moodley 1991; Carter 1995).

Training partners and teams that comprise colleagues who themselves are ethnically, culturally and racially different have become accepted in practice as epitomizing useful role models and symbolically representing the complexity of data that needs to be addressed within the training.

## Students and trainees: selection and motivation

> Change is water flowing under bridges,
> Change is boundaries dissolved,
> Change is being lost in strange readiness to end or to begin,
> Change is challenge to begin ever anew.
> Change is freedom, hardly won to live a new and unpredicted life new shaped.
>
> Clark (1982)

As noted in their book, *Anti-Discriminatory Counselling Practice*, Lago and Smith (2003) indicate that there is no doubt that exposure to the ideas, theories, attitudes and skills that underpin this subject can have disturbing implications for the trainees. As the poem above suggests, 'Change is challenge to begin ever anew.' McLeod (1993: 110) acknowledges that counsellors exhibit a general avoidance of political issues and few attempts, for example, have been made to develop a theoretical understanding of the issues involved in counselling people from different social classes (Pilgrim 1992). Following on from McLeod's observation, it seems likely, also, that trainers of counsellors and psychotherapists also find the challenge of teaching 'diversity' very considerable indeed. Tackling subjects such as equal opportunities, prejudice, stereotyping, power and its many manifestations in social and professional relationships, identity, personal belief systems and so on within the training framework can evoke very complex reactions in the training group, reactions which perhaps many trainers would rather avoid. (See the later chapter by Val Watson for an exposition of these issues, particularly in relation to the experience of black trainees.)

For those students who enrol on longer specialist courses on transcultural therapy a generalized commitment to helping 'others' may not be sufficient motivation to see them through the enormous challenges they will have to face with regard to their own concepts of the world and how it operates. Training in this arena has the potential to go to the core of one's own cultural and racial identity and present demanding questions and disturbing scenarios. In cases of student selection, courses might have to decide upon what criteria trainees are chosen and one of those criteria might usefully be related to the psychology of 'heroic helpers' as defined by Staub (1993). Certainly it is the author's experience that such courses implicitly invite participants to take a position in relation to race relations, immigration matters, issues of power in society and so on. Exposure to the training issues inevitably invites personal introspection at a very deep level. Emotional reactions such as fear, guilt, shame and anxiety may be powerfully evoked (Buckley 2004). High student motivation will certainly be required.

An openness to consider other theoretical and cultural approaches to counselling and helping is certainly advocated by a variety of writers (Lago and Thompson 1989a; Lee and Richardson 1991; Sue *et al.* 1992). This factor may be questioned strongly by students who have attended previous mono-theoretically-based courses. Trainees and their trainers also need to commit themselves to the question of how they might adapt theories and techniques of traditional counselling approaches to meet different cultural needs.

## The training task: empowerment and enablement

Nancy Boyd-Franklin (1989) makes a strong case for the empowerment of therapists through training in order that they may also empower their clients. Indeed, the concept of client empowerment has always been an aim of counselling in general and advocated as being central to any work with refugees (Stringer 1992). Nevertheless, there are substantial contradictions beneath the ideology of empowerment. In short, empowerment cannot be assumed to be a natural outcome of therapy (McLeod 1993).

Troyna (1994) was so concerned about the 'blind faith' assertions of educational researchers in relation to the empowering effects of their research that he wrote a paper advocating caution and more attention to clarity of intent and definition. He cites the work of Jennifer Gore, who argues that empowerment:

carries with it an agent of empowerment (someone or something doing the empowering), a notion of power as property (to em-power implies to give or confer power) and a vision or desired end state (some vision of what it is to be empowered and the possibility of a state of empowerment).

(Gore 1993: 73–4)

Troyna cites other researchers who have usefully drawn a distinction between empowerment and 'giving a voice' (Ellsworth 1989; Gurnah 1992). The two concepts are often used interchangeably but may have quite contradictory outcomes, he argues.

The above paragraphs issue a considerable challenge to trainers and therapists to consider carefully their claims, their intentions and possible outcomes of therapy. Notwithstanding, it is clear that Boyd-Franklin (1989) is concerned to explore how trainee therapists might be enabled to mobilize all their potential for working skilfully and sensitively in transcultural therapeutic settings.

Lago (1994) cites Byham and Cox (1988), management consultants, who define four areas of activity that are required for 'empowerment' to work:

- direction (key result areas, goals, measurements);
- knowledge (skills, training, information, goals);
- resources (tools, materials, facilities, money);
- support (approval, coaching, feedback, encouragement).

Converting the above concepts from a managerial into an educational context we would assert that:

- 'direction' equates to the goals of the training;
- knowledge can be subdivided into beliefs and attitudes, knowledge and skills;
- resources are those required for the training (including clinical placements); and
- support relates to the work of tutors, fellow students and supervisors on the course.

## Multicultural counselling competencies

Sue *et al.* (1992) published a set of 'multicultural counselling competencies' in the USA that have been reproduced in an abbreviated form as Table 8.1. (The abbreviations on the matrix are ours and we apologize for any inaccuracies conveyed by our condensation of the original.) Conceived originally as a

**Table 8.1** Key recommendations for multiculturally skilled counsellors' characteristics

| Dimensions | Counsellor awareness of own assumptions, values and biases | Understanding the world view of the culturally different client | Developing appropriate intervention strategies and techniques |
|---|---|---|---|
| Beliefs and attitudes | Culturally skilled counsellors:<br>• are aware and sensitive to own cultural heritage and to valuing and respecting differences<br>• are aware of how their own cultural background influences psychological processes<br>• are able to recognize their limits<br>• are comfortable with differences between them and clients. | Culturally skilled counsellors:<br>• are aware of their emotional reactions towards other racial and ethnic groups<br>• are aware of their stereotypes and preconceived notions. | Culturally skilled counsellors:<br>• respect clients' spiritual beliefs and values<br>• respect indigenous helping practices<br>• value bilingualism. |
| Knowledge | Culturally skilled counsellors:<br>• have knowledge about their racial/cultural heritage and how it affects definitions of normality and process of counselling<br>• possess knowledge and understanding about the workings of oppression/racism/discrimination (refers to white identity development model)<br>• possess knowledge about their social impact upon others. | Culturally skilled counsellors:<br>• possess specific knowledge and information about the particular group they are working with (refers to the minority identity development model)<br>• understand how race/culture/ethnicity may affect personality formation/vocational choice/psychological disorder/help-seeking behaviour<br>• understand and have knowledge of socio-political influences that impinge upon racial/ethnic minorities. | Culturally skilled counsellors:<br>• have clear knowledge of limits of counselling and how they may clash with minority values<br>• are aware of institutional barriers preventing minorities' access to mental health service |

| Dimensions | Counsellor awareness of own assumptions, values and biases | Understanding the world view of the culturally different client | Developing appropriate intervention strategies and techniques |
|---|---|---|---|
| | | | • understand limits of assessment procedures<br>• have knowledge of minority family structures and community hierarchy. |
| Skills | Culturally skilled counsellors:<br>• seek out educational consultative and training experiences to enrich their understanding<br>• constantly seek to understand themselves as racial/cultural beings and actively seek a non-racist identity. | Culturally skilled counsellors:<br>• should familiarize themselves with relevant research regarding various groups and seek out educational opportunities that enrich their knowledge, understanding and skills<br>• become involved with minority individuals outside the counselling setting so that their perspective is wider-informed. | Culturally skilled counsellors:<br>• have a broad range of help-styles<br>• are able to exercise institutional intervention skills<br>• are willing to consult a wide range of other helpers<br>• take responsibility for interest in language required by the client. |

*Source*: Based on Sue *et al.* 1992.

basis for outlining the need and rationale for a multicultural perspective in counselling, the Professional Standards Committee of the (American) Association for Multicultural Counselling and Development went much further in proposing 31 multicultural counselling competencies and urging the counselling profession in the United States to adopt these as accreditation criteria. Two of the leading journals cooperated on publishing the same article in both their editions as a service to the profession.

The matrix developed by Sue *et al.* (1992) is derived from earlier attempts

to identify specific cross-cultural counselling competencies that have traditionally been divided into three dimensions: beliefs and attitudes;
knowledge; and skills. These three dimensions are set against the three characteristics of, first, counsellor awareness of own assumptions, values and biases,
second, understanding the worlds of the culturally different client, and third,
developing appropriate intervention strategies and techniques.

Ponterotto and Pedersen (1993) cite four instruments that were developed to measure counsellor multicultural competences in terms of attitude,
knowledge and skills (p. 142). They are listed as:

1   Cross Cultural Counseling Inventory (LaFramboise *et al.* 1991).
2   Multicultural Counseling Awareness Scale (Ponterotto *et al.* 1991).
3   Multicultural Counseling Inventory (Sodowsky *et al.* 1992).
4   Multicultural Awareness/Knowledge/Skills Survey (D'Andrea *et al.*
    1991).

The author is unaware of the use of these instruments within the British context, either as tools for self-awareness or as instruments for use within training.
Consequently, no comment is made on the potential 'transferability' of these
to the British counselling context.

For reasons of clarity of presentation, the sections below that depict the
aims of training follow the above example by being divided into the three
major areas of beliefs, knowledge and skill.

## Beliefs, attitudes and awareness

In addition to Sue *et al.* (1992), Webb Johnson (1993), D'Ardenne and Mahtani
(1989) and Lago and Thompson (1989a) have all previously made recommendations concerning training and counselling practice within transcultural
therapy. Not surprisingly, there is considerable agreement across these sources
of the major elements required in any transcultural therapy training.

This first section thus concentrates upon the importance of counsellors'
own sense of who they are culturally and racially and what this means in
terms of their beliefs, attitudes and behaviours. This awareness comes from
developing their understanding and appreciation of the cultural context
within which they have been raised and now live. A recent article by Phoenix
(1994) gives a clue as to the difficulty such an endeavour creates when one
considers the multiple subject positions we all occupy which change over time
and situation. Ponterotto and Pedersen (1993) offer an extensive overview of
the current theories of identity development in the United States. These
models may contribute significantly to trainees' own understanding of where
they position themselves within society.

Training exercises that facilitate this exploration of roots and origins require handling with great sensitivity because of the personal material they might provoke in students (see Lago and Barty 2003 and Patel *et al.* 2000 for descriptions of such exercises). This personal work is really never fully completed and certainly cannot be achieved in an afternoon's training session! It is important that trainers inculcate a view of this personal work as an ongoing element of professional development for therapists.

From such work it is hoped that trainees will gain an awareness of both their own and others' deep cultural, racial and spiritual frameworks of being, thinking and living. This awareness will also

- enhance their understanding of their own stereotypes, assumptions and judgements;
- help them to appreciate the very different psychological and cultural frameworks by which other people live;
- inform their own processes of self-monitoring in relation to negative attitudes they may have whilst conducting transcultural interviews; and
- help them avoid imposing their own frame of reference upon clients.

Skilled tutoring and competent clinical supervision will also assist trainees to appreciate the more subtle and complex areas of this personal dimension and foster understanding of the myriad ways in which unconscious imposition of values can be powerfully transmitted from therapist to client in ways that are neither useful or therapeutic.

Rogers asserts, within his person-centred theory, that 'the organism (person) acts as an organised whole' (Rogers [1951] 1987: 486). The pursuit of awareness being advocated here will hopefully reveal the veracity of the above statement and lead the students to respect the 'organised wholeness' of the culturally different client, a phenomenon quite opposed to the 'invisibility' that many ethnic minority clients experience in this society (Phung 1995).

## Knowledge

This characteristic, like the ones in the preceding and succeeding sections, provides a considerable challenge to the learner, the teacher and the process in which they are engaged. The concept of knowledge, as described here, is of the quality that becomes internalized within the student, not a unit of external facts to be assembled for an examination and then forgotten. The focus here is on how the knowledge informs and illuminates therapist practice.

Sue *et al.* (1992) have considerably developed and expanded this dimension from the sets of suggestions made by the British writers cited in the previous section. This, perhaps, is to be expected as it reflects a set of concerns and research efforts that have been pursued by the therapy professions for much longer in the United States.

To become a transculturally skilled counsellor, students will need to:

- have knowledge about the complex concepts of race, culture, ethnicity and how these relate to their own heritage and thus affect their perceptions of the world;
- gain understanding of the historical and contemporary relations between their own culture and others;
- understand how systems of racism and oppression operate;
- attain specific knowledge about the client group/s they may work with including family systems and community hierarchies;
- understand how race, culture and ethnicity impact upon people's development and inform and motivate their actions in society;
- understand how the processes of the dominant society impact upon its minority group members;
- consider the impact of language difference from clients and construct strategies to deal with this;
- have knowledge of the cultural limits of counselling.

All of the above points are geared towards ensuring that therapists do not misuse their power (personal, role, gender, cultural, racial, institutional) with clients and also that they do not impose culturally biased views or procedures for action that will effectively be harmful to clients.

## Skills

> In sum, skills training should centre around how to incorporate the cultural dynamics and naturally occurring support systems of diverse groups of people into counselling interventions.
>
> (Lee and Richardson 1991)

An underlying, yet core concept within this dimension of skills acquisition is that of becoming and of being perceived as a competent communicator. Rogers (1959) has always stressed that it is not good enough for the therapist to be skilled but that the client has to perceive that the therapist's skills, intentions and commitment are present. Gudykunst (1994) has very usefully described several major themes that underline competent communications skills in cross-cultural encounters. These include the abilities to

- be mindful;
- tolerate ambiguity;
- be able to manage anxiety;

- be able to adapt; and
- empathize.

Indeed, he asserts that the one skill that most consistently emerges in discussions of effective communication with 'strangers' is that of empathy (p. 184).

An interesting pan-historical review of the evolution of human consciousness by Neville (1994) suggests that human beings have a considerable capacity for empathic understanding of their fellows. These span from preverbal sensing through to a fourth dimension perception which he suggests is part of a new, emerging evolutionary phase of human consciousness in the latter part of this century.

However, Jones (1985) urges caution in the unthinking transfer of empathic inference, where one's own feelings and thoughts are used as an index of what another is experiencing. This technique is traditionally based upon a bond of similarity of individuals. Cross-cultural psychotherapy would necessarily be problematic, since empathy defined in terms of understanding others on the basis of shared qualities cannot occur. There is a need for an empathy based on differences, he argues, which would focus the imagination that would transpose itself into another, rather than upon one's own feelings, and in this way achieve a more complete understanding of culturally varied predispositions, personal constructs and experience (p. 178).

D'Ardenne and Mahtani (1999: 48) provide an excellent list of 18 skills deemed appropriate for transcultural therapists. These span the realm of:

- direct skills (listening, linguistic competence, non-verbal, interpretation of expression, organizational and so on);
- commitment to development (of self, of knowledge, of language acquisition and so on);
- competency to recognize the complex issues and reactions within the client;
- skills in involving the client's family and community networks appropriately.

The capacity of counsellors to respond with a range of therapeutic interventions is one that is widely accepted within the North American literature on this subject. Our present understanding is that a much broader range of psychotherapeutic approaches are introduced on counsellor training programmes in the United States and Canada as compared to the UK. Many British courses (as has been stated earlier in the book) tend towards the dissemination of perhaps one particular approach, with the other approaches being addressed only in a subsidiary manner.

Given this broad educational context of counselling training in North

America, the acquisition of a wide range of therapeutic intervention skills may not be as problematic as it might prove in Britain where trainers and supervisors may demonstrate considerable resistance to approaches other than their own. For example, research outcomes of behaviour therapy in the USA clearly show the effectiveness of such approaches in the treatment of clients from any race or ethnic background (Kolko 1987; Paniagua 1994). Various authors argue that this is because these strategies are authoritative, concrete and action-oriented, and emphasize immediate, focused learning factors preferred by certain specific cultural groups (Walker and La Rue 1986; Boyd-Franklin 1989; Paniagua 1994).

Despite this evidence, we believe that ideological differences between adherents of different theoretical persuasions in Britain might prove stumbling blocks to the development of 'multiply skilled' counsellor training. This debate does give insight into the cultural, theoretical and professional differences between North America and Britain. Certainly a range of writings in Britain suggest the successful use of a range of theories with culturally different clients (e.g. D'Ardenne and Mahtani 1989; Kareem and Littlewood 1992; Lago 1992; Eleftheriadou 1994; McDevitt 1994). This availability of different schools of therapists in Britain may be compared to the range of healers in Brazil described in Chapter 7. The difference may occur, however, in the levels of client understanding of what these differences might mean in practice. Because of the relatively short history of counselling in Britain, it is likely that differences between counselling approaches will not be appreciated by a substantial percentage of clients. Perhaps the kernel of resolution to the above seeming differences may be in a statement in Webb Johnson's article (1993: 26): 'Different schools of counselling are not as significant as the attitudes and skills of the individual therapist.' Certainly, much meta-research on clinical outcome supports this view, noting that extra-therapeutic change variables – factors unique to the client (e.g. commitment, motivation to change, etc.) and the quality of the relationship with the therapist are the two most critical elements in accounting for successful therapeutic outcome (discussed in Bozarth 1998).

## Skills for organizational and development work

The general activity of working as a therapist inevitably involves some organizational skills. Therapists often work in organizations and, as such, require good communication and liaison skills. In addition they need to be able to effect good working relationships with referring organizations. These dimensions obviously apply to most therapeutic settings.

Koslow and Salett argue strongly that transcultural therapists need to be able to

- work within the realities and needs of the organization;

- function effectively within that organization; and
- manage the counselling process in organizational settings.

(1989: 150)

This aspect of skills acquisition will hopefully be addressed in the training course and as a result of supervised experience on the counselling placement.

In my previous writing on the subject with Joyce Thompson it was suggested that counsellors who become involved in transcultural counselling may inevitably become involved in training and preventative, educational work within the fields of cross-cultural relations, anti-racism and so on (Lago and Thompson 1989a). The processes of training outlined above and then subsequent clinical transcultural practice will equip and furnish each therapist with extensive knowledge and unique insight for later use in the training domain.

All training courses are limited in the extent to which they may contribute to student development and this latter skill may be only something that can be developed by individuals some time after their training course.

## The use of interactive film material in training

I've come to make a complaint really. Because I'm starting a job next week. I've got a child of three, so I went to see this childminder in my area and I asked her if she would look after my child; it was a white lady and she just looked at me and said 'We don't take black children', and slammed the door in my face.

I've come to see you, perhaps because I think I'm pregnant. I don't know what to do. I mean, me being an Indian girl and pregnant, my mum's gonna kill me, my dad will murder me. Oh, I'm in such a situation. If only I had something I could do about it, I don't want an abortion because I don't believe in them, I don't think they're right. Oh, but maybe that's the only way I can get out of it.

Both quotes from *Multi-racial Videoscenes*, an interactive video produced by Clark and Lago (1981).

The use and value of filmed material has long been recognized in counsellor training. The material supplied to training courses in the UK (in the 1960s and 1970s) was originally furnished by Keele University Careers and Counselling Unit, which ran a film lending library featuring a range of American therapists working with clients and with groups. The British Association for Counselling later purchased this complete library (circa 1980) and later passed over the administration of it to Concorde Films. In the intervening years technology has changed considerably and from the original 16 mm spools of film requiring cine-projectors have come the widespread use of videotapes and videocassette recorders. New materials are now in the form of DVD programmes shown via video projectors.

Of significance in the history of counselling and the use of film has been the pioneering work of the late Dr Norman Kagan on a system that eventually became known as 'Interpersonal Process Recall'. Kagan and his colleagues were able, through the extensive analysis of filmed helping interviews, to identify certain response modes used by counsellors that were consistently helpful to clients. In recognizing, also, that each person in a helping role is differently affected by how 'helpees' present themselves (verbally, physically and emotionally), they derived an interactive technique of using film with training groups to enable trainees to explore their own affective responses to a wide range of interpersonal challenges. Finally, Kagan and his associates refined their methodology to also include a structured system for using audio and video recordings of meetings (counselling interviews, committee meetings, class teaching etc.) as a mechanism for reflection upon and supervision of such sessions.

The second example of Kagan's major contributions referred to above, that of interactive film, became the stimulus and model for the development of an early video training programme entitled *Multi-racial Videoscenes*. Developed by Jean Clark and Colin Lago at De Montfort University, Leicester, this short programme consisted of 16 short vignettes in which people from a range of different cultural and racial backgrounds speak directly to the camera about a troubling incident or emotional situation. Two examples are given as opening quotations to this section. The training group are invited to consider their affective and verbal responses to these potential 'client' statements, having been asked to imagine that they are the counsellor or helper to whom the person on screen is talking. Such apparently simple stimuli generated substantial discussion amongst groups of practitioners from different helping professions on all matters pertinent to this book.

- What would I feel if I had a client presenting these issues to me?
- How would I respond to the client and her issues?
- Would my feelings and verbal responses be congruent with each other or quite different?
- What assumptions are raised in me by the scene?
- If I were in such a situation as the client, how would I react?
- Why do other colleagues in this training group react similarly or differently to me?
- What are the issues there that I may learn from?

(The above video is no longer available but the details have intentionally been included in this second edition as a record of how the stimulus was used within training and in the hope that enthusiastic trainers might envisage the production of new materials using these ideas.)

It can be seen from the above that interactive film techniques have substantial value as a counselling training medium. Stimulated by both Kagan's original idea and the success of *Multi-racial Videoscenes* referred to above, a series of other interactive videos were made during the early 1980s to stimulate training in areas such as working with international students, racism in the church and addressing challenges in multicultural and multiracial organizations.

Recognizing the enormous training potential of film and videos and the paucity of existing materials on this subject, the author, in close association with Joyce Thompson, collaborated on a further video project in association with Leicester University entitled *Issues of Race and Culture in Counselling Settings*. This video continues to be available for hire or sale from Leicester University Audio Visual Aids Unit. A training manual containing the complete transcripts of the interviews together with ideas on how each scene might be discussed within training is available from the author.

The video contains six scenes involving counsellors and clients from same-race/ethnicity and different race/ethnicity backgrounds. The participants shown in the video were friends and colleagues of the producers and had actively been involved in the early work of the RACE division of the British Association for Counselling.

Each of the scenes depicted lasts approximately ten minutes and there was no editing of these interviews. The participants (when acting as clients) were invited to present a concern that was legitimate to their own personal, cultural, ethnic and racial backgrounds. No scripts were offered or written. Each participant in the video is featured twice, once as a counsellor and once as a client. As counsellors, the participants were invited to respond as they would in their normal counselling mode. When the video is shown in training situations trainers are recommended:

- to show the Introduction;
- to have previewed the videotape and read the manual beforehand;
- to have chosen the specific scenes they wish to use for this training session;
- to show each chosen scene, one at a time (not sequentially); and
- after each scene to offer time for the training group to reflect on the proceedings and discuss them.

The introductory notes and transcripts of the first of these interviews now follow. Readers should remember that the following transcript is taken directly from the video, verbatim, and thus should bear in mind that considerable differences exist between the spoken and written word. Communication is enhanced by a wide range of non-verbal and para-linguistic cues (as discussed in Chapter 5), which are obviously absent in the written form. Some of the following sentences, therefore, in the script may convey meanings that are not readily clear.

### Josna and Terri (a black client with a white therapist)

*Spoken introduction to the scene*
'This scene shows the client exercising her right to feel trusting of her counsellor. In the past she has had experience of working with white colleagues, which did not lead to very satisfactory outcomes. In all counselling relationships the process of establishing trust between client and counsellor is crucial. This task might take much longer when those involved are from different cultural and racial backgrounds than it would with people of the same race and the process may also need to be much more explicit.'

*Further background thoughts on this scene*
The following scene could be experienced as a threatening situation for the therapist depending on her level of knowledge, experience, awareness of and comfort with the issues of race and culture.

In this scene the questions posed by the client in order for her to make an informed choice are very explicit. It is important to stress and realize that in many similar situations the client's questions may not be verbalized in such an explicit manner, but we suggest that nevertheless such questions and quandaries may be present in the client's mind and her experience and, even if they are not verbalized, the helper cannot afford to ignore them. Our suggestion is that it would be useful for the therapist to check out if such questions are present. We realize, however, that for many therapists and trainers who have not yet been exposed to the issues of race and culture, little awareness or knowledge may exist that such dilemmas abound and are of great importance to the client.

The transcript of the interview follows; this is followed by a series of questions that may be helpful in contributing to the group's discussion.

*Transcript of the interview*
   Terri: Josna, do you want to tell me why it is you would like to talk to me?
   Josna: Before I start talking to you about something that is disturbing me a
        lot, I feel I need to know a bit more about you. I just got your name
        from the telephone directory and I don't know anything about you. I
        just would like to know a bit more about you before I can really talk to
        you. Have you done any work with black people?
   Terri: Yes I have. Let me just tell you a little bit. My original training was in
        nursing and I have completed a two-year diploma in counselling skills
        in London, which is, in fact, a mixed race course where there are black

and white people on the course. As part of my practice I do work with people from all backgrounds and also people with disabilities. So people can be black, white, Asian and also can have a disability and I work from home. I also train and I do some training in race and culture with a black colleague. I have been doing this for several years now.

Josna: The course that you were talking about, besides having black people in the course itself in terms of the training element, did it have any training on race?

Terri: No. When I started my course in 1977, we were probably one of the beginning courses that were beginning to really be aware of the issue of race and culture and the need to understand more. But there certainly wasn't any training. This was 1977–79. Certainly now, in courses that I run I won't work the course around the course. I usually prefer to do the work with a black colleague so that at least that issue is addressed, and as part of my aims and objectives with people it is stated very clearly that issues of race, colour and language are addressed in the context of my work and for students to own that there are concerns and that certainly as a white woman I own that I am racist and that I need to keep looking at that and need to keep reminding myself.

Josna: How do you deal with the question of race on the courses that you are running?

Terri: I almost want to say head on; by actually making sure that it is overt and not covert and if there is a language that is used and if it is subtle – things like 'well, we feel like that don't we?' it's almost like nudging people to collude. And being aware of words that people will use, of being aware of the need to put in things like roots and origins exercises into things that I run. I have a sense, I feel, we have slightly reversed role. I don't mind being asked but I would also like to know a bit about you as well. I feel I have said things that will help me to understand some of what it is you are really asking me.

Josna: Well, it is just that I have worked with white people. I do work with white people at a professional level and am very aware of the racism that they operate with. I just refuse to be placed in those situations that are going to undermine me. As your client I don't want to receive any racism from you. That is why it is really important for me to check you out. That is what I am doing and I want to know how you operate.

Terri: One of my responses when you say you don't want to receive any racism from me is I am aware I am racist. There are times I may be that way and I would hope that part of my commitment, if I am to work with you, would be that you would also challenge me as I would enable you to work through whatever the issues were. As far as I know,

I am not blatantly racist and, yes, there are times when I get stuck like anybody else and get caught. Hopefully, I am aware enough that I will own that and that I will actually come back to you and say, 'Look, I was reflecting on this and I felt that how I put something across to you was racist.' That is all I can say to you. That is difficult because I don't know in what area other white people, maybe other white women, have been racist to you and how they have used their power. For me, in working with you as a client it is about an empowering and an equal relationship. I am into equality. How does that seem to you?

Josna: I feel that you have given me the right answers and I have had all the right answers from white people before – at the intellectual level – and I don't trust all of that I have to tell you. I do know that if I do decide to have counselling from you and enter into a therapeutic relationship with you that it will be a risk and I will have to see how it goes. For me, it is a big risk and I am not avoiding issues as I try to clarify these very important concerns for me. It is not a block to what the real anxiety may be about. I just feel that it is like buying a house which may look very attractive and solid and it is important to get the structural survey done.

Terri: It sounds like you have been around this way before and have been hurt, that you have actually tried to enter into a contract of looking at issues that are around for you and it has been rather difficult and you have not got what you wanted out of it. Has that only happened with a white person or has that happened with other people?

Josna: I haven't entered a therapeutic relationship. I work with people. I have worked with a lot of people. I have got a lot of experience with working with people as colleagues and have worked together from different areas. I have no problems on a common point of contact. All of that has taught me that these people who appear to be working in the interest of black women and sisterhood are really about a different world completely. It is from those work experiences, and I have seen how counsellors have worked with women that I know, I suppose I am very cautious, I don't want to be treated in that way.

Terri: Your analogy of buying a house and having the survey done – there are so many different types of surveys – you don't know until you have taken the risk to buy. It's like this is what I hear you trying to check out with me. Do I want to buy this commodity you've got? All I can say to you is, what I sense from you, is yes I would like to work with you and I feel it is worthwhile you taking the risk to work with me and should issues come up then we look at those and also look at how they are affecting your life as an Asian woman working with Asian people, with white people, and it's risky. I have the same risk with you. It's not just one sided.

Josna: I'm sure. I know of one therapist who works with quite a lot of black women and has written a book about black women without even getting their permission and writing for them. How do I know that you are not going to use what I say?

Terri: What I do is set up a contract of confidentiality. I do have a supervisor where I take issues that come out of therapy sessions to them, that it remains within the context of you and I, and my supervisor. It is a held confidentiality. It is about trust. That is it and it's you taking a risk on it. It's difficult and I appreciate that. I can feel you are kind of 'How do I know?' You don't know. That is the problem and I really do appreciate what you are saying. It's like 'Am I really going to put myself into this position, with you as a white woman Terri, how's it going to be?' I don't know.

### Suggested questions for consideration

1    Does the client have a right to check out the therapist before making a commitment? (NB Since the production of this video, therapists and their professional organizations have come to acknowledge and stress the importance of clients conducting an exploration with new therapists to assist their choice of who to work with. At the original time of production (1989) this behaviour was less routinized and considered challenging.)

2    How confident is the therapist in being open to questions from the client?

3    In such circumstances how do you feel you would respond?

4    How much information does the therapist need to give to the client to help contribute towards a trusting relationship?

5    How is trust established between client and therapist?

6    Can you identify the range of issues in this scene beyond that of establishing trust?

7    If you felt threatened or inadequate by the client/by the client's questions what would you do?
   •   Refer the client elsewhere?
   •   Take it to supervision?
   •   Gain extra training?
   •   What else?

## Training materials in DVD format

The visual materials discussed above are now very dated, but the training potential of them has not receded. Consequently, it is a joy to be able to refer to the following materials, in DVD format, that have been developed by Dr

Harbrinder Dhillon-Stevens. I quote directly from an email sent to me by Harbrinder.

> Dr Harbrinder Dhillon-Stevens undertook her doctoral research entitled 'Healing Inside and Out: An Examination of Dialogic Encounters in the Area of Anti-oppressive Practice in Counselling and Psychotherapy.' The project investigated issues of anti-oppressive practice (AOP) within the British counselling and psychotherapy professions. It explored how issues of AOP are defined and discussed by counsellors and psychotherapists as well as their values and attitudes towards AOP. Above all, it looks in depth at how AOP enters their work with clients and promotes the concept of a multiple oppression model.
>
> (Dhillon-Stevens 2004a)

The research was conducted through the distribution of an initial exploratory questionnaire, followed by the establishment of an inquiry group that focused on various issues of AOP over eight months (one day a month). The inquiry group explored issues of AOP through role plays between therapist and client. The role plays were critically reflected upon by the individuals involved as well as the other inquirers. All the work of the inquiry group was recorded using video equipment.

Emerging from this research were a number of elements including training DVDs, presentations and publications.

One of the elements, *Healing inside and out*, Volume 1, is an interactive training and teaching DVD resource that contains approximately three hours of material and is the first of an intended series of five DVDs. It has been tested and evaluated for its usefulness within the fields of counselling, psychotherapy and counselling psychology. It can be used in training groups or by individuals, through the self-directed learning section, and can thus promote continuous professional development. It is hoped that it will contribute to the counselling and psychotherapy professions by drawing attention to the value base of these professions and the need for therapists to be aware of philosophical principles and the relationship of these to values and psychotherapy interventions.

DVD technology is an important step in creating a teaching resource that is cutting edge and enhances practitioner learning through interactive relating. The programmes involve the reflection of moment-to-moment internal experiences of the therapists and clients using IPR methodology. (See note in the section above referring to the development of IPR by Dr Norman Kagan.)

Volume 1 focuses on the issues of 'race' and ethnicity. It examines how these issues affect the self-concept of the therapist and client as well as the implications for the therapeutic process. It particularly addresses issues of white identity and what whiteness means to a therapist working with a black client. How do white therapists raise issues about their whiteness and engage in dialogue about whiteness and its implications in the forming of a working alliance?

Other volumes in the series of DVDs consider the following themes:

- disability;
- the use of language and AOP;
- issues of power within the therapeutic relationship;
- AOP in the supervisory relationship.

A training manual accompanies the DVDs to provide guidance for trainers in effectively using the DVD. Exercises and group process issues are also provided. In the interactive section, questions are raised about specific issues covered in the DVD, with possible solutions provided (developed from working with groups in counselling and psychotherapy on these issues). Transcripts of the role play for reference are also provided. An AOP action plan (that can be continually updated) is also included, focusing on:

- development of theory;
- development of practice;
- personal issues for therapy;
- professional issues for supervision;
- identification and monitoring of difficult issues.

## The training task: where, how and with what?

This section addresses, very inadequately the issues of educational approaches and resources that will have to be considered by trainers planning transcultural therapy courses. Many of these aspects will be familiar to trainers already, though the specific demands of the transcultural element may mean a search for new developments in approach and new locations for clinical practice. (A valuable resume of intercultural criteria for mental health training may be found in Pedersen 1985.)

Key themes are listed under the above title of 'where', 'how' and 'with what'.

*Where* (is the training conducted)?
- In the classroom
- In clinical placements
- In supervision (with a culturally different supervisor)
- On visits
- In personal therapy (with a culturally different therapist)

- In training groups and community meetings (see Mearns 1994 for a further explanation of the value of community meetings on training courses)

*How?*
- Lectures
- Seminars (student presented)
- Group discussion
- Multicultural/multiracial communication groups
- Workshops
- Experiential approaches
- Simulated therapeutic interviews/role play/possible audio or tele-visual recordings for later analysis
- Direct therapeutic practice
- Diary keeping
- Research activities
- Reading the literature
- Preparing written assignments
- Case study discussion

*With what?*

Trainers may be hard pressed in locating ideas and resources for conducting experiential sessions. Certainly there exists a lot of room for new developments in this arena. Some suggestions and ideas are listed in the appendix to this chapter and, if pursued, will lead readers to further resources and references.

## Summing up

Much material has not been included within this chapter. The author's own experiences of running short courses on this subject reveal the extent to which the subject matter concerned has the potential to inform as well as upset profoundly participants' views of themselves and others. This was hinted at in the early sections on student motivation and selection. The prospect of stimulating and enabling students to acquire the necessary awareness, knowledge and skills is a daunting one for trainers, especially when one bears in mind the short life and part-time nature of most transcultural counselling courses. This reductionist tendency may be further exacerbated by poverty of resources available to training courses by way of appropriate teaching and learning facilities, and purchase of training media. Some specialist courses are now, inevitably, rather costly, and consequently disadvantage some admirable and talented applicants from poorer backgrounds.

Despite this rather bleak overview, we wish to encourage training organizations to embrace this important dimension of transcultural therapy training.

However short the courses are, even in one-day workshops, potential exists for sowing the seeds of interest and commitment and any multicultural/ multiracial society deserves skilled transcultural therapists.

## Appendix to Chapter 8: a brief list of training resources

### Culture and cultural identity

Baker, K.G. (1989) 'A workshop model for exploring one's cultural identity', in D.R. Koslow and E.P. Salett (eds) *Crossing Cultures in Mental Health*. Washington, DC: Society for Intercultural Education, Training and Research.

Casse, P. (1981) *Training for the Cross Cultural Mind*. Washington, DC: SIETAR.

Fowler, S. M. and Mumford, M. G. (1995) *Intercultural Source Book: Cross Cultural Training Methods*. Yarmouth: ME: Intercultural Press.

Kohls, R. L. (1981) *Developing Intercultural Awareness: A Learning Module Complete with Lesson Plan, Content, Exercises and Handouts*. Washington, DC: Society for Intercultural Education, Training and Research.

Lago, C.O. and Barty, A. (2003) *Working with International Students: A Cross Cultural Training Manual*, 2nd edition. London: United Kingdom Council for Overseas Student Affairs.

### Race and anti-racism

Fernando, S. (2001) *Mental Health, Race and Culture*. London: Palgrave/Macmillan.

Katz, J. (1978) *White Awareness: A Handbook for Anti-Racism Training*. Norman, OK: University of Oklahoma Press.

Parekh, B. (2000) *Rethinking Multiculturalism: Cultural Diversity and Political Theory*. London: Palgrave/Macmillan.

Patel, N., Bennett, E., Dennis, M. *et al.* (2000) *Clinical Psychology, 'Race' and Culture: A Training Manual*. Leicester: BPS Books.

Ponterotto, J.G. and Pedersen, P.B. (1993) *Preventing Prejudice: A Guide for Counselors and Educators*. Newbury Park, CA: Sage Publications.

### Development of cultural/racial identity

Carter, R.T. (1995) *The Influence of Race and Racial Identity in Psychotherapy: Towards a Racially Inclusive Model*. New York: John Wiley.

Helms, J. E. (1990) *Black and White Racial Identity: Theory, Research and Practice*. Westport, CT: Greenwood Press.

Ponterotto, J.G. and Pedersen, P.B. (1993) *Preventing Prejudice: A Guide for Counselors and Educators*. Newbury Park, CA: Sage Publications.

Lago, C.O. (2005) You're a white therapist: have you noticed? *Counselling and Psychotherapy Journal*, April, 16(3).

## Cultural differences in communication

Brislin, R.W., Cushner, K., Cherrie, C. and Young, M. (1986) *Intercultural Interactions: A Practical Guide*. Beverly Hills, CA: Sage Publications.

Gudykunst, W.B. (1994) *Bridging Differences: Effective Intergroup Communication*, 2nd edition. London: Sage Publications.

## Questionnaires

*On cultural assumptions*
Koslow, D. R. and Salett, E.P. (1989) *Crossing Cultures in Mental Health*. Washington, DC: SIETAR, p. 20.

*Values clarification – What do you believe about the human experience?*
McGrath, P. and Axelson, J.A. (1993) *Accessing Awareness and Developing Knowledge: Foundations for Skills in a Multicultural Society*. Monterey, CA: Brooks/Cole.

*Organizational settings*
Koslow and Salett (1989) *op. cit.*, p. 151.

*Client attitudes*
Gopaul McNicol, S.A. (1993) *Working with West Indian Families*. New York: Guilford Press.

*Exploration of biases*
Paniagua, F.A. (1994) *Assessing and Treating Culturally Diverse Clients: A Practical Guide*. London: Sage Publications.

*The use of genograms*
Boyd-Franklin, N. (1989) *Black Families in Therapy: A Multisystems Approach*. New York: Guilford Press.

*Assessment of multicultural competency*
See the relevant section in this chapter for references to four multicultural competency/awareness instruments.

## Training videos

Lago, C.O. and Thompson, J. (1989b) *Issues of Race and Culture in Counselling Settings*. Leicester: Department of Audio Visual Aids, University of Leicester.

Dhillon-Stevens, H. (2004c) *DVD Programmes on Anti Oppressive Practice*. Enquiries to: Dhillon-Stevens Ltd., PO Box 120, Chertsey, Surrey, KT16 9YS.

### Case histories for discussion

Eleftheriadou, Z. (1994) *Transcultural Counselling*. London: Central Books.
Kareem, J. and Littlewood, R. (1992) *Intercultural Therapy, Themes, Interpretations and Practices*. Oxford: Blackwell Scientific.

### Training exercises

Pedersen, P.B. (1994) *A Handbook for Developing Multicultural Awareness*. Alexandria, AV: American Counseling Association.

Please note that many of the references above include training materials.

# 9 Addressing the cultural context of the counselling organization

> I define culture as the collective mental programming of a people . . . it has become crystallized in the institutions these people have built together: their family structures, educational structures, religious organizations, law, literature, settlement patterns, buildings . . .
>
> (Hofstede 1980a)

## Introduction

This chapter focuses upon the practical application of counselling within the organizational context in which it is delivered. In general, there has been a paucity of literature on the counselling context, though recent texts such as the following have attempted to ameliorate this situation: McLeod (1994); Carroll and Walton (1997); Lago and Kitchin (1998); Jordan (2004). In addition, the literature on transcultural counselling has also substantially ignored organizational and systemic issues (Bachner and Rudy 1989). However, they may be the very issues that affect the outcome of the therapy for better or worse. Consequently these dimensions cannot afford to be ignored. The suggestions contained in the following text are directly linked to and influenced by much of the theoretical material introduced in the previous chapters.

The decade that has passed since the first edition of this book has witnessed an extraordinary expansion in the provision of therapeutic services through a variety of organizational settings. More and more counsellors and therapists now work in services that themselves are located within larger organizations, e.g. employee assistance programmes, doctors' surgeries, in-house services for police and other public bodies, and so on. Talking therapy has become an established part of 'managed care'.

The nature of the organizational context within which counselling takes place is crucial in providing a conducive and therapeutic setting for clients.

Hall's (1976a) attention to context and its relationship to meaning (previously discussed in Chapters 4 and 6) further reinforces our view that the location within which the therapy takes place might be for some clients as important as the therapy itself. A survey of clients that we conducted at the University of Sheffield Counselling Service in the late 1990s revealed the (astonishing to us at the time) considerable therapeutic value placed by clients upon their relationship with the reception staff and the ambience and refreshment-making facilities of the service reception area. (In one or two cases, these extra-therapeutic variables were valued more highly than the direct work with the therapists.) The association between place and meaning may be much closer in some cultures than others, though even within a 'low-context' culture such as Britain, the psychological association of churches with worship, surgeries with medicine, schools with learning and so on is a close one. Visitors who feel themselves to be affected by their surroundings regularly attribute words such as 'ambience' or 'atmosphere' to particular settings or buildings. Our intention here is to stimulate organizational thinking on the nature and decoration of buildings and the provision of internal systems that constitute the very context within which the practice of therapy takes place.

In acknowledging this potential power of surroundings upon people's emotional states, it would appear woefully negligent, indeed anti-therapeutic, not to attend to these matters in any counselling setting. Architectural and visual symbols, shapes, colours and textures communicate data to clients and have a power, therefore, to represent the values and intentions of the organization. The following short sections therefore provide some of the dimensions worthy of consideration in designing an atmospherically conducive counselling organization.

## Location of counselling agency

Self-evidently the location of the organization needs to be directly related to the proposed clientele that it aspires to work with and on behalf of. This statement does not imply that this is a simple task to achieve. For example, an agency might 'set up shop' or be offered premises on a busy street, between local shops, in the commercial and social heart of a local community. By contrast, premises might be offered or located some considerable distance from the community the agency hopes to serve.

In the first instance, are potential clients likely to feel able to enter the premises if they fear that neighbours who are out shopping may see them? How acceptable (within the local culture) is the activity of 'going for counselling'? In the second scenario, how easily accessible is the building from the community it is intended to serve? What are the local public transport service facilities like? Has the building got its own car park or are there transport facilities close by? Could clients afford the travel costs? If the agency is open in the evenings is access considered to be safe in relation to street lighting and proximity of transport?

Both discretion and convenience of access are important considerations. As evidenced in Chapter 7, mental ill-health and psychological distress are sources of fear, shame and embarrassment in most, if not all, cultures. It seems prudent, therefore, to anticipate this issue in determining where the agency is to be located. A generally useful operating principle might be to seek a location/building that is sufficiently close to the community it serves to afford reasonably convenient access and that is close to but not in the centre of the community and its 'trade routes' of pedestrian and motorized traffic. All of the above also relates to the critical importance of facilitating disabled access. Gates, narrow footpaths, steps, may all prove formidable barriers to access even the front door of the building. If the agency is also located on the upper floors and there is no lift access, what hope is there? The Disability Discrimination Act has been implemented since the first edition of this text appeared, and the implications of this Act are likely to ensure that much more detail and development, importantly, is dedicated to the facilitation of access and comfort for all users of services.

A further consideration here will be the proximity of the agency to counter-therapeutic facilities. For example, a counselling service geared to assisting those suffering alcohol-related problems might not wish to be next door to an off-licence or pub; similarly it would be inappropriate to site a service concerned with helping sexually abused people close to a sex shop or cinema showing 'adult' films. Though these examples seem far-fetched when written as above, one does come across such scenarios in reality. Less extreme but as terrifyingly frightening for clients was an example, some years ago, of a counselling service in a school where not only was the counsellor's office next to that of the head teacher's, but the head teacher insisted she interview all the children before they saw the counsellor! The result was obvious. No effective counselling occurred.

The use of signs and nameplates are also important. How are potential clients going to know that they have arrived in the right place or what the functions of the agency are? The design, details given and positioning of the signboards and nameplates on the building thus have to be presented clearly. How much information is required? This might vary from a minimum of a very clearly visible street number on or near the front door, if clients have been referred or directed, to much fuller descriptions detailing name, address, purpose, hours of opening, instructions for leaving messages, named personnel and so on. If the agency is located up a side street or contained within rooms within a bigger building, additional signposting giving directions might also be worthy of consideration. To have an appointment and then not be able to locate the agency easily and conveniently could be a source of great distress to new clients, or even a reason not to turn up.

An agency local to one of the authors has a discreet nameplate, bell push and invitation to enter. The agency is situated in a terraced house and the front door may be opened, leading directly into a waiting room. Once there, an internal door, which is kept locked, has instructions for the user and a bell push to signal the client's arrival and bring the receptionist to the (inner) door. Clients do not, therefore, have to wait outside on the street to be let in.

Increasingly, public buildings in cities employ a security system in which the front door is kept locked and access is granted by using the bell push and announcing your arrival through an intercom to the receptionist who then lets you in. Again, what effects might this have upon an already anxious client who also might fear being seen waiting on this specific doorstep? Similarly, agencies may have to consider how they might enhance the sensitivity of general portering and reception staff that are servicing other 'customer' enquiries in larger buildings accommodating different organizations.

The overall ethos of this and some of the later sections is to urge a consideration of the psychological importance of orientation, induction and transition upon clients. The psychological research and literature upon transitional periods in our lives (e.g. going away to university, starting a new job, getting married, suffering bereavement, hospitalization, going on holiday, emigrating etc.) highlights the significant effects of change upon our normal emotional functioning. Though one would hope that approaching a counselling agency, in itself, is not a traumatic transition, it certainly can be so for many. Additionally, clients will already be distressed, for that is the very reason they are coming. Consequently, the primary task to be considered by an agency is that of how to facilitate clients' easy access into the therapeutic process through the appropriate consideration of location, signposting and entry procedures detailed above.

## Publicity, literature and culturally sensitive accessibility

The processes of orientation and induction of clients into the counselling process inevitably commence at the client's initial awareness of the organization's existence. This knowledge may come from friends' conversations, local gossip, mention by referring agencies and available literature distributed by the counselling organization itself. Not all of this referred information may be helpful, or even accurate. However, the counselling organization does have more direct control of its literature and may use this to good effect if it is designed and edited well.

Prior, clear and accurate information helps the client prepare for the initial contact with the organization. Beyond details of location, hours of opening, charges etc., opportunities also exist for describing the procedures of what might happen when a client approaches the service, how the counselling process is conducted, what problems might be helped and other details. In a certain sense, this orienting function of the agency's literature is also an aide to acculturation into the counselling process.

Attention must also be given to the nature of language used in these documents as well as which languages are featured. The former will determine the extent to which professional or technical language is used and the clarity with which it is presented. Which languages to use will, of course, be determined by the languages spoken in the community it is intended to serve.

The consultation process with the community with whom it is hoped the agency will work and the subsequent production of advertising and information materials are critical elements in ensuring that the provision of the service meets the needs of the community. For specific examples of these procedures in action, readers are encouraged to consult Rogers-Saliu and Lipman (2005) and Shoaib and Peel (2003). The first of these two articles provides an account of the work of the African Emotional Service within the Terence Higgins Trust (THT). Realizing that, as an agency, the THT was not seeing a representative sample of clients affected by HIV from African Caribbean communities, a number of potential African clients who wanted counselling but didn't want to use existing services were consulted. As a consequence, several different priorities for service delivery were identified and implemented within the agency. Interestingly, the authors argue that calling the service African Emotional Support immediately made it much more accessible.

> It describes accurately what the service does without using the word 'counselling' (which doesn't translate easily for African communities) and makes no mention of mental health. In the past clients reported being confused and frightened when told they should be referred to a mental health service, as they understood 'mental' to mean 'mad', which has an even greater stigma than HIV within African communities.
>
> (Rogers-Saliu and Lipman 2005: 39)

The research by Shoaib and Peel (2003: 87–94) referred to above was conducted in relation to Kashmiri women's perceptions of their emotional and psychological needs, and access to counselling. They also note, as do Rogers–Saliu and Lipman, that a mental health diagnosis may have serious consequences for Asian people who would appreciate the opportunity of talking to a professional about their emotional distress. Again, the terms 'counselling' and 'mental health' were problematic in this community. Given that honour (*izzat*) and shame (*sharam*) are important concepts within Asian culture and are expressed through actions of women more than men, the confidentiality, accessibility and cultural sensitivity of any therapeutic service available to them would have to be soundly based in organizational as well as practitioner practice. Amongst the recommendations for improved services made by the authors of this article are, first, that services would be improved by the recruitment of a workforce that reflects the community/ies it serves and second, that awareness of services amongst potential users should be addressed at two levels. Training on the issues and awareness of services available should be compulsory for gatekeepers at primary care level, especially GPs, and there should be provision of awareness-raising sessions in the community, again highlighting the services available and the means by which they might be accessed. Needless to say, referral agents and agencies are as critical to service usage in their presentation of the service and the work it does as are the other forms of literature and advertising used.

## Contact, information and communication

The task of facilitating availability and accessibility to services has been some-what enhanced and developed in recent years by the use of technology. Telephone counselling services are used substantially more than face-to-face services by men, a factor that has been recognized for some time. In addition, the emergence of email and internet counselling facilities has been a phenom-enon occurring substantially in the early years of the twenty-first century (Lago *et al.* 1999; Anthony 2000; Goss *et al.* 2001; Bolton *et al.* 2004). The emergence of SMS texting via mobile phones is a further development of tech-nology, a development that had, according to Alan Jamieson, Deputy Chief Executive at BACP, a significant benefit in facilitating the availability of support in Vietnam where road communications had been severely affected but use of mobile phones was the norm (Jamieson 2005).

Given this widespread availability of different technologies, and access to them, it is incumbent upon organizations these days to ensure that informa-tion about their services and contact details are available and accurate. In recent addresses to BACP regional consultations for members (York 2004, London 2005, Bristol 2005), Alan Jamieson, Deputy Chief Executive of BACP, has discussed the challenges of diversity to the organization. Stressing the point that people are entitled to have access to information and organizations in a setting and form that meets their needs, he has listed some of the technical developments that have been adopted by BACP and other agencies. These include:

- provision of a website with the facility of increasing the font size for visually impaired persons;
- provision of the journals (on request) in tape and disc format, with

the capacity (in the disc form) for the information to be manipulated to suit the user;

- the option of corresponding with the organization in Braille and 'moon' formats;
- an information line that can be accessed via telephone, email and minicom;
- Welsh and English versions of the journal. (The provision of different languages by counselling organizations, both for information and for counselling, is a point that deserves repetition here!);
- provision of induction loop facilities for the hearing impaired in reception and counselling rooms;
- the availability and provision of sign language signers;
- the provision of compatible software, e.g. Jaws/ Dragon-word and text combinations.

Making services accessible requires an active commitment, a sensitive listening to client needs and an imaginative capacity to respond appropriately to need and demand. Some of the above facilities are a direct recognition of the wide range of client needs and, if not met, only serve to increase the multiple oppressions that many clients may experience. (See the later chapter by Shaindl and Diamond, also Dhillon-Stevens (2005) and Moodley (2003a).)

## Internal decor and style

In moving our attention from the outside of the building to the interior, we have already discussed the possibility and ease of movement for the client from the street into the building. The quality of reception, as evidenced by the decor as well as the receptionist, will have a significant impact on clients and their sense of comfort in this new situation.

All cultures have conventions related to hospitality. These conventions influence both design and layout of buildings as well as informing inter-personal behaviours. The whole of this chapter is concerned with considering how counselling organizations can create the conditions (physical, psychological and emotional) within which successful therapy can occur. In attempting to ease the transition of clients from the outer world to their inner world, counselling personnel (reception staff as well as therapists) will need to consider the impact of the environment and interview rooms as well as their own modes of greeting clients. This factor critically applies to the reception staff who may often not get help, staff training, support or guidance to carry out their task which is so vital to enabling the successful transition from street to therapy. Special courses for the reception staff and involving them in staff meetings can be useful mechanisms to enhance their knowledge and improvement of practice. Indeed, it is not unknown that their impact upon the client might be much more than the therapist's!

Achieving a balance between appropriate and formal surroundings consistent with public service and providing a more intimate and culturally appropriate setting is a considerable challenge to those staff charged with the interior design. Many features of the reception area and interview rooms will require consideration and are listed below.

- Colour and design of wall covering (paint, wallpaper) and complementary colours of ceilings/woodwork.
- Use of floor coverings/carpets/tiles etc.
- Style, comfort and layout of furniture conducive to putting clients at ease.
- Visual images – posters, calendars, paintings, statues, models, icons, notices.
- Plants and fresh flowers.
- Lighting – electric, candles, central, bright, dimmed, sidelights etc?
- Location and storage of leaflets and other information.
- Heating – source of, fireplace, radiators etc.
- Smell – wood polish, neutral, incense, fresh air spray, pot-pourri etc.
- Availability of refreshments – water, orange juice, tea, coffee, biscuits (or not).
- Convenient and signed access to toilets.
- The reception desk needs to be 'protected' or regularly monitored to ensure that any confidential material is not easily exposed to clients. This concern needs to include correspondence, word processor screens and so on.

The above list does not imply an unthinking application of all these elements. However, these elements do each require consideration in relation to the overall purposes of the organization and the client group that it hopes to serve. Decisions might be taken, for example, to use cushions instead of chairs or to invite clients to leave their shoes at the door. Some agencies provide slip-on slippers for clients to use. What is the case for these decisions and are there any contrary tendencies that will also have to be catered for?

The choice of visual images can also be problematic. How might the images selected contribute to the client's sense of comfort, familiarity and of being respected? Culture-specific images unrelated to the culture of the client group may have little impact. For example, a poster of an impressionist painting or a framed photograph of people at the Royal Ascot race meeting on Lady's Day may reflect staff values but bear little relation to clients' lives! Images of sacred buildings, historic sites, religious deities will all have impact, as will photographs of people. A certain understanding or sensitivity toward the underlying messages and values transmitted by such images is certainly required in deciding what goes on the walls and why.

Though brief, the propositions in the above paragraph are certainly not easy to resolve in practice. Nevertheless, a basic survey of clients using a counselling service as early as the 1970s revealed their discomfort in using an agency that had no culturally relevant images to them as a group.

## People matters

> Discriminatory practices result from ways in which the services are organized – selection procedures, points of comparison for promotion etc. (in the case of staff) and diagnostic processes, selective criteria for types of treatment, indicators of dangerousness etc. (in the case of patients). Racism may have direct advantage for the dominant white population in that, for example, the exclusion of black staff from management, and the easing out of black patients from time consuming types of 'sophisticated' treatment modalities or their labelling as (psychiatrically) dangerous allows white society to continue its dominance.
>
> (Fernando 1988)

In Chapter 2 a short organizational case study was given in which the complex issues of inequality were raised within the structure of a counselling agency. Using that case study as a basis, the following sections depict some of the key issues that will require attention in any agency where transcultural therapy is to be offered.

### Management structures

How is the agency to be managed? There are many varieties of management practice that range from voluntary committees on the one hand to named, salaried heads or directors on the other. In between, various combinations of these practices might also involve the consultation of and management by staff groups and user groups.

Several important questions relating to the essential work of the agency underpin the above structures.

- Who is involved?
- What is/are their function/s?
- What power do they have?
- Where does the formal decision making lie?
- Where does the informal decision making lie?

- Are the selection procedures for all staff fair, transparent and in accordance with equal opportunities legislation and the management of diversity philosophy? (See NCVO 2003 for further details.)

## Establishment of policy

Inevitably, there is often a very strong relationship between the establishment of policy and the management structure of an organization. Policy may precede practice and/or be generated and modified by practice. Central to these processes must be a concern for the optimum delivery of the therapeutic endeavour to the community it is designed to serve. Attention therefore needs to be focused on the involvement of this community within the policy setting functions and reviews of service delivery.

An organization will inevitably reflect the culture within which it is embedded and the cultural mores held by organizational members. Where organizations may be composed of members originating from differing cultural/ethnic backgrounds and (in the case of counselling) where the counsellors may have been schooled in different systems of theory, there is likely to be the development of a very complex organizational subculture; a subculture that will have to seek to contain tensions and disagreements between the various cultural, personal, theoretical and practice-based positions held by staff in the service of optimum delivery to clients.

The establishment of policy and good practice, in consultation with the client community and with cognisance of the decision-making machinery and the effects of group dynamics upon everyone involved, are all factors which contribute to the complexity of this task. A further dimension of this already challenging scenario is that of the funding sources of the agency and the extent to which funders determine its activities.

## The counselling team

How are they selected? By what criteria? Who are they? What span of age range, race, ethnicity, culture, gender, faith do they represent? How are they trained? Is the training in-house, external, full-time, part-time, compulsory, short-term, long-term, theoretically homogeneous or diverse, and so on? Such a huge range of questions appears daunting. Nevertheless the patterns of selection and training will influence therapeutic outcomes for clients who use the agency.

Within these two dimensions of selection and training also lie decisions about the employment and involvement of, or liaison with, other forms of helpers, e.g. traditional healers, religious elders etc. In short, how might the counselling agency extend its capacity to respond sensitively and therapeutically to the client demands placed upon it?

### Monitoring outcomes of therapy

The training that most counsellors will have received, a point made elsewhere in this book, will have been derived from Eurocentric models of therapy. Larson (1982) argues that traditionally trained counsellors tend to believe they are competent enough to adapt to any differences among clients and serve their best interests. However, several authors have challenged this false assumption of believed efficacy by researching client experiences of therapy (Thomas and Sillen 1972; Ridley 1995). Consequently an important and often neglected professional activity within most counselling agencies is that of monitoring counsellor effectiveness and client satisfaction. Both quantative and qualitative analysis of client usage of the service will provide the counselling organization with valuable data as to the development of future policy, practice and further training.

This 'feedback loop' of client experience into the organizational process is desirable in all therapeutic situations but in the delivery of transcultural therapy we would argue that it is vital. The very complexity of transcultural therapy demands that counsellor assumptions of helpfulness are not a sufficient basis upon which to establish future practice.

## Concluding thoughts

The quote by Hofstede at the beginning of this chapter points us to the dynamic maelstrom of tendencies that support and reinforce beliefs and practices that make a specific culture. This chapter has attempted an examination of the culture of a counselling organization and provokes the central questions of its suitability to the culturally different clients that use the service. All methods of assessing efficacy and sensitivity of the counselling practice in relation to cultural difference have to be valued and taken note of.

This bold résumé raises many difficulties and challenges to the organization and the various people within it. To be open to constant challenge and to attempt modifications to procedures and practice may be an enormous source of stress for the practitioners. Nevertheless this pales into insignificance when compared with the imposed stresses upon culturally and racially different clients of uninformed, insensitive and inappropriate methods of therapy.

The organization (and the therapists within it) concerned to offer a transcultural service must have clear aims and high commitment to the groups of people they wish to serve, accompanied by professional reflectiveness and integrity.

# 10 Supervision and consultancy: supporting the needs of therapists in multicultural and multiracial settings

> ... and there is no requirement for counsellors to be trained as supervisors before undertaking the role of supervisor to other counsellors.
>
> (Thompson 1991)

## Introduction

The above quote is taken from the introduction to Joyce Thompson's research into the manner in which the issues of race and culture are dealt with on training courses in supervision. Her findings, discussed later in the chapter, revealed a general lack of attention to these issues but an accompanying enthusiasm for their inclusion on future courses. There has certainly been a marked and substantial increase in the provision of courses on supervision in the decade since the first edition was published, but this author is not aware of many courses dedicated to the exploration of supervision focusing on multicultural/multiracial therapeutic issues.

The British Association for Counselling and Psychotherapy has in recent years created a scheme for the recognition of supervisors. The increasing professionalization and standardization of counselling/psychotherapy in Britain has given rise to the publication of new texts that are concerned to stimulate the enhancement of psychotherapeutic supervisory practice. (See, for example, Hawkins and Shohet 1989; Dryden and Thorne 1991; Langs 1994; Shipton 1997; Carroll and Holloway 1999; Gilbert and Evans 2000; Scaife 2001.)

A clear consensus exists in both the American and British literature that clinical supervision is one of the most important ingredients in the training and ongoing development of counsellors and psychotherapists. This consensus prevails across various psychotherapeutic disciplines such as social work, psychology and psychiatry (Loganbill *et al.* 1982).

Ivey (1982) used supervision as a variable within the micro-counselling approach in teaching basic counselling skills to Masters degree students in counselling and guidance. Under experiential conditions it was determined that students who worked with a supervisor in their group performed significantly better than those who did not.

Despite an increasing number of books and articles emerging about supervision, the empirical research on supervision is rather circumscribed. Most of the research is restricted to a truncated range of psychotherapists' experience, examining trainees rather than advanced psychotherapists (Holloway and Horsford 1983).

Earlier literature and research in the United States revealed that:

- supervision was one of the top five activities psychologists engaged in (Garfield and Kurtz 1976);
- more than two-thirds of counselling psychologists provided clinical supervision (Fitzgerald and Osipow 1986, quoted in Thompson 1991);
- fewer than 10 to 15 per cent of supervisors had trained in supervision (Hess 1982); and
- little was known about how supervisors assume the supervisory role, and the full extent of supervisors' responsibilities and legal liabilities were not necessarily evident to supervisees or supervisors (Loganbill *et al.* 1982).

In addition, McCarthy *et al.* (1988) asserted that there is no standard literature or solid theoretical base of syllabus for supervision. Carroll (1988) also noted that supervision was still tied to counselling theory despite its efforts to become a discipline of its own, yet he believed strongly that it was on the verge of a professional breakthrough in Britain.

The earlier literature in Britain in the 1980s did not emphasize the need for formal training in supervision or the examination of variables such as race and culture in the therapeutic relationship (Carroll 1988; Hawkins and Shohet 1989; Proctor 1989; Dryden and Thorne 1991). Nevertheless Shohet and Wilmot do note in Dryden and Thorne 1991 that race, age, sex, ideology, boundaries, power, control and confidentiality could all be issues that block the progress of the supervisor/supervisee relationship (p. 88).

## What is supervision?

'The primary purpose of supervision is to ensure that the counsellor is addressing the needs of the client': this statement is taken from the original Code of Ethics and Practice for Supervisors that was current at the publication of the first edition of this text. This focus upon the client's needs continues to be of paramount importance, as evidenced in the new BACP Ethical Framework, specific points from which are cited later in the chapter.

The following definition of supervision is taken from the *Dictionary of Counselling* (Feltham and Dryden 1993):

> Supervision, literally the overseeing of a counsellor's work, protects the client and supports the counsellor. Regarded as a professional and ethical necessity for practising counsellors, supervision takes various forms but all address key elements of a counsellor's work; its professional and ethical boundaries; the competence and continuing professional and personal development of counsellors; the skilful and purposeful use of therapeutic techniques; client material and client–counsellor interaction; the well-being of counsellors themselves. Counselling itself being an emergent profession, supervision is a relatively recent discipline within counselling. Models of supervision differ according to the orientations of counsellor and supervisor . . .

Forms of supervision may include one-to-one, peer and group situations. A relationship that can be conceptualized as triangular is created when supervision is undertaken by therapists to enhance their work with their client. (See Figure 10.1.) The figure depicts the therapeutic relationship that exists between counsellor and client and the supervisory relationship between counsellor and supervisor. The broken line between supervisor and client is indicative of the purpose and process of supervision, namely that first,

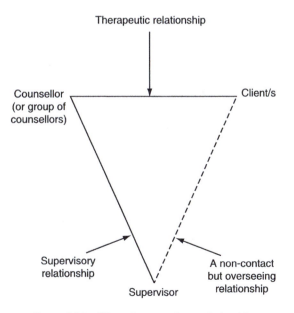

**Figure 10.1** Triangular supervisory relationship.

through the supervisory relationship with the counsellor, the supervisor ensures that the needs of the client are addressed sensitively and ethically and second, that there is no direct contact between supervisor and client.

The complete text of this book is geared towards the exploration of the complex issues that exist when counsellor and client hail from different racial, ethnic and cultural origins. With the addition of a supervisory component to the therapists' work in transcultural counselling comes a new range of complex challenges. Writers have observed that disregarding the influence of cultural factors on the supervisory relationship can contribute to considerable conflict in the supervision process (Guitterez 1982; Cook 1983). Earlier findings by Vandervolk (1974) in the USA revealed that prior to any supervision black supervisees anticipated less supervisor empathy, respect and congruence than white supervisees. With such apprehension being experienced by black supervisees it would be reassuring to report that white supervisors' attitudes were positively oriented towards black supervisees. However, Helms (1982) found that a predominantly white sample of supervisors perceived that supervisees 'of colour' (a term widely used in the USA and meant to include Asian, black and Hispanic people) were less able to accept constructive criticism, less open to self-examination and more likely to have problems keeping appointments than white supervisees. In contrast to white supervisees' self-evaluations, supervisees of colour evaluated themselves more positively on these dimensions than their supervisors did.

In reporting the above findings, Joyce Thompson goes on to say that:

> It seems therefore that Helms' findings indicate that cross-culturally/ cross-racially mixed dyads are more conflictual than racially homogeneous dyads and that supervisors may also contribute to this conflict. If either speculation is true then we may expect visible racial/ cultural group supervisees to experience considerable discomfort or dissatisfaction with cross-cultural/cross-racial supervision.
>
> (Thompson 1991)

Dhingra (n.d.), in acknowledging the higher incidence of white supervisors and challenges posed to black supervisees, produced two lists articulating key issues for practitioners in both roles. These were derived from Fong and Lease (in Pope-Davis and Coleman 1997).

- *Issues for black supervisees*
  Invalidated as a person, issues of trust, feeling vulnerable, reinforcement of social reality, low expectations, difficulty in challenging power issues, more struggle and hard work, living up to expectations to be 'the same', lack of meaningful relationship, ineffective response to needs of black client, premature ending.

- *Issues for white supervisors*
  Unintentional racism, white privileges, avoidance or minimiza-
  tion, guarded and defensive, assumed similarity, power imbalance,
  communication issues, denial of own cultural values, reinforcement
  of oppression, effect on empathic understanding, own needs vs
  supervisees', feeling deficient, questioning credibility.

Within both lists, reference is made to the imbalances of power inherent
within society at large and which can inevitably be played out in professional
relationships, including those of counsellor/client and counsellor/supervisor.
Consistent with the theme of triangular relationships featured in this chapter
is a further triangle detailed by Ryde (2000), who articulates the complex
power dynamics presents in cross-cultural supervision. These are: role power,
cultural power and individual power. Role power alludes to the power inherent
in the role of supervisor and cultural power to the power of the dominant
ethnic grouping, usually someone who was born within the white western
majority group. This power, Ryde asserts, is emphasized if that person is male,
middle-class, heterosexual and able-bodied. Individual power, she explains,
points to the particular power of the individual's personality, which may be
over and above that given to the person through role or culture. When all
three different sources of power are brought together in the same person the
effect may be quite overwhelming.

A further triangular configuration is considered by Ryde in her reference
to Karpman's work (1968) on the dynamics of the 'persecutor/victim/rescuer'
triangle. These dynamic roles, once established, can get played out within
the client/counsellor/supervisor relationship. All of the above indicate how
valuable it is for supervisors to also have their supervisory work supervised, a
point made most strongly within the BACP Ethical Framework.

## The triangular supervisory relationship – extending the concepts

Within the above paragraphs we have already alluded to triangular relationships that have differing transcultural dimensions. For example, just using the
simpler descriptive terms of black and white this triangular relationship looks
like Figure 10.2. In the figure the trans-identity element is embodied in the
counsellor–client dyad and in Figure 10.3 the counsellor–supervisor relationship. Thompson (1991) conceptualized a further six different combinations of
this triangular relationship (see Figure 10.4).

Much has already been said in previous chapters about the many levels
of potential misunderstanding, the effects of prejudice and stereotyping,
the impact of language and so on that may occur within the cross-ethnic

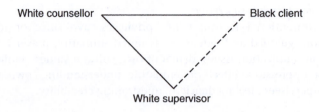

Figure 10.2   The racial complexity of the triangular supervisory relationship (i).

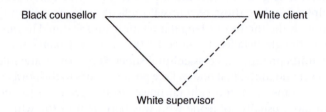

Figure 10.3   The racial complexity of the triangular supervisory relationship (ii).

relationship. All of these phenomena apply as much to the supervisory relationship as they do to the therapeutic relationship. The white supervisor working with a white counsellor who is discussing her work with a black client may have not begun to think about or indeed raise his own awareness of the implications surrounding transcultural counselling. His method of responding to the counsellor's concerns will be informed by his normal theoretical perspective and consequently will not take into account any data that pertains to the client's cultural and racial self. Similarly the white supervisor with a black counsellor already has a transcultural supervisory relationship potentially beset with difficulty as described by Thompson (above).

Despite considerable changes in the decade since the first edition was published, it is still generally the case that the majority of supervisors are likely to be white, a factor that generally impoverishes the potential for more extensive development of therapists in the field and consequently may affect the levels of sensitivity, skill and knowledge counsellors are able to bring to their work with clients.

Supervisors, when consulted by counsellors from different racial or cultural origins to their own or when consulted about clients who are culturally or racially different, will be under pressure to attempt to understand the presented dynamics and story. If untrained and/or insensitive to this arena, all they have to offer is the 'same as usual' responses geared to their present understanding. It is likely that they will be keen to be seen to be of professional use to the counsellor and this pressure may well lead them to present themselves as more knowledgeable, more aware and more informed than they really are on these issues. Likewise, the less secure and/or perhaps trainee

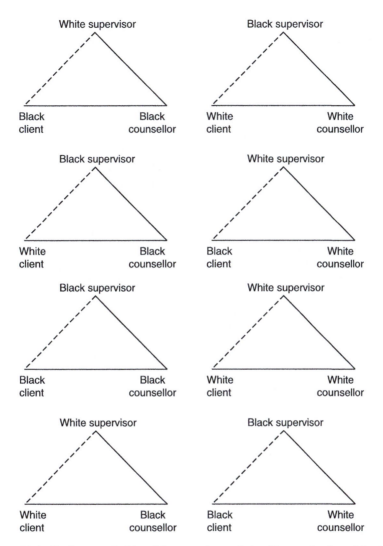

**Figure 10.4** Further complexities of the supervisory relationship: matrix of possible triads.

counsellor will be keen to impress the supervisor and similarly put on a front of 'knowingness' and competence.

This overall scenario now looks like a not too honourable or honest relationship in which both participants are engaged in impressing one another sufficiently in order to retain both self-esteem and esteem in the face of the other. These collusive dynamics are extremely subtle and at best might eventually contribute towards the creation of a more trusting secure relationship between counsellor and supervisor where real differences and ignorance might be honestly shared. Unfortunately, the same dynamics might be perpetuated and thus become corrosive, dishonest and ultimately of little benefit to the counsellor and certainly not protective enough of the needs of the culturally or racially different client.

The above scenario, which sketches the possibility of an 'inauthentic' encounter between supervisor and therapist (for reasons more connected to the creation of a harmonious working relationship), formed the basis of a chapter by Lago and Thompson (in Shipton 1997: 119–30). In this developed conceptualization of the triangular supervisory relationship where differences in identity are present, the idea of inauthentic communication was introduced as being inherent in and between the communications of all three participants – the client, the therapist and the supervisor. This extended conceptual model was based upon the idea of the presentation of a self to the world that ensures, at minimum, a safety and at best an acceptability of the communicator by others. This acceptable part of the person has been termed the 'proxy self'. In an oppressive society it is argued that those who are oppressed have to develop such psychological mechanisms, particularly in their dealings with those who represent oppression, in order to survive.

Presented diagrammatically, the above triangles (Figures 10.2, 10.3 and 10.4) depicting client, therapist and supervisor were then joined by curved lines (rather than the straight lines in the diagrams above) to symbolize that each set of communications (between client and therapist and between therapist and supervisor) was beset with the potential of 'inauthentic' communication and perception. (See Fig 10.5 overleaf) It is recognized, of course, that such phenomena are inherently present in all therapeutic and supervisory relationships, but with the addition of differential identities, then the possibility of substantive misunderstandings, perceptions and projections between each of the participants in this triangular relationship are very considerable indeed.

## The demands on supervisors, professionally and educationally

The disproportionately high number of white supervisors reflects in part the fact that smaller numbers of black people initially enter counselling training and even fewer go on to become supervisors. This makes it professionally incumbent upon supervisors to develop their own skills in this specific arena. Atkinson (1985) suggested that supervisors need to have

- some general knowledge about the racial/cultural identity process;
- information about cultural norms and conflicts between black and whites; and

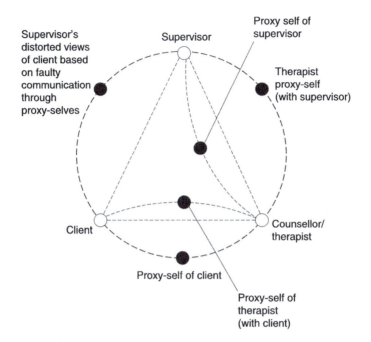

**Figure 10.5**    The 'curved' triangular supervisory relationship.

- a willingness to address how trainees/counsellors manage their anxiety in situations where differences are present (see also Atkinson 1985).

Hunt (1987) suggests that a culturally sensitive supervisor understands the differences in transcultural counselling and can help trainees learn facilitative behaviours in transcultural interactions.

Notwithstanding the above assertions, it seems reasonable to assume that many supervisors, who themselves may have trained as therapists quite a few years ago, will not have been exposed to these issues within their own training or indeed in their clinical practice with clients and will therefore not be sufficiently sensitive or informed about them in the supervisory process.

All of the above leads us to conclude that specialist training of supervisors in these areas is of utmost urgency. Supervisors have a potentially enormous impact upon counsellors and their practice. The significance of their role can be equated to that of their trainers in the creation of sound professional and ethical practice.

## Suggestions and guidelines for supervisory practice

In supervisor training Thompson suggests the following issues as worthy of exploration:

- Power in the counselling/supervisory relationship.
- Perceived power and colonial history and its implications for effective practice.
- Counter-transference issues between counsellor and client and between counsellor and supervisor.
- Parallel process issues between supervisor and supervisee.
- The danger of collusion and over-identification with counsellors and between counsellors and clients.
- The importance of role models and positive images.
- The facts and mechanisms of racism and the effects of oppression.
- Black people's expectations of white people.
- White people's expectations of black people.
- Black/white people's perceptions and expectations of other black/white people in differing roles.
- Advantages and disadvantages of working in same race triads (counsellor, client, supervisor).

Shukla Dhingra (n.d.), inspired by ideas in Pope-Davis and Coleman (1997), produced the following list of suggestions for cross-cultural supervision

- Record sessions.
- Use role play and feedback within supervision.
- Examine one's own values and beliefs.
- Examine one's theoretical model.
- Understand the counsellor's (the supervisee's) key cultural values.
- Explore the cultural meaning of (your and their) world views.
- Pay attention to power dynamics.
- Plan discussion of each other's culture.
- Clarify communication styles.
- Challenge supervisee's cultural assumptions.
- Maintain ongoing self-assessment.
- Acknowledge racism.
- Pay attention to the supervisory process.

Ryde (2000), using the seven modes of supervision introduced by Hawkins and Shohet (1989), converts these into dimensions for consideration within the cross-cultural supervisory relationship. They are as follows:

- Mode 1: A focus on the culture of the client and her context. This includes attending to possible culture-specific behaviours (e.g. avoidance of eye contact).
- Mode 2: Finding ways of responding to the cultural differences and the hidden cultural assumptions implicit in the supervisee's interventions.
- Mode 3: The culture inherent in the relationship between the client and the supervisee. How the cultural material manifests in the process of the work; any 'unconscious supervision' (Casement 1985) which might correct the approach to the work.
- Mode 4: A focus on the cultural assumptions of the supervisee. Also the counter-transference of the supervisee, which seems to be responding to the cultural material, e.g. racist fantasies.
- Mode 5: Cultural difficulties experienced in the here-and-now cultural dynamics between client and supervisee and how they are mirrored in the supervision relationship.
- Mode 6: The supervisor attending to her own cultural assumptions and her own counter-transference, which seem to arise as a result of the cultural material.
- Mode 7: The wider context in which the work is done, particularly organizational, social and political.

All of the above will also require contextualizing within the supervisor's own theoretical model. Again, the implications of this sentence are very considerable indeed despite its few words!

As mentioned earlier, the development of theoretical models of supervision is still in its early stages. Many supervisors inevitably employ their theoretical models of therapy within the supervisory process. Similar to the challenge facing therapists, supervisors also have to consider carefully how the many dimensions of difference (of cultural, racial and linguistic difference, power differences, of racial identity and so on), all described elsewhere in this book, can be incorporated appropriately into their professional task of supervision.

Let us return to the statement of purpose taken from the BACP Ethical Framework:

- Practitioners (supervisors) are responsible for clarifying who holds responsibility for the work with the client.
- There is a general obligation for (supervisors) to receive supervision/ consultative support independently of any managerial relationships.
- Supervisors . . . have a responsibility to maintain and enhance good practice by practitioners, to protect clients from poor practice and to acquire the attitudes, skills and knowledge required by their role.

The implications of this statement are clear and far-reaching.

The supervisor might be working with a counsellor who is relatively unaware of these issues yet who has one or several clients who are culturally and racially different. If the supervisor seeks to fulfil his professional commitment in such circumstances, his task is formidable. He will have to employ some of the following methods and strategies to support and educate the counsellor: teaching, information provision, knowledge of relevant texts, ideas about relevant referral resources, a fund of pertinent metaphors and stories, a willingness to pursue joint learning with the supervisee, a willingness to go beyond his own cultural and theoretical boundaries, a willingness to consult further expertise and so on.

The above methods imply that the supervisor of 'transcultural' therapists must have sufficient personal knowledge and preferably personal experience acquired through personal, clinical and training experiences to meet these very high professional demands.

The timely relevance and pertinence of Thompson's research is evidenced in the above paragraph. Supervisors of 'transcultural' therapists need to be extremely knowledgeable, clinically very experienced and open to much new learning if they are to measure up to the important task assigned them within the wider demands of the 'transcultural' therapy relationship.

# 11  The challenge of research

The field of cross-cultural counselling has received relatively little attention in the research literature. In addition, many counselling agencies and individual counsellors in private practice have so many clients applying from their majority cultural group that there is little incentive for them to develop expertise in cross-cultural work. The multicultural nature of contemporary society, and the existence of large groups of dispossessed exiles and refugees experiencing profound hopelessness and loss, make this an increasingly important area for future investment in theory, research and practice.

(McLeod 1993: 118)

Research in counselling with black and ethnic minority clients, like therapy practice with these groups, is marginal, under-funded and not taken seriously by the mainstream counselling and psychotherapy research community.

(Moodley 2003a)

## Challenge and complexity

There are two overarching dimensions to this chapter on research. The first revolves around the theme of complexity of task and the second encompasses the fact that so much needs to be done.

A variety of research projects have been carried out in the United States and Canada over several decades. (For an elaboration of the issues confronting and being addressed by the research community in the United States and Canada, consult the later chapter by Moodley and Vontress.) In the first edition of this book it was noted that 'very little research, to our knowledge, had been completed in Britain'. This point was further confirmed in an article by Jewel (1994) and underlined by the absence of citations in a handbook of research (Sutton 1987). From time to time, the author has been consulted by counselling students in the UK and elsewhere, wishing to write projects on this subject. Most frequently, these studies have been based on literature reviews and reflections on transcultural counselling practice. In some instances the writers have offered case studies combined with commentary and critique. All of the above efforts have been of value as they have contributed to a growing awareness, knowledge and literature upon the subject.

Research activity within the UK has increased considerably since the publication of the first edition. Much of this activity has been carried out by a growing number of therapists undertaking postgraduate courses at Masters and Doctorate degree levels. In addition, an increasing number of articles are being published in the counselling and psychotherapy journals. In particular, the emergence of the quarterly journal *Counselling and Psychotherapy Research* (CPR), published by BACP since 2001, and the incorporation of an annual research conference (organized under the auspices of BACP), have significantly stimulated relevant research within the multicultural counselling arena. Regular research reports are included on multicultural counselling in CPR and one edition (June 2003, 3(2)) was dedicated completely to the subject. The assertion (in the first edition of this book) that so much needs to be done, both generally and most specifically in Britain, still holds true, though the above trend is very much to be welcomed.

In responding to the above challenge, the issue of complexity of task then confronts the potential researcher. Who do you study? What do you investigate? How do you go about it? Where? How are the results evaluated? Let us briefly take each of these questions and address their implications.

Who is studied? This question is central to the whole task and emanates from a need for researchers to achieve a working definition of the transcultural counselling relationship. The culture, race and ethnicity of both counsellor and client will have immense significance, as will, of course, their differences or similarities in religious orientation, class, gender, language, income level, role and so on. The possible number of combinations of counsellor–client dyads is huge and a mechanism for tolerating or managing this variety of variables will constitute a major challenge.

What is investigated? The purpose of the research will also require much consideration. The task might variously be focused on the communication interaction, the impact of different theoretical styles, an exploration of the effects of projection and counter-transference, perceived levels of counsellor understanding, outcome measures for the client and so on.

The implementation of the necessary research procedures will also constitute a great challenge. How, for example, will counsellors and clients be invited and contracted into the research programme? The demands of ethical practice in this regard alone are considerable. The participants might be subjected to a variety of research procedures such as the following: pre- and post-interview questionnaires, subsequent researcher-led interviews and the use of external evaluators to 'rate' the efficacy of therapeutic procedures. All of these research approaches inevitably introduce further sub-sets of procedural quandaries for the researcher. Many of the challenges referred to above are inevitable and inherent in the more generalized arena of research in counselling and psychotherapy and these have been confronted over several decades now by research practitioners. Research instruments and questionnaires have been developed over time and tested for reliability. Ethical guidelines have been established and mechanisms and procedures for evaluating the impact of counselling upon clients have been created.

The above sets of procedures, however, may not be applied so easily to the transcultural therapeutic relationship. For example, if diagnostic evaluations are used, do they apply or can they be interpreted accurately by the client who is culturally different to the investigator who devised the categories? The inappropriate use of questionnaires applied blindly across races has long been of real and very justified concern as to the racist inferences drawn from the results (Szasz 1970, 1971). In addition, the very motives that drive the researcher cannot be ignored, as research is certainly not a 'neutral' activity (Lehmann 1994).

The above brief examination of the complexities facing the researcher of transcultural counselling are admirably summed up by Sue (1988): 'Not enough research has been conducted, and published research suffers from methodological and conceptual limitations' (cited in Jewel 1994: 17). A further dimension deserves notice at this point. The majority of research work on this subject has been conducted in North America. Though it is considered inadequate (as suggested above), it nevertheless, by virtue of its very existence, dominates and determines theoretical discourse and clinical practice. What is required is a substantial research effort set within the context of British therapeutic practice and British culture. Previous research is obviously profoundly useful but researchers must not be blind to the cultural context within which it was carried out and how that constitutes a different base for interpreting and understanding the outcomes.

## Hypotheses for research

Sundberg constructed a very useful set of 15 'proto-hypotheses' that would lead towards research in intercultural counselling (Pedersen *et al.* 1981). He deliberately used the term 'proto-hypotheses' as they were far from having operational definitions. He also acknowledged that many of these points would be seen to be similar for any kind of counselling, though recognizing their particular application within the transcultural counselling dyad. His main points are summarized as follows:

- Mutuality of purposes and helping expectations

- – Counsellors require awareness of different cultures' help-seeking behaviours.
- – The more similar the goals envisaged for counselling between counsellor and client, the more effective therapy will be.
- – The more similar both client and counsellor are towards a whole range of relationship values the more effective therapy will be (e.g. dependency, power, authority etc.)
- – The more specific the client's concerns are, the more likely she can be helped.
- Developing the counsellor's intercultural understanding and communication skills
  - – The counsellor needs to know about socialization processes in the client's culture.
  - – Counsellor effectiveness will be enhanced by the counsellor's sensitivity to communication and awareness of other cultures' communication styles.
  - – Previous background and training in transcultural interactions will enhance counsellor effectiveness.
- Developing the client's intercultural attitudes and skills
  - – The less familiar the client is with the counselling process the more the counsellor will need to inform the client about it.
- Cultural considerations of the client's areas of action
  - – Effectiveness will be increased when mutual knowledge exists about the client's previous assumptive framework in relation to the present and future fields of action.
  - – Effectiveness is enhanced by understanding the client's relationship to relevant cultures and significant cultural reference group members.
  - – Counsellors need to appreciate the processes of adaptation required in moving across cultures.
  - – Extended consideration of the client's present living situation and, as a consequence of this, possible decisions after counselling is required.
  - – Despite great differences there are some common elements across cultures and clients, e.g. counsellor flexibility of response, client capacity to tolerate anxiety etc.
  - – Culture-specific methods will be more effective with certain groups than others.
  - – The counsellor needs to respect the client as an individual with her own competences and resources.

These 'proto-hypotheses' are worthy of contemplation. However, they also reflect an historic set of conceptualizations defined by the American cultural context of that time. Very scant attention, for example, is given to the effects of race in terms of racism, power inequalities in society, counsellor-projected attitudes and so on. This focus has been taken in some of the later American research (cited in Jewel) but has been more centrally adopted as a matter of great concern within the British context (Lago and Thompson 1989a).

Jackson and Meadows (1991) advocate three principal aims of research that are directly related to their notion of the deep underlying structures of culture. Their concern is to stimulate a deeper understanding of the underlying conceptual cultural systems that may be utilized to inform counsellor sensitivity and therapeutic interventions. They also argue 'that research efforts grounded in well-conceived cultural frameworks that are culturally specific have the potential for resolving issues of scientific cultural bias'.

Much of the literature on multicultural counselling, training and research has been dominated by a suboptimal conceptual system, assert Speight *et al.* (1991). In their article advocating a redefinition of multicultural counselling they explain that there have been two major differing tendencies in the literature. Described as 'etic' and 'emic', the first perspective refers to the universal approach in multicultural theory, practice and research. In research the etic approach emphasizes the development of explanatory constructs applicable to all cultures. The etic approach has merit but a problem of 'imposed etics' arises when explanatory constructs in a particular culture are assumed to be universal and are applied to other cultures without establishing cross-cultural equivalency. Sue (1981) has specifically criticized 'imposed etics' as leading to:

- a pathological view of ethnic group members;
- a genetic deficiency view of ethnic group members;
- a culturally deficient view of ethnic group members; and
- a culturally different view of ethnic group members.

(Cited in Speight *et al.* 1991)

The 'emic' approach, by contrast, refers to the culturally specific approach which has been prevalent within anthropological literature and attempts to understand different groups in their own terms rather than by contrast to other reference groups. An emic approach to research thus focuses on understanding behaviour and experience from within the cultural context in which it occurs. From a positive perspective this approach can portray the relationship between an individual and her society but there is a contrary tendency to overemphasize the influence of culture upon the individual and thus minimize all other human factors.

Moving from the question posed by Sue *et al.* (1982), 'How can a counsellor and client who differ from each other effectively work together?', Speight *et al.* (1991) develop an optimal theory that is derived from earlier work by Kluckholm and Murray (1953), Cox (1982) and Ibrahim (1985) and is also described as having its roots in ancient, traditional African culture.

These influences are explained as follows. Kluckholm and Murray (1953) established a basic paradigm when they argued that every person is like all other persons, is only like some other persons and is also like no other person. Thirty years later Cox (1982) produced a diagram of three intersecting circles in which individual uniqueness, human universality and cultural specificity are representative of the interactive components influencing humans. To fully understand individuals it is necessary to understand the unique and simultaneous influences of these three domains upon individuals' world views, and it is this understanding that Ibrahim (1985) said is necessary for counselling to be effective (Speight *et al.* 1991).

The ancient roots of optimal theory are traced back to the beginnings of human culture where differences are fully integrated into a holistic picture of the individual. This influence is also combined with recent contemporary writings taking a transcendental perspective of universality.

From this theoretical perspective Speight *et al.* (1991) urge that optimal theory research, which is directed towards understanding rather than controlling or predicting, has to grapple with the influences of individual experience and uniqueness, human universal tenets and cultural specificity. They suggest that researchers might use research approaches that involve naturalistic-ethnographic, phenomenological and cybernetic research paradigms to illuminate meaning and subjective experience.

Certainly the above recognition of human complexity reflects the clinical experience of this author who has had both successful and unsuccessful experiences of counselling clients from both near and far, culturally and racially speaking. These experiences have led me to consider the interrelationship between culture and personality and to hypothesize that some people in many cultures, because of their personality type, might be more drawn towards insight-producing, dialogue-based helping than other forms of assistance. By contrast, racially and culturally similar clients to the counsellors, because of their personality, do not find the counselling approach as effective as other approaches. These contrary indications can also exist within cultural milieux that value and reinforce psychotherapeutic interventions or tend towards other helping interventions.

## Racial and ethnic identity development

The majority of race awareness exercises and prejudice prevention programmes are not solidly grounded in accepted theory of interracial interactions. For this reason, many of them have met with only limited success. However, in the past decade research on racial and ethnic identity development has enabled us to bring a new under-standing to the nature of prejudice. Racial identity theory serves as a solid foundation for studying the origins, nature and prevention of prejudice.

(Pontoretto and Pedersen 1993)

The above quote constitutes the first paragraph of the Introduction to the second part of a book on the prevention of prejudice. Racial and ethnic iden-tity development has been described by one American academic theorist as 'being at the leading edge of thinking on multicultural counselling in the United States at the present time' (Lee 1994).

A range of models of identity development has now been developed within the United States. In short, these are models that attempt to describe a developmental process that human beings may proceed through in their quest to achieve a healthy sense of racial and ethnic identity. Feeling good about who we are enables us to respect and value others. Consequently the counsel-lor's own sense of racial identity development becomes an important if not determining component in the cross-cultural counselling relationship.

A range of models have now been developed and the following two are described as examples.

First, Helms's White Racial Consciousness Model (1984) suggests five stages of development: contact, disintegration, reintegration, psuedo-independent and autonomy.

- The *contact* stage is characterized by an unawareness of self as a racial being, a tendency to ignore differences, an awareness that minorities exist yet searching for resolution through withdrawal.
- *Disintegration* involves becoming aware of racism, which leads to guilt, depression and negative feelings. There exists a sense of being caught between internal standards of human decency and external cultural expectations. Responses to this dilemma lead to over-identification with black people, the development of paternalistic attitudes towards them or a retreat into white culture.
- *Reintegration* is typified by hostility towards minorities and positive bias in favour of own racial group.
- Stage four, *the pseudo-independent* stage, is marked by an increasing interest in racial group similarities and differences accompanied by an intellectual acceptance of other groups. Limited cross-racial inter-actions or relationships with special black people are a feature also of this stage.
- The stage of *autonomy* is reached when racial differences and similar-

ities are accepted and respected. This is accompanied by a perception that does not equate differences with deficiencies and an active seeking of opportunities for cross-racial interactions.

The second model to be described is based upon the work of Atkinson *et al.* (1989) and has been termed the Minority Identity Development Model. Again, a five-stage model has been adopted, in this order: conformity, dissonance, resistance and immersion, introspection, and synergetic articulation and awareness.

- The first stage of *conformity* is typified by members of minority groups identifying more strongly with dominant culture values, accompanied by a lack of awareness of an ethnic perspective. Negative attitudes are exhibited towards self and others of ethnic group origin and there is an acceptance of and belief in dominant group stereotypes about self and others.
- During the *dissonance* stage, people experience confusion and conflict about their previously held values and they become aware of issues involving racism, sexism, oppression etc. Feeling anger and loss they search for own-group role models with whom to identify.
- The third stage of *resistance and immersion* involves active rejection and distrust of the dominant culture and greater identification with own culture. The immersion into their own culture involves interest in own group history, traditions, foods, language etc. A motivation to exhibit activist behaviour that is geared to challenging oppression emerges, as well as a possible wish to separate from the dominant culture.
- The fourth stage of *introspection* involves a questioning of their rigid rejection of the dominant group's values resulting in experiences of conflict and confusion regarding loyalty to one's own cultural group and personal autonomy. This is a struggle for self-awareness.
- *Synergetic articulation and awareness* represent a stage of resolution of the above conflicts and offers a sense of fulfilment regarding personal cultural identity. Appreciation of other cultural groups as well as dominant group values is experienced, combined with a motivation to eliminate all forms of oppression.

Other models developed in this area include the Phinney Model of Adolescent Ethnic Identity Development, Cross's Model of Black Identity Development, Kim's Model of Asian-American Identity Development and Arce's Model of Chicano Development. Hardiman (1982) developed a white identity development model based on the analysis of six autobiographies written by white Americans. (These are all referenced and discussed in Ponterotto and Pedersen 1993.) All of this development and research work has been completed within the cultural context of the United States and no equivalent work has been carried out to our knowledge in the British context, a challenge itself to British researchers.

Speight *et al.* (1991) cite several references that criticize these ethnic and racial identity development models as oversimplifying and relying on the notion of ethnic–cultural–racial pride. There are few models, they add, that address the complexity of individuals occupying positions of multiple oppression in society (e.g. persons of mixed-race heritage or of minority group heritage combined with, for example, non-dominant sexual preferences). This complexity of occupancy of multiple social positions within society requires 'researchers and therapists to interrogate their own position as much as those of their respondents and clients' (Phoenix 1994). Diamond and Gillis consider the complexity of multiple diversity in Chapter 16 of this book.

Jewel's (1994) evaluation of multicultural counselling research includes a substantive section on research into racial identity development. He quotes Sue (1988), who points out that ethnicity *per se* tells us little about the attitudes, values, experiences and behaviour of individuals, therapists or clients who interact in a therapy session. Any research into ethnicity matching between client and therapist is likely to produce weak or conflicting results. However, the meaning of ethnicity as it relates to perception, expectations, cultural and linguistic fluency upon the client and therapist may have more potential. Carter (1995) makes the point strongly in noting that it is not our ethnic identity as such that matters, but rather our psychological relationship with that identity that is critical.

Helms and Carter have carried out a wide variety of research based on the white racial identity model that has included linking racial identity attitudes to counsellor preferences and including demographic (social class) effects. They have also attempted to establish theoretical models of how white clients respond to black counsellors (cited in Jewel 1994). Carter (1995) published a seminal work providing extensive research evidence in the employment of identity development models within counselling and psychotherapy and positing a 'racially inclusive' model in clinical treatment. The data generated from the therapeutic dyads and relationship type studies conducted by Carter suggested that

> a therapist's actions (i.e. intentions) and affects, perhaps because of his/her position of power, have a greater impact on the psychotherapy process than a client's reactions. These findings strongly indicate the importance of training a therapist to explore the meanings and significance of his/her own race and to understand how race influences perceptions of self and the client.
>
> (Carter 1995: 228)

The two identity development models described above were introduced to the participants on a British training workshop in the Summer of 1994 and were enthusiastically received as a useful set of conceptualizations for counsellor consideration. Lee, at the same conference, referred to the possibility of assessing the differential levels of counsellor and client attainment on the development models as a way of further understanding the possible dynamics that might emerge during therapy (Lee 1994). Useful research therefore is not only required on generating cultural identity models for the British context but also on their value within the transcultural therapy process. A notable recent contribution to this development has been made by Tuckwell (2002), who considers the challenges of white racial identity on therapists in the British context (see also Chapter 15 of this book).

## Research, clinical effectiveness and training

Since the publication of the first edition of this text, as mentioned in the opening paragraphs to this chapter, the expansion of research practice in counselling and psychotherapy in the UK has been considerable. The quarterly journal *Counselling and Psychotherapy Research* frequently contains pertinent articles on this subject and, in one issue (June 2003), the whole publication was devoted to 'Culture and Therapy'. Some key texts published in CPJ include: West and Abu Talib (2002); Dhillon and Ubhi (2003); McKenzie-Mavinga (2003); Moodley (2003b); Pattison (2003); Shoaib and Peel (2003); Alleyne (2004); and Chantler and Smailes (2004).

This expansion in the UK research field has been stimulated by the emergence of counselling, psychotherapy and clinical psychology doctoral programmes within the last decade. One particular research study within this context was that conducted by Dr Jessica Buckley (2004) on 'Cross-ethnic therapeutic relationships'. This was a qualitative study of white therapists' experiences of working with clients from different ethnic origins. This study substantiated many of the points that have been made earlier in this text: that working across ethnicities

- raises powerful emotional issues;
- challenges fundamental therapist assumptions;
- evokes guilt and shame;
- invokes emotional disconnection from the issues presented;
- induces careful use of language;
- extends the time to build trust;
- encourages therapist avoidance of issues.

It also confirms that:

- the need existed for therapists to talk safely about racism and associated issues;
- therapists commonly searched for 'associative identification' statuses with their clients (e.g. both being female, both having children, etc.); and
- cross-ethnic therapeutic work is frequently experienced as a struggle.

Lee and Richardson (1991), from the substantially advanced American position on research, specify four major domains for research development. Underpinning these, they remind us that research evidence must guide multi-cultural counselling practice. Their four goals comprise the following:

- Toward empirical validation of the continuously evolving notions about multicultural counselling and human development. Not only is new research required on counselling process and outcomes but empirical evidence is also required to support ideas about the effectiveness of indigenous models of helping and the development of culturally responsive counselling interventions.
- Culturally diverse notions of normal human development and investigations that assess mental health outcomes in relation to person–environment interactions among different groups need to be conducted.
- Empirical investigations should be initiated to produce inventories that assess significant developmental aspects of specific cultural groups.
- Research efforts should be structured to investigate intra-group differences among people. The majority of research evidence has been gathered without consideration of differences in factors such as level of ethnic identity, level of acculturation or socio-economic status.

The link between research and training is obviously an important relationship, in which research can inform trainees and they in their turn may be stimulated towards new research. Research is also required on the efficacy of the training process itself in producing knowledgeable, aware and skilled counsellors. A research study by D'Andrea *et al.* (1991) cited by Jewel (1994) suggested, for example, 'it is more difficult to promote the acquisition of multicultural counselling skills than to improve students' cross-cultural awareness and knowledge' (p. 25).

A particular dichotomy exists between the general emphases of traditional counsellor training and transcultural counselling courses. The particular circumstances in Britain surrounding training have to be taken into account here as well (see Chapter 8). But, generally speaking, traditional counselling courses encourage inner awareness, study of therapeutic process, theoretical perspective and the enhancement of skills. Most courses do not concentrate on societal issues, personality types or specific clinical disorders that may be presented by clients. The focus is on the therapeutic process, whoever the client may be.

Short courses on transcultural therapy tend to encourage participants' understandings of various client groups, their relative position in society, the complex issues of personal and institutional power and mechanisms of racism. Awareness training is geared towards comprehending the implications of projection, stereotyping, transference issues and so on. The focus here is on societal understanding with specific client groups, not on therapeutic process and skills. This tension between the two types of training is an interesting one.

Some training developments within transcultural counselling courses have included experimentation with role play scenarios (similar to traditional counselling training) and use of video materials (Clark and Lago 1981). Pedersen's triad model, first developed in the 1970s, has had some impact upon the training, though less so in Britain, and has subsequently been developed further (Pedersen 1988). Research on the efficacy of specific training procedures and how these may contribute to ensuring an appropriate balance between knowledge, awareness and skills development in counselling students is urgently required.

## Summing up

The whole research and training endeavour within transcultural counselling is subsumed by a deep concern for ethical practice in relation to all clients living within a multiracial society. From an ethical perspective, 'counsellors and psychotherapists are obligated to protect clients from potential harm and prevent harm wherever possible (beneficence) and are equally responsible for not inflicting harm upon clients (non-maleficence)' (Lee and Kurilla 1993: 4). This book addresses the substance of the very real challenges facing counsellors in a multiracial and multicultural society. We are concerned that counselling and psychotherapy does not become a further oppressive or damaging instrument of society but that it continues to aspire to be an appropriately liberating and therapeutic force for any troubled individuals, families or groups seeking psychological help and emotional support.

# 12 Updating the models of identity development

## Courtland C. Lee

Understanding the complex role of culture is a major challenge in counselling practice. Knowledge of cultural realities has become a professional imperative, as counsellors encounter increasingly diverse client groups. The purpose of this chapter is to present counsellors with a basic understanding of a key aspect of that knowledge base. It provides a conceptual framework for understanding one of the most important dynamics that must be considered in counselling practice – cultural identity development. It can be asserted that understanding how individuals develop an identity as a cultural being may be the basis for effective counselling across cultures. While much has been written about various aspects of cultural identity development, this chapter is an attempt to synthesize knowledge about this important construct.

## Cultural identity defined

Cultural identity refers to an individual's sense of belonging to a cultural group and the part of one's personality that is attributable to cultural group membership. Cultural identity may be considered as the inner vision that a person possesses of himself as a member of a cultural group and as a unique human being. It forms the core of the beliefs, social forms, and personality dimensions that characterize distinct cultural realities and world view for an individual. Cultural identity development is a major determinant of a person's attitudes toward herself, others of the same cultural group, others of a different cultural group, and members of a dominant cultural group (Sue *et al.* 1996).

## The multidimensional nature of culture

Cultural identity must be understood within the context of the multidimensional nature of culture. Culture can be broadly defined as any group of people who identify or associate with one another on the basis of some common purpose, need or similarity of background. Given this definition, and within sociological and anthropological perspectives, culture can be conceptualized along a number of important dimensions. Culture can be considered from a demographic perspective with respect to such things as gender, age or place of residence. It can also be conceptualized from a status perspective encompassing such things as socioeconomic status, educational level or disability status. Culture can also be seen from an affiliational perspective including both an individual's formal and informal affiliations. Finally, culture can be conceptualized from an ethnographic perspective encompassing such things as race/ethnicity, nationality, sexual orientation, language and religion.

It is important to note that an individual exists at all times in every dimension of culture. At any given time, people make meaning for their lives from various cultural dimensions. For this reason, it must be understood that people are developing an identity from a number of cultural perspectives.

## Developmental models of cultural identity

The development of cultural identity has been theorized within the context of these dimensions of culture. Given this, there are developmental models that explain various aspects of cultural identity including: racial/ethnic identity (Atkinson *et al.* 1993; Cross 1995; Helms 1995); homosexual/gay/lesbian/ bisexual identity (Cass 1979; Coleman 1982; Troiden 1988; McCarn and Fassinger 1996; Marszalek and Cashwell 1999); feminist and womanist identity (Downing and Roush 1985; Ossana *et al.* 1992); biracial identity (Poston 1990; Kerwin and Ponterotto 1995); and disability identity (Vash 1981; Gill 1997).

Cultural identity development occurs in a milieu characterized by complex social interaction amongst groups of people. Therefore, it is important to point out that most models of cultural identity development have been developed in a context in which one group of people has been in a position of economic, political and social dominance whilst another group has been in a subordinate position. Specifically, one group has generally enjoyed cultural privilege and has been idealized and favoured in a common relationship with other cultural groups. This sense of cultural superiority has had an effect on the cultural identity development both of individuals within that group and of those who are not. For example, whites have traditionally enjoyed cultural privilege in their relationship with people of colour (McIntosh 1989). Likewise, heterosexuals have been in a dominant and privileged cultural and social position with respect to gay, lesbian and bisexual individuals. The cultural privilege inherent in the dominant–subordinate relationship profoundly influence the attitudes of members of the dominant cultural group toward members of the subordinate group. Likewise, the perceptions of this cultural privilege held by people from subordinate groups profoundly influence attitudes they hold of themselves and of members of the dominant group (Atkinson *et al.* 1993; Helms 1995; Sue *et al.* 1996).

The various aspects of cultural identity have traditionally been conceptualized as developing through an evolutionary linear stage process (Cass 1979; Downing and Roush 1985; Poston 1990; Atkinson *et al.* 1993; Cross 1995) or, more recently, as a dynamic personality status process in which cultural information is simultaneously interpreted and internalized at a variety of levels (Helms 1995). Though theorists have presented different speculations about the specifics, the stages or levels of cultural identity development for people in subordinate groups appear to progress in the following manner (Sue *et al.* 1996):

- *Stage/Phase 1:* An individual experiences naivety about his cultural realities and those of other people. He may have limited awareness of himself as a cultural being. Significantly, he may engage in depreciation of his cultural group realities and demonstrate an uncompromising appreciation of the dominant cultural group.
- *Stage/Phase 2:* An individual encounters the reality of cultural issues, either his own and/or those of other cultural groups. This reality triggers dissonance about identity as one's sense of naivety, appreciation and depreciation, or lack of awareness is impacted by racism, sexism, homophobia, ableism and so on.
- *Stage/Phase 3:* An individual fully embraces his cultural realities and attempts to relate fully to other members of his cultural group. This acceptance is often accompanied by a total rejection of the realities of the dominant cultural group.
- *Stage/Phase 4:* An individual reflects on the meaning of himself as a cultural being. He generally questions the nature of the complete acceptance of his cultural group and the categorical rejection of the realities of the dominant cultural group.
- *Stage/Phase 5:* An individual internalizes his awareness of self as a cultural being. This internalization is accompanied by an appreciation of his cultural group and a selective appreciation of the dominant cultural group.

Conversely, the process of cultural identity development for individuals in dominant groups generally seems to progress through the following stages or phases (Hardiman 1982; Rowe *et al.* 1994; Helms 1995; Sue and Sue 2003):

- *Stage/Phase 1:* An individual has limited awareness or appreciation of herself as a cultural being. A person has limited knowledge of other cultural groups. At some level, a person feels that his or her culture is superior to other cultures, particularly those in a subordinate social position. Key aspects of culture are naively considered to be unimportant factors in human relationships. There is limited aware-ness of sociopolitical influences regarding racism, sexism, ableism, homophobia and so on.

- *Stage/Phase 2:* At some level, an individual is forced to acknowledge aspects of herself as a cultural being. A person develops an intellectual acceptance of other cultural realities. A person may also develop guilt over her privileged cultural status with respect to other groups.
- *Stage/Phase 3:* An individual fully experiences herself as a cultural being. A person questions or challenges her own cultural privilege. The guilt about her privileged status leads to an overidentification with subordinate cultural groups and a possible denigration of aspects of her own culture.
- *Stage/Phase 4:* An individual engages in an honest appraisal of herself as a cultural being. A person becomes introspective and assesses the categorical nature of her overidentification with subordinate groups and denigration of her own culture.
- *Stage/Phase 5:* An individual develops new levels of understanding about herself as a cultural being. A person actively seeks true relation-ships with diverse cultural groups. A person becomes fully aware of sociopolitical influences regarding racism, sexism, ableism, homo-phobia and so on, and becomes fully committed to eradicating oppression.

Whilst there may be significant variation in these stages or phases for those in both dominant and subordinate groups depending on the aspect of culture that is being considered, it is important to note that not everyone proceeds in a linear fashion through any cultural identity process. Environ-mental considerations including family dynamics and general life experiences make it possible that individuals may start their development at any stage or phase of this process. Additionally, as an individual progresses through the stages or phases of cultural identity development, it is possible that experi-ences with racism, sexism, ableism, homophobia or other systemic factors of oppression may cause him to regress to an earlier level of development.

## Implications of cultural identity development for counselling across cultures

The attitudes and perceptions that people develop about themselves and others as cultural beings have important implications for counselling for both counsellor and client. Perceptions of one's place in a cultural group and one's attitudes about other cultural groups can significantly impact upon thoughts, feelings and behaviour. Therefore, cultural identity must be factored into the counselling relationship as well as into counselling intervention. An understanding of cultural identity may form the framework for culturally responsive counselling.

## Cultural identity and counsellor self-awareness

Culturally responsive counselling must start with counsellor self-awareness. A culturally responsive counsellor has a set of attitudes and beliefs that grow out of self-awareness. These must focus on her view of herself as a cultural being. Such a counsellor is aware of the dynamics of her own cultural realities. This produces a strong identity with one's people and helps to bring a deeper personal feeling of belonging and meaning in life.

Additionally, culturally responsive counsellors are aware of their own cultural values and biases and their origins. They are also aware of the origin or source of most of their views toward members of other cultural groups.

The key point is that culturally responsive counsellors explore such issues in an attempt to discern their own stage or phase of cultural identity. It is important to discover how inherent values and potential biases of a particular stage or phase of identity development might impact upon clients who are culturally different. Such self-exploration leads to self-awareness, which is crucial in developing a set of personal attitudes and beliefs to guide multicultural counselling intervention. Culturally responsive counsellors are sensitive to cultural differences because they are aware of their own stage or phase of identity development.

## Cultural identity as a vehicle for understanding clients

The following case study is presented to illustrate the significance of cultural identity development to culturally responsive counselling intervention. The case considers culture from a race/ethnicity perspective.

---

## CASE STUDY

### Paulette

Paulette is a 19-year-old black woman who is a second year student at a prestigious university in the United States. She is the daughter of a municipal court judge and a prominent physician. She grew up in an affluent neighbourhood in the suburbs of a major American city.

Paulette has spent her entire life in a white world. Throughout her childhood, hers was the only black family in her neighbourhood. She had always attended exclusive private schools where she had been the only black student. All of her friends were white. When she started dating, all of her boyfriends were also white. The social and recreational activities that she engaged in were those of affluent white youth. The only contact she had with other black people and their culture occurred when she visited her relatives at family functions.

While growing up, Paulette's parents impressed upon her how important it was to avoid what they referred to as 'common' black people. For example, she was forbidden by her parents to go into the nearby city because too many 'rough' black people lived there and it was dangerous. In addition, she constantly heard her parents talk about black people and their activities in very negative terms.

When she entered the university all of her friends were white. She had no contact at all with other black students on campus. In fact, the other black students refused to have anything to do with Paulette, because they thought she 'acted white'.

One day during her second year, Paulette went into a shop with several of her friends. While her friends went to the counter to pay for their purchases, Paulette browsed at a magazine rack. While the white male shop assistant was taking money from her friends, he noticed Paulette by the magazines. He said to her friends, 'What does your little nigger friend over there want?'

While Paulette's friends laughed at this remark, it had a profoundly negative effect on her. This was the first time she had ever heard the term 'nigger' used in reference to her. Significantly, it was the first time in her life that Paulette was confronted with the fact that she was black.

After this event Paulette began to have trouble eating, sleeping and studying. She claimed that when she looked in the mirror she did not know who was looking back at her. She stated that she did not want to be around white people any more, but she did not fit in with the black students. She suddenly did not know where she belonged racially. When she told her roommate that she wished she were dead, the roommate took her to the university counselling centre.

### Case analysis

Paulette's seeming depression and possible suicidal ideation have as their basis a crisis of identity. Three assumptions concerning cultural identity development in a racial/ethnic context are evident in this case. First, Paulette's upbringing and socialization would suggest that, as a black person, she is in an early stage or phase of cultural identity development. Her attitudes toward black people are ill-formed at best, negative at worst. Second, she has a strong identification with white people and the dynamics of their culture. Since she was raised in this culture, she has come to internalize the attitudes and values associated with a white racial identity.

Third, however, while her low level of black identity appears relatively stable, it is by no means permanent. The stability of her stage of black identity was shattered when the shop assistant forced her, albeit in an ignorant and cruel fashion, to acknowledge the reality of who she actually is. However, she had no frame of reference as a black person. Her depression stems from not knowing her racial identity. Her identification with white culture has been shattered and she has no cultural identity as a black person. This dissonance has placed her in psychological distress. Importantly, this dissonance can be the impetus for movement to higher stages or phases of cultural identity development.

### Counselling direction with Paulette

Counselling intervention with Paulette must be predicated on an understanding of her challenges related to cultural identity. She must be assisted in working through her issues of racial identity development. Counselling must focus on facilitating her movement through stages or phases of racial identity development to a place where she is able to affirm herself as a black person. Her perception that she shares a common cultural heritage with black people must be enhanced.

In actual counselling work with Paulette this can be accomplished through several important steps. The first step consists of bibliotherapy. Paulette can be introduced to a black cultural experience through the writings of black women writers such as Maya Angelou, Nikki Giovanni and Toni Morrison. Counselling sessions might consist of discussions of Paulette's thoughts and feelings about the ideas and experiences presented in the works of these writers. As Paulette's cultural consciousness with respect to race/ethnicity begins to increase, the second step is to involve her in black cultural activities. This will provide her with an opportunity to interact socially with a black peer group.

As her black identity continues to evolve, the third step should focus on getting Paulette involved in activities in the black community. She might be encouraged to join a black church and participate in social and civic activities in the community.

The final step in the process should involved working through any anger she might feel toward her parents. As Paulette's black identity hopefully continues to evolve, she may become increasingly angry toward her parents. She may feel that they have denied her heritage by raising her in the manner in which they did. As Paulette becomes aware of her racial identity, she may also better understood her parents' stage of cultural identity development with respect to race.

The goal of counselling is to help Paulette reach a stage in her racial identity development where she is able to affirm herself as a black person. She should be able to interact with people from all racial and cultural backgrounds motivated by a sense of pride and self-validation as a young black woman. She should also become confident enough to confront her parents about issues related to her early socialization that she feels have stifled her racial identity development.

It is important to point out that in order to be responsive to presenting issues such as those of Paulette, counsellors must have a thorough knowledge of cultural identity development. It is necessary that they understand the dynamics and issues of their own stage of racial identity development. In a case such as this, culturally responsive counselling is predicated on a counsellor, regardless of racial background, having evolved to a relatively advanced stage of racial identity development.

---

## Conclusions

The case of Paulette underscores the importance of developing the awareness, knowledge and skills for culturally responsive counselling intervention in diverse societies. It also demonstrates the important relationship of the construct of cultural identity to optimal mental health and psychosocial development. Assessing stages of cultural identity development can serve as an important vehicle for understanding the reality and issues confronting clients. Basic to an appreciation of cultural identity development on the part of clients is counsellor self-awareness. As cultural identity development theory implies, effective cross-cultural counselling intervention is enhanced when counsellors work on the evolution of their own cultural attitudes and perceptions.

# 13  Key issues for black counselling practitioners in the UK, with particular reference to their experiences in professional training

## Val Watson

Contemporary writing and discussion on the training of counsellors in the United Kingdom have generally taken a back seat. In particular, work relating to issues of 'race', culture, ethnicity and diversity has occupied a small space in counselling literature. Recently, Lago and Thompson (1996), Banks (1999), Palmer (1999), Tuckwell (2002), Lawrence (2003), McLeod (2003) and McKenzie-Mavinga (2003) have dealt with the issues of 'race' and culture and the implications for the training of counsellors and psychotherapists. D'Ardenne and Mahtani (1989), Ridley (1995), Lago and Thompson (1996), Palmer and Laungani (1999) and Moodley (2000a, 2000b) highlight the hegemonic dominance of European counselling theory within UK counsellor education and the potential for perpetual misunderstanding of minority ethnic clients through the exclusive and often uncritical study of European theory in training programmes.

Feltham (1997) and Hall and Moodley (2001) have criticized the continued support of the core-theoretical model for counselling training by national organizations such as the British Association for Counselling and Psychotherapy; this limits opportunity for a pluralist perspective. McLeod (2003) advocates an approach where the counsellor is less attached to one theory, adopting an attitude of 'cultural naïveté' and respectful curiosity.

Merry and Lusty (1999) state that taking account of the presumed preferences of people from different cultural groups may compromise the theoretical basis and orientation of counselling work. Their view may articulate the fears of counsellor educators in general.

This chapter focuses on some key issues affecting black counselling practitioners in the United Kingdom, with reference to their formative experiences whilst in training. A brief summary of the UK counselling and psychotherapy training context is followed by an exploration of black counsellors' experience of training and practice using qualitative research findings (Watson 2004), and contributions made by counselling and psychotherapy practitioner-researchers currently engaged in the debate. The chapter concludes by outlining some of the challenges facing black counsellors in their work, noting the implications these may have for clients and the training of therapists in general.

An essentialist argument of the distinctiveness of black counsellors' training experience is not claimed here. Issues raised in this chapter may be applicable to individuals who identify as being part of other minority groupings within society. The majority of the black counsellors who participated in the research referred to in this chapter resisted the notion of an 'assertion of common oppression' (hooks 1982), which implies parity of experience of oppression amongst minority groups. The counsellors argued that their experience of racism and the legacy of slavery, colonization and oppression led them to conclude that this experience has a particular effect on therapeutic relationships and counselling practice in the UK.

## Counselling training and practice contexts

An estimated 2.5 million people claimed to be using counselling or counselling skills in their work (Persaud 1996), with 270,000 working within the voluntary sector and 30,000 in independent practice. Coldridge and Mickelborough (2003) note the Royal College of General Practice survey reporting that 51 per cent of GP practices in England and Wales were offering counselling services, constituting an increase of 20 per cent since 1992.

Available statistics do not quantify access to training or therapy by ethnicity, gender or any other category. There are over 900 counselling courses available for study in the UK. The indicators are that a substantial number of people pursue counselling and psychotherapy training through part-time study via further and higher education, voluntary organizations and private institutions.

The familiar profile of the therapist as white, female, middle-aged and middle-class persists. Membership figures available from the British Association for Counselling and Psychotherapy in March 2004 suggest that female therapists are in the majority. Research findings show that few black counsellors are working in or contemplating working solely in independent practice. Most are working in the statutory services, the voluntary sector, education and a range of medical settings or a combination of these.

## Fear in the training room

As well as fascination and interest, the issues that emerge when black and white counsellors are together in training have a significant component of fear and dislike, verging on loathing of each other and themselves. Fanon (1967) observed that the black person is a 'phobogenic object', capable of stimulating anxiety in white people. McInnis (2002), Jones (2001) and others support the research evidence referred to in this chapter which showed that the presence alone of a black person often provokes responses of fear and awe in training and work settings. This was rarely acknowledged openly but often emerged as an issue in situations of conflict.

## The black counsellor's experience of training and practice – some research findings

### Selection and recruitment

Gillon (2002) and Kearney (2003) are critical of the ways in which recruitment, selection and training processes disadvantage and invalidate the experiences and values of trainees from lower socio-economic backgrounds, favouring the promotion of white middle-class values. Black counselling trainees originating from deprived socio-economic backgrounds are at a further disadvantage, training in circumstances where their ethnicity, experience and existence are likely to be denied and their access to professional networks and opportunities post-qualification may be limited.

Research evidence indicates that black counselling trainees were likely to be in the minority (often of one) on most training courses in the United Kingdom. This was so even on courses based in city areas with a recognized high minority ethnic population. Exceptions were courses specifically devised for black counsellors or trainees.

Most of the research participants possessed other professional qualifications and saw counselling as a tool for personal and social transformation. They wanted to be involved in improving black mental health provision including access to talking therapies. This was often inspired by professional or personal experience and their knowledge of national statistics recording the over-representation of black people in the mental health system.

### Black counsellors' perceptions of trainers

Research participants reported that trainers' initial enthusiasm for their arrival trainees changed to viewing their presence as a problem, which placed additional demands on them as trainers who already felt pressurized by the requirements of their task. Trainers were characterized by black counsellors as impatient and resistant to the raising of issues relating to 'race' and culture. Reported accounts showed that they did little to meet black counsellors' needs and in some cases contributed to their difficulties.

## Assessment

Black counsellors believed that they had to work harder, if not twice as hard as their white peers to prove their competence as counsellors. The origin of this notion seemed to be intergenerational and applied to all fields of work. Black counsellors recounted that they were often subject to assertions from their tutors/trainers and insinuations from peers that they were receiving preferential treatment through a form of affirmative action, or that their work was sub-standard.

Some research participants stated that they felt insecure throughout their training because they experienced the course assessment process as idiosyncratic, unfathomable and highly subjective in terms of understanding and conforming to accepted white cultural norms. Group work projects, counselling skills assessments and presentations often exposed language, syntax and cultural differences between black and white trainees which in some cases affected the choices made by individuals for group membership and group work tasks.

## The training experience

Recollecting their training experiences, black and white counsellors include descriptors ranging in emotional heat from 'challenging', 'enlightening', 'fantastic' and 'life changing' to 'gruelling', 'a nightmare', 'scary' and 'ghastly'. Such phrases have poignant significance when accompanied or contrasted with descriptions of experiences of isolation or exclusion as a minority member of a training group.

Generally, the research participants had presumed that counselling training attracted applicants who were politically and socially aware of the sources and impact of racism. They were optimistic that the training course would raise awareness about cultural and racial issues, sensitizing the behaviour of participants. These assumptions were dispelled and replaced by feelings of shock and disappointment at the ignorance (in some cases wilful ignorance) of peers and trainers who regarded the black trainee as an exotic object of study or a source of expertise on issues relating to black people. Over half of the 44 black counsellors involved in the research (Watson 2004) were asked to provide specialist input on 'race' and culture for peers during or immediately after qualifying as therapists. This request was made on the basis of their ethnicity rather than proven knowledge and skills as a trainer.

Generally, black counsellor research participants viewed the training environment as an unsafe place in which to explore issues of 'race', or express feelings of vulnerability. The incidents in training that they remembered as significant invariably contained a racial component. They anticipated that racism (personal and institutionalized) would be a regular feature of their life, training and work experience.

### Recurring themes

Listed amongst black counsellors' fears and experiences were the fear of:

- being scapegoated;
- being excluded;
- being misunderstood;
- being discounted or not believed;
- being labelled/pathologized as difficult, aggressive, fearsome and/or dangerous;
- being visible or invisible;
- being accused of having a chip on their shoulder;
- feeling powerless;
- being judged as incompetent or incapable.

These themes are identified as significant for black people elsewhere in medical settings (McInnis 2002; Alleyne 2004), educational settings (Callender 1997; Osler 1997; Jones 2001) and management settings (Douglas 1998) in describing their learning, training and work experiences.

As their training progressed, black counsellors were aware of the dual tension of being seen as 'not being black enough' by members of their minority ethnic community and, simultaneously, being 'too black' and therefore not conforming to the expectations of the white counselling professional community. They were concerned that in meeting expectations and requirements of the white counselling community there was a risk of losing their black identity and connection; an identity which in many cases had been hard won or learned (Hall 1996), and was still in the process of development enhanced in part by the continuous self-awareness work of counselling training.

## Addressing 'race' and culture in training

Trainee black counsellors found that course prospectus claims that issues of 'race', diversity and culture would be part of the training were misleading and rarely lived up to even basic expectations. Their experience was that training input on issues of 'race', culture and difference were often bolted on in the closing stages of the course or at the insistence of trainees. Whilst acknowledging that other minority group concerns were similarly treated, their perception was that input on, say, sexual orientation, disability or spirituality was more readily welcomed. Trainee members who identified with the minority group highlighted for specialist input expressed similar nervousness and criticism about the training provided.

Advanced notice of input on issues of 'race', culture and diversity evoked a mixture of foreboding and optimism amongst black and white trainees. Black trainees' anticipation of being humiliated or experiencing anger often materialized, creating temporary or longer-term difficulties in their relationships with their white peers and trainers.

The examples below of experiential exercises offered in training since 2001 show how the use of inappropriate material and poor facilitation by unthinking tutors/trainers can alienate black trainees, leaving them unable to retain trust in the competence of the trainer as well as potentially damaging group relations:

- Case study vignettes were issued for group discussion and reflection; all of the case study clients, except for one entitled 'black female client', had a first and family name. The inference that could be drawn from this exercise was that black clients do not need names; generic labels were sufficient. The black trainee counsellor who challenged this was accused by her peers and tutors/trainers of making an unnecessary fuss.
- In a guided visualization exercise a tutor asked participants to imagine that they had become black and to explore their feelings of anger, fear and sadness. Apart from ignoring the presence of the black trainee participating in the exercise, the assumption by the trainer that feelings of anger, fear and sadness would naturally arise demonstrated extreme insensitivity and a lack of understanding, empathy and cultural competence.

In an all-white training group, would objections have been raised about these two exercises?

- In an expressive arts exercise a counsellor drew a black rock, to symbolize herself as strong and solid. Feedback from her white peers was that the image she had created was 'scary' and 'sinister'. They were puzzled by her explanations and offered alternative interpretations linked to feelings of depression and latent anger.

Some black counsellors described how their white peers professed a liking for them as individuals and at the same time insisted that they would not tolerate black people as neighbours, threatening relocation if this occurred. Black counsellors heard their peers repeat and concur with stereotypes about black people being socially and intellectually inadequate with a propensity for criminal drug-related activity. Weeks and even months after the bombing of the Twin Towers in North America in 2001 some counsellor research participants were quizzed about their links and sympathies with Muslim 'terrorism'.

Although a small number of counsellors did report and reflect on the sensitive and effective ways in which 'race' and culture had been addressed, on the whole the experience was a negative one. Black counsellors felt the need to be continually vigilant and remained apprehensive about the inclusion of topical issues and debates which included race and the potential for the mishandling of discussion groups by tutors/trainers.

Research participants were often frustrated by the superficial, ill-informed discussion arising from training input addressing issues of 'race'. In their view, white trainees and tutors/trainers regularly became defensive and tearful when such matters formed part of the learning agenda as a means of deflecting attention away from a deeper exploration. Schwartz and Parker (2002) support this claim, observing that in training sessions that address 'race' and oppression the shame and guilt of white trainees negatively affects their ability to empathize with others. Bergerson (2003) refers to this occurrence as reclamation of the 'pivotal focus' whereby the social, historical and political power of white members of a group can force or steer discussion inward towards the relatively safer realms of dealing with white people's guilt rather than challenging racism and internalized racism.

What the research participants witnessed was their white peers' and trainers' fear of the black trainee; fear of discussing or confronting their own racism; fear of exciting the disapproval of group members; fear of saying the wrong thing. Thus, there was limited opportunity for black counsellors to learn, explore or be challenged about their knowledge and understanding of 'race' and diversity issues as it applies to them and their clients. According to the research these phenomena were not identified or referred to in training by trainers. Black counsellors were expected to deal with the painful outcomes of such training events as best as they could.

Recently black and white racial identity development models such as those devised by Helms (1995) have been used as part of the discussion on race. Thompson (2003) and others are critical of this, insisting that such models serve to 'make white people feel better about themselves', presenting a skewed version of healthy black identity development. Root (2000) argues against an anachronistic and oppositional black–white binary, offering an alternative model which takes account of demographic changes reflecting the increasing number of individuals who claim mixed heritage. This perspective is of particular importance in the UK as statistics show a 75 per cent rise in the 1990s of the number of people who identify as 'mixed race' or dual heritage.

## Visiting black trainers

Whilst there is some logic in inviting a black trainer to provide training on 'race', there is a danger that they will be perceived to have expertise on matters of 'race' alone.

The research suggests that it is likely that they will encounter and be required to mediate the wrath, fear and resistance of the training group as well as the manifestations of guilt and shame that emerge from the training. The black trainer is placed on a flimsy pedestal with high expectations from black and white trainees to meet the needs of all, usually on a one-off basis.

Overall, black counsellors found the presence of the visiting black trainer affirming and challenging. Some trainees were concerned about how the assessed effectiveness of the trainer might reflect on the way in which the subject matter was received. They were also mindful that they must deal with the repercussions of the trainer's visit within the training group. The significance of internalized racism of the black trainer and black trainee was rarely prepared for or discussed.

### Black counsellors as embodiments of power and strength

Black counsellors reported that they were often characterized by their white peers and tutors/trainers as powerful, strong, dangerous, difficult, resentful and obsessed with 'race' and 'race' matters. Black female counsellors believed themselves to be frequently cast in a maternal role, expected to contain group anxiety and anger or to raise matters of high risk in the group that others dared not do.

Black male counsellors, almost always in the minority in training, described how they felt obliged to minimize their gender and ethnicity and thus avoid confrontations with their female peers and tutors/trainers. They talked of working hard to challenge the black male stereotype. Many were keen to act as role models for other black men in their community, post qualification, and acknowledged enhanced appreciation of male–female relations as a result of their training experience.

### Hiding and using silence for survival

The research evidence revealed that many black counsellors felt under siege during training and chose to hide or repress parts of themselves in order to 'survive'. Cleminson (1997/98) and Uwahemu (2004) suggest that this is the learned behaviour of people who have survived oppression, slavery and colonization.

Black counsellors made extensive use of silence as a means of conserving energy, thus avoiding conflict with their white peers. They stated forcefully that their goal was to gain a counselling qualification, not to educate their white peers. Denying their feelings and responses by silencing themselves was seen as a small price to pay. The use of silence allowed them to 'tune out' offensive comments made by their peers. They believed that their silence made them less vulnerable to attack or intrusive questioning. By remaining silent, black trainees unintentionally provoked interest and 'fear' amongst their white peers who relied on continual verbal feedback to monitor relationships with others regarding silence as withholding.

As a participant in training groups I have experienced that my silence is considered more noteworthy than that of other equally reticent white participants. Verbalizing my observations of this difference in treatment does little to change the perceptions or fantasies of some white participants that I have more important contributions to make.

### Rendering 'race' invisible

Research by Thompson and Jenal (1994) and Dhillon and Ubhi (2003) refers to the ways in which the impact of 'race' can be minimized in the white counsellor–black client relationship. In these, black clients tended not to mention 'race' and did not necessarily connect personal crises or impaired social functioning with racial incidents they may have experienced, thereby letting their counsellor and themselves 'off the hook' of exploring the impact of racism or the therapist's own racism. They also suggest that black clients learn to recognize and negotiate their counsellors' 'non-racial' or 'race'-avoidant postures, realizing that issues of 'race' are not for exploration or are too difficult within the relationship.

It is possible that black counsellors learn 'race-avoidant' postures in training which are then replicated in their work with black and white clients. This could have a significant impact on the black counsellor–black client relationship, especially if there are expectations of compatibility based on apparent ethnic match. This is complicated further if counsellor and or client are unaware of their internalized racism, do not identify as black, or see 'race' as an issue in their life experience.

### Internalized racism

Exploration of racial identity development and knowledge of the damaging effects of internalized racism (black self-hatred) is important for black and white trainees. Lawrence (2003) asserts that monitoring internalized racism is a 'daily challenge' for the black counsellor in training and qualified practice. Identifying and addressing internalized racism in the black trainee counsellor is, I suspect, not detected in many training environments as trainers are largely unaware of its existence. However, by not interrupting or challenging what they hear, black counsellors could begin to absorb negative images and messages about black people, accepting these as valid and accurate, internalizing the racism and oppression they experience rather than rejecting it. Clearly, this has implications for black counsellors' relationship with black and white clients.

## Challenges facing black counsellors in their work

### Hard to be seen as professional

Moodley and Dhingra (1998) note that the position of black client was easier for white people to accept than that of black counsellor: this was supported by research findings (Watson 2004), and the common training materials used also supported this assumption. Through their training and everyday experiences, black counsellors learnt how they are perceived by white people. They used this understanding in their work with white and black clients, recognizing that the majority of their clients in their professional work were likely to be white. Black counsellors involved in the research described critical incidents where they experienced subtle rather than blatant racism from clients and colleagues and were unable to challenge or name these events as such. Alleyne (2004) refers to such incidents as examples of 'micro-aggression', which are particularly damaging in their cumulative effect and can encourage internalized racism.

### Training issues and the future

Black and white trainees need a learning environment facilitated by tutors/ trainers who have an understanding of their own racial identity, and are capable of dealing with issues of 'race' and culture effectively.

Discussion at the recruitment stage about black trainees' needs invites joint reflection between the trainer and trainee about how those needs could be met. This would include acknowledgement of black trainees' prior experience of racism and sensitive preparedness for racism that the trainee may experience during training. Counselling trainees whose apparent ethnicity is not considered by them to be an issue may find such an introduction challenging and unnecessary but it could begin important dialogue about the relevance of 'race' or racism in their lives and future professional practice.

Recognition from tutors/trainers and trainees that black counsellors may need to distance themselves from the training group at times for reasons of emotional safety could be a positive addition to the black trainee's experience. In examples known to the writer, tutors/trainers have encouraged the formation of support groups for minority students. Black counsellors have also formed support networks (including therapy and supervision) outside the training group.

Research evidence indicates that the complexity of the situations that arise for black and white trainees is not necessarily illuminated or enhanced by their time in training. McKenzie-Mavinga (2003) suggests that this is because issues of race are not addressed in a 'normative way'. She proposes that the study of historical perspectives to explore black issues and the impact of racism and oppression encourages dialogue and debate in a training group rather than high levels of emotional angst and/or resistance. Further, Lago and Thompson (2002) have shown the usefulness of exploring the dynamics of black–white dyadic relationships in counselling and supervision as a training device.

## The future of counsellor training

### Trainers and training

Insufficient attention has been given to the training of the trainer.

No significant attempt has been made to examine the role and competence threshold of the trainer on a national basis, probably because this area of investigation is complex and contentious. Although some trainers have teaching or training qualifications, current evidence suggests that their preparation for training is based on their experience as trainees with the possible additional support from experienced supervisors or co-trainers. As Clarkson and Nippoda (1998) suggest, trainers tend to train therapists in their own image. Evidence of critique or active debate which identifies good and poor practice is scant. An investigation into counselling training with consideration given to monitoring and auditing its provision is overdue.

### Implications for black clients and black trainees

Black counsellors are likely to receive personal therapy and supervision from white practitioners. This experience directly influences their professional development. Counsellors and supervisors (black or white) who ignore the potential implications of race, racism and internalized racism endanger the therapeutic growth of the client. The arguments for ethnic matching of client and counsellor are persuasive but often impractical. Other ways need to be found to offer black clients opportunities to experience the healing potential of counselling. The recruitment of black trainers to deliver on all aspects of counselling training may influence future debates on training and practice issues.

# 14 Upon being a white therapist: have you noticed?

## Colin Lago

Whiteness, as a set of normative cultural practices, is visible most clearly to those it definitively excludes and those to whom it does violence. Those who are housed securely within its borders usually do not examine it.

(Frankenberg 1993: 228)

The invisibility of whiteness as a racial position in white (which is to say dominant) discourse is of a piece with its ubiquity ... Research – into books, museums, the press, advertising, films, television, software – repeatedly shows that in Western representation whites are overwhelmingly and disproportionately predominant, have the central and elaborated roles, and above all are placed as the norm, the ordinary, the standard.

(Dyer 1997: 3)

There is no more powerful position than that of being 'just' human. The claim to power is the claim to speak for the commonality of humanity. Raced people can't do that – they can only speak for their race. But non-raced people can, for they do not represent the interests of a race. The point of seeing the racing of whites is to dislodge them/us from the position of power, with all the inequities, oppression, privileges and sufferings in its train, dislodging them/us by undercutting the authority with which they/we speak and act in and on the world.

(Dyer 1997: 2)

## Introduction

The quotations offered above provide a piercing glimpse into the breadth and depth of what 'whiteness' is and how it is constituted. Indeed, because I have been 'reading around' this subject in recent months, I believe I could have provided a chapter just consisting of such quotes upon which readers would be invited to reflect and, where possible, which they would discuss with friends and colleagues. (As you may see, I have not written such a chapter, as I feared it would be so unusual in style that it may not be published!) Nevertheless, I have included a considerable number of quotes, for they are elegantly articulated, clear and to the point.

What is it to be white? What is it to be white in a multiracial/multicultural society? What is whiteness? What is it to be a white therapist? What are the effects of whiteness upon our work?

These and other questions of this sort have troubled me for a long time and increasingly so in recent years. One year ago, a colleague (Sheila Haugh) and I offered a weekend course/workshop on this subject and attracted approximately a dozen participants. This year we only received four applications. Of course there may be many perfectly rational reasons for this reduction of interest (e.g. there are too many competing short courses/workshops for counsellors, the advertising wasn't pitched right or in the right journals and so on), but nevertheless it is interesting to reflect on the reasons for this low take-up. My own hypothesis inevitably has to acknowledge the very serious levels of apprehension, fear and guilt that this subject potentially raises in white people and there is reluctance, therefore, to address this complex, often obscure yet devastatingly powerful aspect of society and identity.

Gill Tuckwell, in her recent groundbreaking book (2002), quotes several writers who have examined the dynamics that can arise in the various therapeutic dyads of white therapist–black client, black therapist–white client, black therapist–black client pairings. She cites Thomas (1992), who points out that 'while the working through of feelings about whiteness is not yet an issue in a white therapist–white client relationship, feelings about blackness are an inescapable part of the black patient–black therapist dyad'. *Tuckwell continues,* 'At the heart of the discussion of transferential processes, applied to racial dynamics, lies the notion of therapy as a social process, in which therapy is likely to evoke the same values and assumptions about blackness and whiteness as those in society as a whole.'

## Why should we examine whiteness?

Following on from this notion of therapy as a social process, thus making it a further arena in which larger society's dynamics are inevitably present, Carter provides data, both from his studies of therapeutic dyads and from relationship type studies, that suggest that a therapist's actions (i.e. intentions) and affects, perhaps because of their position of power, have a greater impact on the psychotherapy process than the client's reactions (Carter 1995: 228). These findings, Carter asserts, 'strongly indicate the importance of training a therapist to explore the meaning and significance of their own race and to understand how race influences perceptions of self and the client'.

Peggy McIntosh, from her own pursuit of understanding how her whiteness affected her life experiences, listed 46: 'Special circumstances and conditions I experience which I did not earn but which I have been made to feel are mine by birth, by citizenship and by virtue of being a conscientious law abiding "normal" person of good will' (McIntosh 1988: 5–9).

Amongst her statements appear the following:

- I can choose accommodation without fearing that people of my 'race' cannot get in or will be mistreated in the places I have chosen.
- I can be sure that if I need legal or medical help, my 'race' will not work against me.
- If my day, week or year is going badly, I need not ask of each negative episode or situation whether it has 'racial' overtones.
- I can do well in a challenging situation without being called a credit to my 'race'.
- I can turn on the television or open the front page of the newspaper and see people of my 'race' widely represented.

The sheer inequity of the above statements (and the remaining 41 in her original list) compared to the everyday experiences of 'non-white' people is shockingly obvious.

Adding the above societal positioning of whiteness to Carotenuto's definition of therapists power presents a graphic picture of the (societally and professionally reinforced) white therapists' potential for power (see page 39).

Decoding 'whiteness' has proved a challenging and elusive task, a point that is made time and again in the edited text *White Reign* (Kincheloe *et al.* 1998). For example,

- Even though no one at this point really knows exactly what whiteness is, most observers agree that it is intimately involved with issues of power and power difference between white and non-white people.

  Kincheloe *et al.* 1998: 4)

- This collective white denial of privilege inhibits questions and public reflection on how being white may provide benefits.

  (Kincheloe *et al.* 1998: 15)

- One difficulty in studying the white self is that, until recently, it was an invisible and non-researched category, even difficult to name and not perceived as a distinctive racial identity. Even today, most white Americans either do not think about their whiteness at all or else think of it as a positive or neutral category.

  (Vera *et al.* 1995, cited in Kincheloe *et al.* 1998: 78)

- White skin privilege and the advantages that accompany it are not necessarily obvious to those who are white and middle class.

(McIntosh 1998, cited in Kincheloe et al. 1998: 80)

Even the sub heading for Chapter 5 of this book is 'The Invisibility of Whiteness' (Kincheloe et al. 1998: 77).

An examination of 'whiteness' holds the potential for illumination of the skin colour as an identity within society alongside other identities. Whiteness frequently operates as a veil that conceals and thus disguises its essence. Whiteness is manifestly not just a blank sheet or a sphere of neutrality, as is often implied, but clearly occupies a position in relation to others, and most often (always?) that position is one of relatively greater societal power.

This author also believes that substantial change will not occur until such time as the majority group (and its members) fully recognizes and appreciates the conditions and circumstances created for others by its (their) present way of being. Studying whiteness is more than timely. This concern was already being explored in the 1970s and 1980s in the UK, but is an issue that seems to have been pushed away again from close examination for many years, with perhaps the issues of 'difference' and 'diversity' presently taking centre stage. This chapter asks you not just to pursue a description of the 'different', but rather to explore from what position you are looking and judging. In other words, continue to 'know thyself'.

## So what is it to be white?

Almost 20 years ago, two colleagues (Jean Clark and Shantu Watt) and I used to run an evening class course at Leicester University (that was, incidentally, tied in as an optional study course to the Diploma in Counselling being headed there by Michael Jacobs). An experiential exercise that we used to conduct there involved the exploration of the processes and stages of transition of oppressed groups from the earliest moments of sensing something was 'not quite right' through to striving for and achieving recognition of their felt injustices and thus gaining a sense of parity within society. Such societal change processes are often played out over long periods of time, throwing up, in the process, visionaries, leaders, symbols, arguments, new concepts and metaphors, all challenging to the prevailing attitudes and mores of the time. Within any such historical period of change, the dominant group has seldom, if ever, initiated this movement. For those within it there is no problem, nor, indeed, even an inkling that there might be a problem. However, as the critique grows and begins to achieve recognition, the dominant group is then forced to begin to recognize the challenges (and hopefully accept the truths) as presented. A prime example of such a transitional process is given next.

Perhaps one of the most significant developments in social history during the last 100 years or so was the evolution of the women's movement, from the early days of suffragettes seeking to obtain the vote to women seeking equal pay and, promotion prospects and, most importantly, equality of opportunity with men. This long-term process was strengthened and informed through the raising of consciousness through meeting, relating, uniting, talking and writing.

Male society keenly felt the challenges presented by the women's movement and the effects that it began to achieve over time, attitudinally, socially, industrially and politically. In the latter decades of the last century, some men started and joined men's groups to begin to explore questions for themselves about what it was to be male in contemporary society. Some of these men's groups, as did the women's groups before them, inevitably pursued their discussions along the line of the 'compare and contrast with the "other" model', but this is only one way and does not necessarily lead to the revelation of the essence of that which is sought. At worst, it may only lead to the clarification of what one is not!

This traditional transitional process, as indicated earlier, is fuelled by the cumulative experiences of injustice and powerlessness in members of the minority group, strong motivators to inspire and energize steps to change. By contrast, where groups already occupy the power position, where might they find the energy to understand themselves? Certainly, the exercise referred to above revealed how those members of majority groups who become sensitive to the expressed needs of the minority group can become themselves, for a time, also subject to ridicule and alienation. Barriers to such exploration can therefore be most potent.

## Whiteness, ideology and contradictions

Whiteness often operates in a manner explained by Marx when he described the function of ideologies as concealing the contradictions that lay beneath them. From the perspective of whiteness as a veil, a norm, a neutral zone in which all is apparently possible, then clearly there are a multitude of other contradictory dimensions not being recognized or confronted.

The contrast between the position of being white and not recognizing the 'invisible weightless rucksack' described by McIntosh (1988) ('of special provisions, assurances, tools, maps, guides, codebooks, passports, visas, clothes, compass, emergency gear and blank cheques' that accompany the colour) and being 'non-white' is stark. For those who are not white, who suffer discrimination, the effects go very deep, leading to what West has described as a 'collective clinical depression' (1993: 17).

As Dupont Joshua has noted, racism works from the outside in, from society to the individual's internalization of those values. If society continually sends out messages that you are a second-class citizen, this accumulated message inevitably impacts upon the self-esteem and self-worth of those individuals in receipt of such messages.

Carrying the rucksack of invisible white privilege, the white person can hike through life without much awareness of these impacts. Suffering the implications and behaviours of white societal institutions, on the other hand, can only increase the sensitivity and pain of those not carrying the same rucksack.

## A postscript – dangers and challenges

> The goal here is not to elicit white feelings of guilt for white racism but to encourage insight into the nature of historical oppression and its contemporary manifestations.
>
> (Kincheloe *et al.* 1998: 19)

The overall thrust of this chapter is to encourage and urge white colleagues to undertake a process of reflection and introspection into what their whiteness means, implies, communicates, symbolizes and so on. However, an inherent danger, lurking within this pursuit of white identity awareness, is the reaffirmation (for some) of feelings of superiority over others as a reaction to or defence from the pain of their discovery. This urge to examine whiteness is therefore a thrust to situating whiteness alongside other identities, not to reassert its dominant power position.

As a profession grounded upon the premise of the necessity for awareness generated through reflection, introspection, therapy and group work, we (white therapists) need to embrace these wider meanings and understandings of ourselves and our identities that are embedded in and determined by society.

What about starting your own whiteness awareness group?

# 15 Specific issues for white counsellors

*Gill Tuckwell*

The significance of whiteness as a racial position has been largely discounted until recent years. For white people in the western world, perceptions of race have usually focused on black groups, thus enabling white groups to avoid the challenging, and at times painful, experience of exploring aspects of their own white identity. This predilection within society has been reflected in the counselling profession, where white counsellors have given minimal consideration to the implications of whiteness on their interactions in the counselling room. This chapter seeks to redress the silence about whiteness and address particular issues that are pertinent to white counsellors. Organized in three sections, the chapter discusses the following areas: the influence of the social context on the development of white racial attitudes; the central importance of self-awareness for white counsellors; and the relevance of white racial identity to counselling practice. In this way, the chapter draws on the conventional components of counsellor training by highlighting the need for theoretical knowledge, self-awareness and effective counselling skills.

## Understanding the social context

The social context is particularly important for understanding the development of racial thinking in the western world, for it was here that the concept of 'race' was devised. The use of race as a classification system for human beings dates back to the period of extensive European travel to Africa, Asia and North America in the eighteenth century when white Europeans were impelled to prove their innate superiority over the black indigenous peoples they sought to conquer and enslave. Many racial theories were expounded at this time with the aim of defining discrete racial types based on anatomical differences such as skin colour, hair type or eye shape (Jahoda 1999). Inherent in these theories was the hypothesis that these physical differences were indicators of intellectual capacity, as reflected by brain size and other biological traits. Many white theorists were thus concerned with craniological measurement in a quest to provide scientific proof that white populations had superior mental functioning to black populations. However, the idea of biologically determined racial types was refuted in 1859 by the publication of Charles Darwin's *The Origin of Species*. In this revolutionary work, Darwin identified the human race (*Homo sapiens*) as a single species with gradual and continuous variations within the species rather than distinct racial types. The drive by white imperialists to prove their innate superiority over black people, and thus justify practices of racial domination and control, could no longer be substantiated on scientific grounds after this time.

Despite the lack of empirical evidence for defining pure racial groups, notions about race and supposed racial differences in intellectual ability and behaviour have continued to be prevalent in western thinking. This unwillingness to abandon misconceptions about racial constructs must therefore be understood in sociopolitical and psychological terms by examining the function that these ill-founded assumptions serve at both a societal and a personal level.

From a sociopolitical perspective, it has been seen that race is essentially a system of classification in which groups of people are assigned relative positions in the social hierarchy. Issues of power and control are thus inherent in racial categorization, and white people, as the instigators and beneficiaries of this system of social stratification, clearly have a vested interest in preserving the political and economic advantages conferred on them. Many of the institutions in the western world were created from the material benefits of the slave trade and colonization for the dominant white group, and embedded within institutional structures and practices are notions of white supremacy and black subservience (Malik 1996; Tuckwell 2002). While successive acts of legislation in the UK over several decades have vetoed overt racist behaviour and discrimination, the historical legacy of white racial superiority continues to operate at an institutional level, often through policies and mechanisms that are subtly discriminatory. Whereas race, in biological terms, is not a valid concept, its manifestation in various forms of racism remains a potent force in society. The complex and contradictory nature of race has been summarized by Fernando (1996: 8) in the following way: 'Race, as we generally conceptualise it, is a biological myth but a social reality and as such is a very powerful signifier of individual and group behaviour.'

The significance of race within the structures and systems of society and its power in influencing the everyday reality of different groups of people has, in turn, had a profound cumulative effect at a psychological level. From their respective positions in the social hierarchy, black populations and white populations have had radically different experiences over generations, and these have impacted on the collective memory. A number of black writers (Fanon 1967; Lipsky 1987; Akbar 1996; Alleyne 1998) have drawn attention to the transgenerational trauma of slavery and internalized racial oppression for black people. Alleyne (1998: 44) argued:

> No black person has been spared the effects of racial oppression ... [w]e have carried in our collective and individual psyches a history of enslavement and racial oppression through the generations. This powerful intrapsychic experience has profoundly influenced our relationship with ourselves and with the white other, and it has shaped our determination.

By contrast, white people have been much slower to recognize and acknowledge the far-reaching impact of our historic role as a colonial oppressor, and the damaging effects of white supremacist attitudes for ourselves as well as for black people. This process of denial has been compounded by the requirements of the politically correct era in which white people are increasingly socialized to comply with legislative and organizational policies while primitive feelings and beliefs about race in the inner world may remain unchallenged. Drawing on powerful imagery relating to the colonial past, Morgan (1998) referred to the idea of an 'internal colonizer' who continues to inhabit a corner of the minds of white people, and whose negative responses towards the black other may be involuntarily evoked at times of pressure or vulnerability.

Despite the proliferation of changes that has taken place in social, political and economic life since the days of slavery and colonialism, deep-seated racial attitudes and beliefs reverberate in both subtle and complex ways at different levels of society. On the one hand, the false division between black and white that was highlighted by Darwin on biological grounds is reflected in the socio-political arena. The contemporary postmodern world, with its emphasis on pluralism and diversity, delights in fluidity and ambiguity, and the demarcation between black communities and white communities has in many ways become less distinct. Traditional boundaries relating to gender, culture, race and social class are blurred as individuals are exposed to alternative options and a whole range of lifestyle choices. On the other hand, the function of race in shaping life chances and influencing relative access to power and resources is highly significant in a society that continues to give meaning to racial differentials. In this determining context, racial assumptions and stereotypes abound, and internalized beliefs about the inherent power of whiteness continue to hold sway. As a social process, counselling is subject to the same values and assumptions about blackness and whiteness that pervade the wider society. For white counsellors to avoid the inadvertent replication of prevailing societal attitudes and power imbalances between black groups and white groups requires specific understanding of white racial identity and the development of self-awareness from a racial perspective.

## Developing white racial awareness

It has been argued that the enduring nature of race stretches beyond its every-day usage as a descriptive characteristic and lies predominantly in its force within societal and psychological functioning. With its historical roots in colonization and oppression, the contrived notion of race has enabled white people to concentrate on the supposed deficiencies of black groups and thus avoid the need for self-examination or self-doubt. This focus, which serves to maintain white authority and privilege, leads to some very real difficulties for white people in looking at ourselves and addressing these issues both person-ally and collectively. The overriding present-day challenge centres on the need for us to redefine whiteness, both acknowledging oppressive acts of the past and developing a secure sense of white identity that is free of the colonial overtones of conferred power and superiority. This process requires willing-ness for deep reflection and a re-examination of our thoughts, feelings and behaviour.

For many white people, the idea of being white is an unfamiliar concept, conveying minimal sense of personal identity or collective meaning. In the history of race, it is noticeable that white people have rarely spoken about being white. The paradoxical nature of white people's relationship with their own racial identity was highlighted by Carter (1997: 198) in the following way: 'The predominant comment of Whites is that they are not aware of them-selves as White. This is interesting when one considers the fact that Whites, specifically Europeans and Americans, essentially created racial classification and the ideological and sociopolitical meanings associated with race.' Having grown out of the historical construction of race, the silence about whiteness preserves the traditional position of white authority in which white character-istics, values, customs and traditions are seen as the unquestioned norm, serving as a reference point for defining and labelling other groups. Whilst this may not be conscious or intentional on the part of white people, it never-theless reflects notions of white superiority that have been passed down the generations. The journey into white awareness starts with a recognition of the implications of this silence about being white and an initial step from denial to ownership of our whiteness. This acknowledgement, which brings us face to face with the discomfort of our part in the history of racial domination, as well as our ongoing racist inclinations, is a crucial stage in releasing the unspoken power of whiteness.

The historical legacy of conferred power lies at the heart of white people's experience and awareness of being white. As part of the dominant majority in western societies over many generations, we are used to having status and influence on our side and this has left deeply engrained assumptions about our entitlement to power and privilege. Using compelling imagery, McIntosh

(1988: 94–5) referred to white privilege as 'an invisible knapsack of special provisions, assurances, tools, maps, guides, codebooks, passports, visas, clothes, compass, emergency gear, and blank checks.' These special provisions and assurances, comprising 46 conditions identified by McIntosh as regular experiences for white people, include the following:

- the freedom to live our lives most of the time fairly well assured that we will not be harassed or discriminated against on grounds of our race;
- seeing people of our race widely and positively represented in the media;
- not having to educate people about racial issues or speak for all members of our racial group;
- being able to make mistakes in public and not have people put this down to our race;
- being able to discuss issues of race without fearing negative consequences for ourselves.

Carrying this invisible rucksack of white privilege, white people can hike through life with little recognition of their protected status and little incentive to oppose the racial hierarchy.

The transgenerational position of power and privilege for white people has had a profound impact on our internalized feelings and beliefs, both about ourselves and the black other. These beliefs and attitudes are complex and ambiguous, often revealing a disparity between consciously held principles about racial equality and intense racist feelings that emanate from the unconscious. In this way, notions of white supremacy and overt acts of racism may be abhorred and strongly condemned while primitive racist impulses continue to prevail at an unconscious level. Writing from her own experience, Morgan (1998) discussed the tenacity of these racial processes:

> For me to think differently about my place in the world and the privileges it has brought me requires an undoing of a well-laid system of assumptions about myself. The fact that those assumptions existed and continue to exist does not make me an inherently bad person, but to break through their limitations is hard work.
>
> (Morgan 1998: 54)

This hard work reflects the pervasiveness of our internal racist tendencies, which evoke painful feelings associated with guilt and shame. Morgan further suggested that for white people who strive to be non-racist there is a twofold trauma in facing our own racism: we are confronted not only with negative racist impulses that lie beneath the veneer of political correctness but also with our drive to deny them out of guilt and shame.

The complex interweaving of guilt and shame represents a major source of discomfort and confusion for white people in the journey into white awareness. At the most basic level, this guilt and shame derives from historic acts of atrocity committed in the name of white supremacy. Discussing the collective internalized effects of oppression on black groups and white groups, Fanon (1967: 231) concluded that 'the disaster of the man of color lies in the fact that he was enslaved. The disaster and the inhumanity of the white man lie in the fact that somewhere he has killed man.' In the wake of our historic role as colonial oppressor, successive layers of guilt and shame are intermeshed in white attitudes and responses in relation to the black other, and these are often hard for us to acknowledge and make sense of. Complicated reactions relating to guilt and shame may be intertwined in the following situations:

- getting in touch with our deep-seated racist impulses and feelings;
- benefiting from societal racism and enjoying privileges at the expense of others;
- recognizing our wish to justify ourselves and deny our internal racist tendencies;
- experiencing ambivalence about the fight against racism and the concomitant risks to our own position of self-interest;
- fearing criticism and being seen as racist;
- wanting to feel better about ourselves and develop a more positive sense of our own white identity.

There is no easy way to resolving ambiguous feelings about our whiteness. The route to establishing a more meaningful and creative sense of white identity is both long and gradual, and requires emotional engagement as well as a willingness to push out the perimeter of our understanding. Clearly, history cannot be rewritten, and the shame and degradation of past acts of white supremacy cannot be expunged. The most fitting atonement for our collective past would be demonstrated by an active resolve to examine and address our racial attitudes and actions in the present. This would not only be beneficial to ourselves but also would undoubtedly enhance our interactions with our black counterparts who, frequently, are weary of our retreat into shame and guilt. Emphasizing the process of symbiosis which operates between white people and black people at different levels of society, Ellis (2004: 41) suggested that 'when white society ignores their own basic feelings and needs . . . black society's needs will also go unmet . . . Healthy societies take responsibility for their own psychological, emotional and physiological needs, while respecting those of others.' This responsibility for ourselves, and commitment to serious long-term reflection and action, would mark a radical departure in the struggle against racism.

If we are to overcome the internal racist within us, and find release from the guilt, fear and shame that bind us, we need to meet the 'shadow' side of our psyche, and begin to integrate the acceptable and the unacceptable parts of ourselves. Human beings are capable of great feats of fortitude, love and compassion as well as acts of cowardice, hatred and cruelty. Learning to embrace our positive traits at a psychological level without resorting to the complacency of our societal position would enable us to confront the ruthless racist within. This process, which may pose a threat to our current position of privilege and status, would also promote healing for our ontological insecurity and enable greater psychological well-being in the future. Helms (1992) stressed the significant psychological benefits for white people in raising awareness of their whiteness and developing a healthy white identity:

- the White person can look in the mirror and like and respect the reflected person;
- the White person can look in the mirror and see a White person without also seeing guilt, anger, and confusion;
- the White person can know that he or she obtained privileges and benefits from society because he or she 'was qualified' rather than because he or she is the 'best' color;
- the White person can approach the world from a mentally healthy perspective rather than having to deny, distort, or avoid the realities of the world;
- the White person can learn to pity those who can only love themselves by hating others;
- the White person can be a person who does not survive via hatred;
- the White person will be a more complete human being.

(Helms 1992: 96)

Increased racial awareness will, in turn, enable white counsellors to work more competently with racial dynamics in the counselling room and to be available to the needs of their clients.

## Working with racial issues in counselling

The organization and practice of counselling in the western world is rooted in the dominant values of Euro-American societies such as individual autonomy and personal achievement. Only slowly are efforts being made to overcome the white Eurocentric bias in the counselling profession, and address issues of difference within the professional associations, ethical codes of practice, training programmes and ongoing professional development. Issues of power and dominance at a professional level may be mirrored in counselling interactions, where there is an asymmetry of power between the role of the practitioner and the role of the client. Where the counsellor is white, there is a particular tendency to enact the traditional role of the white professional and to reinforce the norms and values of the wider society. Specific action is therefore needed by white counsellors to explore their own racial attitudes and beliefs and to challenge the dominant white ethos of the counselling profession. This actional approach was highlighted by Ridley (1995), who pointed out that racism is often unintentional, and may be caused by inaction as much as by direct forms of racist behaviour. He suggested that while counsellors may wish to act in a non-racist way, by their failure to accept responsibility for addressing racial issues, they may end up perpetuating the discriminatory practices they seek to avoid. The emphasis on action is discussed below in relation to four basic areas.

### Being aware of one's own racial identity

At the heart of racially aware practice lies the counsellor's willingness to focus on self and to explore her own racial constructs at a subjective level. Since white people have generally been socialized to disregard their whiteness, their sense of their own racial identity has frequently been absent as a component of the counselling relationship. As a result, white counsellors have often avoided their uncomfortable feelings and insecurities about race either by disregarding racial matters or by concentrating unduly on the client's racial or cultural material. As white counsellors, we can only work freely with racial issues with our clients when we recognize the significance of our racial identity and become more comfortable with our own whiteness. Effective integration of racial material in the counselling process is therefore related to the counsellor's level of racial awareness, and her motivation to extend her understanding and competence in this area. The level of awareness will determine the action or inaction taken by the counsellor, leading to radically different outcomes which, in turn, impact positively or negatively on the level of awareness. The significance of counsellor awareness and motivation on the counselling process and outcome is illustrated in Figure 15.1 in relation to self, the client material and the counselling relationship.

For white counsellors, the capacity to break through the barriers of our social conditioning begins with a willingness to face and challenge deep-seated feelings engendered by whiteness and blackness. Only as we engage at a visceral level with uncomfortable and emotionally charged issues will we be free enough to articulate racial matters meaningfully with our clients and work at depth with racial dynamics in the counselling process.

### Understanding issues of power

In earlier sections it was seen that the history of race has led to deeply internalized assumptions about white supremacy and black subservience. Few people in the western world have escaped this indoctrination, which is continually enacted in manifestations of white dominance at various levels of society. For white counsellors, issues of white dominance and power may be played out – often unintentionally – in individual attitudes and in the systems and structures of the counselling profession.

In view of the widespread tendency for white people to associate racial matters with black people, it is often assumed that race is only relevant in interracial situations as, for example, in a white counsellor–black client dyad. While issues of power are highly pertinent in black–white interactions, they

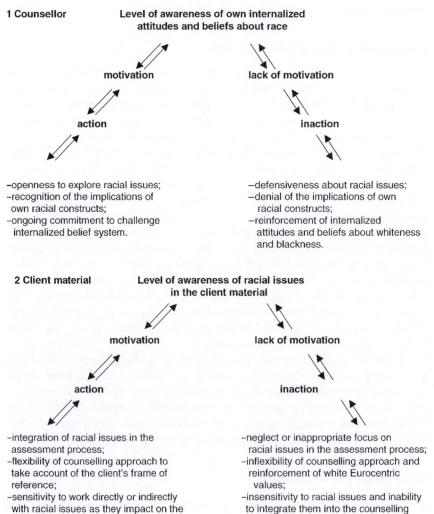

**1 Counsellor**

**Level of awareness of own internalized attitudes and beliefs about race**

**motivation**

**lack of motivation**

**action**

**inaction**

–openness to explore racial issues;
–recognition of the implications of own racial constructs;
–ongoing commitment to challenge internalized belief system.

–defensiveness about racial issues;
–denial of the implications of own racial constructs;
–reinforcement of internalized attitudes and beliefs about whiteness and blackness.

**2 Client material**

**Level of awareness of racial issues in the client material**

**motivation**

**lack of motivation**

**action**

**inaction**

–integration of racial issues in the assessment process;
–flexibility of counselling approach to take account of the client's frame of reference;
–sensitivity to work directly or indirectly with racial issues as they impact on the counselling process.

–neglect or inappropriate focus on racial issues in the assessment process;
–inflexibility of counselling approach and reinforcement of white Eurocentric values;
–insensitivity to racial issues and inability to integrate them into the counselling process.

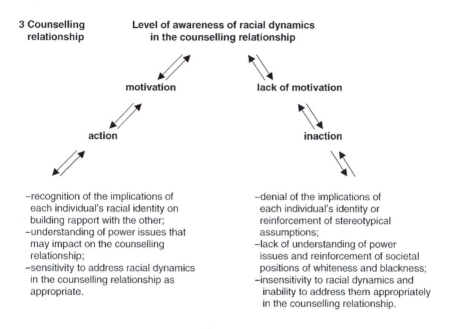

**Figure 15.1**    The significance of racial awareness on the counselling process and outcome.

are equally relevant in all-white situations where there is a particular danger of white collusion by promoting systems and practices that work to the advantage of the white majority and the disadvantage of the absent black minority. Too often have white people relied on black people to take on the burden of change in organizations, and this has been as evident in the counselling profession as elsewhere. With white people occupying the majority of senior positions, there is a specific role for white practitioners and organizers in challenging the white bias of the counselling profession. Issues of power need to be addressed in the following areas:

- the structures and systems of organizations such as professional associations, counselling agencies and training institutions, which have a direct role in determining who enters the profession;
- the regulation of the profession at national and international levels through the establishment of ethical codes of practice and accreditation procedures, which impact on the values and ethos of the profession;
- the formulation of policies and procedures in counselling agencies, which have practical responsibility for the delivery of appropriate counselling services for a diverse client population;
- the content and process of training, supervision and ongoing

professional development of counselling practitioners, whose personal attitudes and professional competence have a major influence on their face-to-face interactions with their clients;

- the stimulation of critical reflection and open debate about theoretical issues and current professional concerns, through ongoing research and articles in counselling journals.

A radical reappraisal of these systems and practices would challenge the white status quo and open the way for a redistribution of power within the profession. Such measures would greatly enhance the credibility and relevance of counselling services for a diverse client population.

### Developing racially aware practice

With the premise that each of us is a racial person whose experiences have been shaped by our position in the social hierarchy, the development of racially aware practice requires an understanding of the influence of race on individual experience rather than a specific set of skills (Helms and Richardson 1997). This is necessarily a gradual and time-consuming process that requires wisdom and ongoing attention as counsellors seek to integrate racial awareness and understanding in their practice. Broad principles for competent practice include sensitivity to the interaction between intrapsychic and sociopolitical experiences, flexibility of approach and an appropriate communication style. These areas are discussed below.

Racial sensitivity requires that appropriate attention is given to race factors in the client material, avoiding the extremes of colour blindness (in which race is denied or avoided) and colour consciousness (in which race is over-emphasized). The challenge for the counsellor is to be able to understand the complex and subtle ways in which racial dynamics may be interwoven in the client's presenting difficulties and incorporate these in the assessment and ongoing counselling process. Stressing the fact that race is often manifested indirectly rather than directly in the client's presentation, Carter (1995: 232) suggested that 'a therapist must learn about and understand the sociopolitical ramifications of a client's racial group membership and must reflect on how the client has integrated race in his or her intrapsychic dynamics'. The interaction between psychological and sociopolitical aspects may be considered in the following example.

---

In a supervision session between a white supervisor and a white supervisee, the supervisee presented her work with a black client in a workplace counselling service. In the counselling session, the client had described feeling low and depressed. As well as domestic difficulties and the recent death of her mother, she was also unhappy at work, and felt unable to fit in with colleagues in her work team. She had requested – for the second time – a move to a different team. In the supervision session, the supervisee concentrated on the client's individual circumstances and at one point, in response to an exploratory intervention from the supervisor, emphatically said 'It's not about race.' The supervisor, while acknowledging the pressures of the client's immediate circumstances, drew the supervisee's attention to issues of racial socialization and sociopolitical forces that are unavoidably part of individual and collective experiences in a racially constructed world. From this perspective, the client's personal circumstances and psychological symptoms could be viewed within a racial context, taking account of possible racial oppression in the workplace and the effects of black internalized oppression on self-esteem and interpersonal functioning. Understanding these processes, which have been described more fully in the first section of this chapter, enabled the supervisee to move beyond her colour-blind approach and consider the influence of underlying racial dynamics, including her own position as a white counsellor. Only then could she draw on racial understanding to inform her practice, and incorporate racial dynamics into the work with her client, whether explicitly or implicitly.

---

The complex interaction of racial processes on psychological functioning and sociopolitical reality has profound implications for the counselling style and approach. In view of the lack of focus on race factors in all the mainstream theoretical approaches to counselling, counsellors cannot rely on any single approach to address the multi-layered aspects of race. This calls for some flexibility in approach, as counsellors apply their own insight and awareness of racial matters and cultural differences to their counselling practice. This flexibility must be balanced by a thorough understanding of the basic tenets of counselling, giving heed to clear boundaries and an explicit working agreement. This flexible approach may be used to facilitate the counselling relationship and construct a style of communication that is appropriate to the client's presentation and cultural frame of reference. These issues are illustrated in the example below.

---

In a live training workshop, a white female counsellor conducted an initial assessment session with a black female client of refugee status. Major issues for the client included attachment, separation and loss. In describing her sadness about loss of contact with her grandchildren, the client asked the counsellor if she had grandchildren, how old they were, and how often she saw them. Sensing this was an important area in building rapport with this client, the counsellor adopted a more self-disclosing style than her usual approach, saying that her grandchildren lived some way away and she was not able to see them as often as she would have wished. In the feedback session following the counselling simulation, the client said that the counsellor's warmth and openness about herself at this moment in the session had been the changing point for her in building trust with a counsellor whose racial and cultural background and life experiences were very different from her own. The counsellor's self-disclosure in this situation had been a means of establishing some common ground and finding some shared emotions.

---

The examples that have been given highlight many of the issues that have been raised in this chapter. It has been argued that the silence about whiteness reinforces notions of white supremacy, and an active approach is needed by white counsellors to contest these assumptions at both an individual and a professional level. Only as we engage in a process of self-reflection will we recognize ourselves as racial people and challenge the socially conditioned posture of white dominance. This will have a profound effect on our capacity to address racial dynamics with our clients, whether black or white, and increase our competence in providing relevant counselling services for the pluralistic social reality of the twenty-first century.

# 16 Approaching multiple diversity: addressing the intersections of class, gender, sexual orientation and different abilities

*Shaindl Lin Diamond and Joseph Roy Gillis*

## Introduction

Discourse on multiculturalism within most professional psychology bodies suggests that counselling professionals should learn about the specificities of various cultures in order to gain competence for working with what has been termed the *culturally different* (Sue and Sue 1999). This approach is reflected in most contemporary textbooks on multicultural psychology, which often include complete chapters devoted to explaining the histories, lifestyles and values of specific cultural groups and how these factors might influence or interfere with the therapeutic process (Sue and Sue 2003; France *et al.* 2004). Knowledge about the background and history of various minority groups certainly can be beneficial to psychologists, but it is not generally realistic to impart more than a superficial understanding of culture that amounts to little more than stereotypes and generalizations. In addition, this approach to understanding diversity fails to address the intersectionality of human identity.

In this chapter, current multicultural discourse based on binary constructs and essentialized notions of difference will be problematized for these very reasons. It will be argued that simplistic formulae explaining human identity can never account for the complex and contradictory nature of intersectionality. Instead of proposing a new model of identity that would include class, gender, sexual orientation and disability as discrete categories, a poststructural analysis of difference will be introduced. According to this analysis, human identity is shaped by an interplay of forces that determine how unique individuals experience themselves and the world around them. This perspective will hopefully challenge readers' current conceptualizations of identity constructs and will raise further questions about how singular identity constructs are infused with all other aspects of the self.

There are many problems associated with examining single groups in isolation from one another. The increasingly diverse demographics of the United Kingdom make it very difficult for professionals to develop complex understandings of specific minority groups in their historic or current realities. In addition, even when academics take time to study a culture in depth, they risk interpreting the other's experience with a colonial gaze. For example, Orientalism has been criticized by a number of theorists for being 'a western system of thought and/or an academic discipline which projects ontological and epistemological distinctions between the Orient and the Occident, and European concepts and values onto the body of the oriental other' (Sullivan 2003: 60). In psychology, Orientalism might present colonial interpretations of 'Oriental' individuals as factual accounts that will in turn inform clinical interpretations of client identities. For example, the informed practitioner might expect the 'Oriental' man to be more feminine, weak, passive and asexual or the 'Oriental' woman to be more exotic or 'eager to be dominated' (Sullivan 2003; Wilchins 2004).

These stereotypes can be perpetuated and legitimated within academic discourse, so as to naturalize colonial understandings of race, gender and sexuality of the 'Oriental' other, while completely overlooking complex cultural histories and differences (Sullivan 2003). Within the current structure of mainstream psychology, a westernized discipline that is committed to seeking out scientific (totalitarian) truth, it may be impossible to teach multicultural knowledge that is not steeped in implicit colonial, racist, patriarchal and heterosexist discourses.

## Identity development models – values and critiques

This is evident in considering the interpretation of client identities using any number of psychological identity formation models (Atkinson *et al.* 1993, Minority Development Model; Cross 1971, 1978, 1991, Nigrescence Model; Katz 1989a, White Ethnic Identity and Worldview; Sabnani *et al.* 1991, White Racial Identity Development; Sue and Sue 1999, Black and White Racial/ Cultural Identity Development Model). For example, Atkinson *et al.* (1993) created a five-stage Minority Development Model to explain how experiences of oppression impact the identity formation of all minority groups. The model stages include:

1   *Conformity*, when a minority individual prefers dominant cultural values over those of his own culture;

2 *Dissonance*, when events occur which lead the minority individual to question the superiority of the dominant culture;

3 *Resistance and immersion*, when the individual completely immerses himself in minority culture and rejects dominant culture;

4 *Introspection*, when the individual begins to feel more comfortable with his sense of identity and no longer views every aspect of the dominant culture as negative; and

5 *Synergistic*, when the individual appreciates the self, other members of minority cultures, and some members of the dominant culture.

Such conceptualizations of minority identity exist only in relation to dominant white identity, and this way of thinking can easily lead to essentialist notions of what it means to be black or white. Although the model's developmental concepts may offer an important contribution to our understanding of difference, it is always problematic to construct racial or cultural identity based on the binary division of white/black.

In addition, these models fail to capture the complex identity formation process of those individuals who occupy multiple positions of oppression or privilege. Using this model, consider the interpretation of a black gay man's identity development, focusing on the sexual orientation aspect of his identity. The Minority Development Model of Identity Formation fails to take into account the specific reasons why a black gay man might not want to reveal his sexuality and may choose instead to identify with another part of his self. Some possible reasons for his reluctance to be public about his sexual orientation are that he may not want to endanger the support of his family as a buffer against an otherwise racist environment or that he may feel that he does not want to expose himself to the heterosexism within his ethnic community. It is clear how such identity formation models are based on singular accounts of minority experience, and all those who do not fit the stereotypes of the group are alienated. In a way, these models pit minority identities against each other, to determine which identification is more formative and consequently in need of more attention.

Also central to these identity formation theories and models is an understanding of social inequality between cultural groups and how inequality impacts identity and lived experience. According to this ideology, material inequalities between groups are caused by the privileging of Eurocentric, patriarchal and heterosexist modes of knowledge within western institutions. Many multicultural proponents (Prilleltensky 1994; Sue 2001; Vera and Speight 2003) respond to this power imbalance by advocating for the equality of various cultures, which will ultimately be achieved by integrating knowledges about different cultural groups within western institutions. This analysis of 'between-group' power organizes marginalized groups into discrete entities, each faced with separate problems originating from different root causes. On the surface, this logic might appear to make perfect sense – a black person is oppressed by racism; a woman is oppressed by sexism; a queer person is oppressed by heterosexism; a disabled person is oppressed by ableism.

In fact, throughout history, marginalized groups of people have endorsed this very logic to form social movements to combat oppressive systems. This identity-based political organizing begins with the group analysing its experience of oppression and moves towards a 'reclaiming, redescription, or transformation of previously stigmatized accounts of group membership' (Heyes 2002). Instead of accepting previously determined ideas, theories and language as determined by the dominant group about the marginalized group's inferiority, the marginalized group transforms its 'sense of self and community, often through consciousness-raising' (Heyes 2002).

Identity politics has been very successful in some ways as a theoretical and practical tool for combating oppressive systems, but its underlying ideology shares many of the same problems as contemporary multicultural psychological discourse when it comes to theorizing identity. Clearly, the whole of an individual's identity and experience cannot be represented by one dimension of that person's membership of one group. Because identity politics in its simplest form is the organization of a group based on one aspect of its identity, this puts pressure on the individual to identify primarily with this one aspect, even though in reality people define themselves in relation to their multiple identities (Heyes 2002). Taking this criticism one step further, this pressure to give priority to and identify with only one aspect of one's identity further marginalizes other identities and experiences that are not dominant within the group.

Eradicating one form of oppression will not liberate all members of the oppressed group, as many suffer from compound forms of marginalization (Combahee River Collective 2000; Moodley 2003a). Burnham (2001: 2) writes:

> The dynamism of the relationships among race, class and gender arises from the fact that, while each has its own unique social logic, polarizes different social forces, and generates distinct, characteristic institutional and cultural modalities, each is also, simultaneously, a constituent and formative factor in the development of others.

Thus, the ways in which oppression and privilege shape identity and lived experience cannot be dissected into neat, simplistic categories, nor can this process be understood utilizing conceptual tools based on a categorical approach. It is not as though a person becomes intelligible through a simple description of a number of discrete base identities. Identity categories such as race, sexual orientation, gender, class and ability level do not exist independently from one another, but rather function together as part of an interconnected system. As Gloria Anzaldua states, 'Identity is not a bunch of little cubby holes stuffed respectively with intellect, sex, race, class, vocation, gender. Identity flows between, over aspects of a person. Identity is a process' (1998: 263–276).

## The challenge of addressing multiple diversity

Although there is a clear need to address multiple differences within the individual, it has proved difficult for multicultural theorists to move beyond an identity politics ideology. At its worst, multicultural psychology continues to construct the individual based primarily on membership of one 'culturally different' group, and individuals are forced to mould their identities and liberationist politics in relation to this imposed definition of self. The danger of disassociating identity constructs such as race, gender, sexuality or ability level in this way, focusing singularly on one identity construct, is the likelihood of producing discourses that are at least implicitly ableist, heterosexist, sexist or racist.

Constrained by this model, marginalized groups within the discipline of psychology are often resistant to recognizing other oppressions for fear of losing resources for combating their own. In fact, this has already happened in the field of multicultural psychology, where many theorists fear that adopting a broad definition of multiculturalism will lead to the marginalization of issues related to racism. As prominent multicultural psychologist Sue explains,

> . . . this stance is not intended to negate the importance of the many cultural dimensions to human identity but notes the greater discomfort that many psychologists experience in dealing with issues of race rather than other sociodemographic differences. As a result, race becomes less salient and allows us to avoid addressing problems of racial prejudice, racial discrimination, and systemic racial oppression.
> (2001: 792)

It is understandable that some multicultural psychologists are not ready to let go of a more exclusive definition of multiculturalism, given the prominence of racism in contemporary society. However, individuals who are marginalized on other bases are facing many of the same challenges within the discipline as racialized people. They are voicing feelings of neglect and invisibility within the current framework of multicultural psychology (Olkin 2002; Carr & Sloan 2003; Gillis 2003). Mohr (2002) argues that when the multicultural movement emphasizes the experiences of groups that are widely accepted as diverse or multicultural, while ignoring other minority groups, it risks conveying the message that some groups are more worthy of study than other groups, which . . . can lead to feelings of marginalization, invisibility, and discrimination among individuals who are associated in some way with the excluded categories.

(Mohr 2002: 2)

In an attempt to remedy some of the tensions among marginalized groups, many multicultural theorists have begun to grapple with issues of multiple identities and experiences of oppression. Still, for the most part, the struggle to understand difference has not significantly shifted away from an identity politics model, but rather theorists are now conceptualizing client experience in terms of multiple (but still discrete) identity categories. This discourse continues to be limited by those identity constructs that are named and recognized as oppressed positions – for example, constructs based on racial identity, ethnic identity, sexual identity, gender identity, class identity and so on. Under this rubric, a person who is black is oppressed, and a person who is black and disabled is doubly oppressed. Therefore, this individual is more oppressed than the former individual. Likewise, a person who is black, gay and disabled is triply oppressed and is therefore even more oppressed.

There are a number of problems inherent to this additive approach to identity and oppression based on the ideology of identity politics. By relying on the same simplistic identity constructs, this in fact reinforces the hierarchy of oppressions, as if there were multiple, discrete identities that cross over one another without ever coming into direct contact. This approach completely fails to recognize the complex and contradictory differences among the hypothetical individuals described above. For example, how is race classed? How is sexuality raced? How is disability gendered? There is no attention paid to how the lived experience of one oppressed identity category is infused with all other aspects that shape the individual (Sullivan 2003).

In a personal account of her identity, feminist author Nomy Lamm (1995) reflects on these very issues. She considers how all the oppressed positions she occupies in a sexist, ableist, heterosexist, fatist society interact with the privileged aspects of her lived experience to shape her personality/being:

> When I think about all the marks I have against me in this society, I am amazed that I haven't turned into some worthless lump of shit. Fatkikecripplecuntqueer. In a nutshell. But then I have to take into account the fact that I'm an articulate, white, middle-class college kid, and that provides me with a hell of a lot of privilege and opportunity for dealing with my oppression that may not be available to other oppressed people. And since my personality/being isn't divided up into a privileged part and an oppressed part, I have to deal with the ways that these things interact, counterbalance and sometimes

overshadow each other. For example, I was born with one leg. I guess it's a big deal, but it's never worked into my body image in the same way that being fat has. And what does it mean to be a white woman as opposed to a woman of color? A middle-class fat girl as opposed to a poor fat girl? What does it mean to be fat, physically disabled and bisexual? (Or fat, disabled, and sexual at all?)

(Lamm 1995)

Nomy Lamm's (1995) description of her identity and the questions she raises illustrate how differently individuals can experience various social locations. It is clear that the heterogeneous, contradictory and complex constructs and discourses that shape Nomy Lamm as a subject cannot be dissected into discrete identities that simply exist side by side, without points of interconnection.

The complexities that shape human experience are rarely captured in current psychological discourse on diversity and multiculturalism. Perhaps the oversimplification of culture is inherent to the fundamental logic of multiculturalism, which conceptualizes culture as a result of different kinds of people, living in different geographic locations, rather than as 'social formations constructed as totalities' (Cotter *et al.* 1992). Culture and other sociodemographic categories take on fixed and rigid meanings and are defined by the characteristics that are decided to be essential to any given group. In this way, multiculturalism ascribes to an ideology of liberal pluralism, where cultures are considered different but of equal value, and each cultural group needs to struggle for representation within societal institutions. Within the limits of multiculturalism and identity politics discourse, the boundaries that define identity and liberationist politics restrict therapists and their clients from defining identities and conceptualizations of self.

Issues of race, class, gender, sexuality and other constructs intersect, interconnect and impact individual identities in unique ways. These categories are not discrete entities. Any given construct of identity will play out differently in each person's life, depending on the many other factors constructing her social experience, making it impossible to make assumptions about the individual based on her single group membership. The underlying message here is that there are no knowable characteristics attributed to specific heritages, sexualities or genders that the psychologist can depend on to interpret the individual client's experience (Walcott 2003). This is not to say that therapists should ignore the material effects of sexism, racism, heterosexism and ableism in society. On the contrary, such an analysis should be at the forefront of our minds as we interpret problems in living experienced by clients. However, in the context of therapy, it is important to address the multiplicity and intersectionality of our clients' identities and understand that we cannot assume knowledge of their lived experience based on their identification with any particular group.

If current multicultural discourses are limiting people and their thera-peutic work, by enclosing them in overly simplistic theories and definitions of self, where can we turn as therapists? Perhaps it is useful to consider how it is that multicultural discourse in psychology has come to theorize identity in this way. How is it that certain differences are highlighted as being more sig-nificant than others? How did these particular differences become so ingrained that they came to be seen as defining characteristics?

## Poststructural analysis

These questions can be examined through a poststructural analysis – not in a pursuit for ultimate truths about human identity, but rather in seeking to develop more sophisticated understandings of the multiplitous subject. The poststructural approach to difference is dissimilar to multicultural discourse in psychology that has evolved within a modernist framework that seeks totali-tarian truths to explain the human psyche under the meta-narrative[1] of humanism. Poststructural theorists have challenged basic concepts that are produced and perpetuated within modernist discourse, such as 'truth', 'mean-ing', 'subjectivity', 'power' and 'freedom' (Derrida 1976; Foucault 1978; Wilchins 2004).

Within the poststructural framework, the liberationist agenda and the very notion that humans are destined to evolve towards some enlightened state are scrutinized (Sullivan 2003). These humanist assumptions are seen to be based on the ideal of a single, universal end goal, which will be experienced and interpreted by all individuals in the same manner. In this way, the meta-narrative of humanism leaves little opportunity for understanding the differ-ences, complexities or ambiguities that remain outside modernist knowledge – or in psychoanalysis terms, outside the conscious realm – and the subject is thus determined by that which is already named.

The problem with language is that it works through a process of exclusion, rooted in polemical relationships based on simplistic good/bad, natural/ unnatural, superior/inferior or normal/pathological formulae (Wilchins 2004). The subject is constructed on a spectrum, with the 'good' at one end and the 'bad' at the other. The 'good' category is always placed at the centre of examination, and all subject positions that deviate from this category are viewed, to some degree, as 'inferior', 'pathological' or 'unnatural'. The 'good' subject is left unquestioned, never to be redefined, whilst the meanings of its derivative subjects are constantly under judgement and reconsideration, as people are progressing towards 'better' knowledge (Wilchins 2004).

In this way, the words used to describe different identity categories do not represent objective reality. Rather, these categorizations are designed to organize the world in a particular way, to perform social actions and, more specifically, to maintain dominance of the dominant group over the marginalized (Sampson 1993). As critical theorist Edwards (1991) explains:

> . . . it would not be possible to establish the existence of named objects, bodily actions and significances in the physical world, or in behaviour, prior to the construction of such naming practices, since it is essentially through and for those practices that the categories are brought into existence.

This approach helps us to understand that, for example, a homosexual identity is not some 'natural, inherent, essential property' of a person *per se*, but is rather 'to be constituted as a person on the basis of certain socially marked characteristics defined in relation to and in the service of the dominant heterosexist ethic' (Sampson 1993: 1223). In other words, organizing the diverse sexualities existing in the population into a binary dichotomy is not simply given in the natural order of things, but by organizing sexuality in this manner, the dominant heterosexual group can reinforce its own normality and define the homosexual group as the other (Foucault 1978; Butler 1990). Similarly, organizing gender identities into a dichotomy of male/female is not merely given by the natural order, but this binary system offers a simplistic way of organizing our world, in which the dominant male group can reinforce its power over the female group. The same approach can be applied to any dichotomous identity construct (i.e. white/black; able-bodied/disabled).

The poststructuralist focus on reaching beyond the dichotomous constructions of modernist discourse, or moving beyond the limits of knowledge, can have a paralysing effect, leaving actors with no stable reference point for naming oppressive practices (Diamond 2005). However, this exercise in deconstructing categories that are generally taken for granted is not meant to question the reality of how the existence of these categories impacts our lives. Deconstruction is a political tool that reveals how truth is constructed in specific contexts at particular times, rather than some transcendent reality to be left unchallenged (Derrida 1976; Wilchins 2004). For example, as seen in the above illustration, because heterosexuality is a 'truth-effect'[2] of modernist knowledge, its dominant position and organization are contestable and therefore susceptible to change (Sullivan 2003). Rethinking the categories that are at the basis of our identities can help actors understand how these constructions are maintaining power differentials between dominant and marginalized groups of people. Without examining these categories that are so often left unquestioned, marginalized groups of people are at a disadvantage for defining their own realities, as they are left with a discourse that supports the hegemony that they wish to challenge (Sampson 1993).

This brand of poststructuralist deconstruction can help clients to examine critically how they are constructed as different, inferior, unnatural or pathological in relation to 'the norm that is defined and upheld by white supremacy, patriarchy, and capitalism' (Clare 2001: 361). Consider, for example, disability theorist Eli Clare's (2001) account of his early experiences of dealing with his difference:

> My first experience of queerness centered not on sexuality or gender, but on disability. Early on, I understood my body to be irrevocably different from those of my neighbours, playmates, siblings. Shaky; off-balance; speech hard to understand; a body that moved slow, wrists cocked at odd angles, muscles knotted with tremors . . . I heard: 'wrong, broken, in need of repair, unacceptably queer' every day, as my classmates called out cripple, retard, monkey; as people I met gawked at me; as strangers on the street asked, 'What's your defect?'; as my own parents grew impatient with my slow, clumsy ways.

Clare (2001) goes on further to explain how he came to believe that his 'body was utterly wrong', to the extent that he wanted to cut off his right arm so that it would not shake. This example demonstrates how 'dominant cultural narratives are internalized, psychically invested, and become part of one's sense of self and one's way of knowing, experiencing, and interacting with the world and others' (Sullivan 2003: 61).

Clare's (2001) story clearly illustrates the importance of working through the internalized oppression and shame infused in identity categories constructed within modernist discourses. Feminist psychologists and other critical psychologists understand that the individual is inextricable from his or her context, whether one is dealing with problems in the therapy room or in another situation (Burstow 1992; Prilleltensky 1994; Vera and Speight 2003). Certainly, actors need to focus on changing the material, external conditions maintaining oppression. However, therapy, by its very nature, offers a site for individuals to concentrate on understanding and (re)constructing their subjectivities. Overcoming negative self-perceptions – such as 'I am inferior', 'I am sick', 'I am immoral' or 'I am wrong' – represents an important political and therapeutic process that necessarily involves the deconstruction of hegemonic definitions of identity. Clare (2001: 363) concludes this in his story, as he writes: 'Our bodies – or, more accurately, what we believe about our bodies – need to change so that they don't become storage sites, traps, for the very oppression we want to eradicate. For me, this work is about shattering the belief that my body is wrong.'

The poststructuralist philosophy for social change is based on the 'local and specific', the 'differences within and between people' and 'the ways in which these are constructed and lived' (Sullivan 2003). As queer theorist Wilchins (2004: 42) writes, 'The void of not-knowing is fertile with potentiality.' Deconstruction of named identity constructs makes space for differences and alternatives, the excluded and the erased (Derrida 1976; Wilchins 2004). Rather than constituting difference only in terms of the degrees of difference from the 'normal', poststructuralism aims at bringing forth differences, complexities and ambiguities from the fertile place of not-knowing. It is in this place that actors can begin to overcome the paralysis caused by totalitarian truths, which can never account for the potentiality of multiplicity.

Over the past 30 years, theories and models of racial and cultural identity development have become critical to the theory, research and practice of multicultural psychology and psychotherapy. These models have brought important concepts, such as oppression, privilege and power, into the realm of psychology and our understanding of human diversity. Perhaps the most salient information coming from these models is the critical process of therapists becoming aware of internalized dominant cultural values and assumptions that will necessarily impact the therapeutic process. However, as demonstrated in this chapter, constructing racial or cultural difference based solely on a process defined by binary constructions is very problematic and fails to address the complex forces that shape unique individuals. In our theoretical quest to understand the intersections of multiple diversities, a poststructuralist analysis may be useful in helping professionals to think 'outside the box' and to remain open to the infinite possibilities that our clients present to us. This perspective offers one strategy for addressing the complexities and contradictions implicated in human identity. It is evident that examining difference using poststructuralist theory will not lead psychologists and clients to simple (totalitarian) truths about themselves or their identities, but at least it will not trap us within limiting discourses that define identity, lived experience and solutions to complex issues in fixed and confining ways. Of course, it is important that therapists develop an awareness of how race, gender, sexuality or ability level might impact one's experience, and we can develop these understandings through reading and by immersing ourselves in the struggles of oppressed people. However, in the therapy room, we should let clients lead us to understand their social locations and how various forces have come to shape their lived experiences in unique ways. This is not to assume that clients have access to knowledge about all the discourses and forces that have shaped their being. Rather, this analysis prepares us to come with an openness to take part in a journey of discovering how unique individuals make sense of their social realities and being in the world.

## Notes

1    In poststructuralism, a meta-narrative is 'a grand overarching account, or all-encompassing story, which is thought to give order to the historical

record, and to justify the existence of social institutions and authorities' (Wikipedia 2005).

2    A 'truth-effect' occurs through the repetition of a claim. As a claim is repeated, it becomes more familiar until it eventually solidifies into a truth. Once a claim is accepted as a truth, people no longer question its validity, despite the absence of evidence to support it.

# 17 Race and culture in counselling research

## Roy Moodley and Clemmont Vontress

Research in counselling with black and ethnic minority clients, like therapy practice with these groups, is marginal, underfunded and not taken seriously by the mainstream counselling and psychotherapy research community (Moodley 2003a). While counselling and psychotherapy, generally, demonstrate a high level of sophistication in theory, practice and research, especially in the cognitive-behaviour and process experiential therapies (see, for example, Toukmanian and Rennie 1992; Dryden 1996; Roth and Fonagy 1996), multicultural or cross-cultural counselling and psychotherapy, on the other hand, is considered the 'second cousin', reinforcing the prevailing myths about appropriateness and relevance of therapy to these groups (see Fernando 1988). This ultimately leads to the paucity of knowledge on many of the critical experiences of black and ethnic minority clients. Moodley (2003a) outlines a number of reasons for this paucity. Amongst them are: lack of interest by the research and professional community, the lack of appropriate culturally sensitive research methods and the confusions and complexities surrounding the concept of multicultural counselling. These have made a difficult situation problematic especially when it comes to writing research proposals, defining the populations under study and applying for funding.

However, in recent years, the increased interest in multicultural/cross-cultural counselling has caused an explosion of empirical research, particularly in North America, on a variety of therapeutic issues relating to black and ethnic minority groups. Whilst the focus has been on how culture is part of the process, a wide variety of variables have also been looked at. For example, Ponterotto *et al.* (2002) reviewed 114 studies published between 1995 and 2000 in the six key refereed journals in North America: *Journal of Counseling Psychology*; *Journal of Counseling and Development*; the *Counseling Psychologist*; *Journal of College Student Development*; *Journal of Multicultural Counseling and Development*; and *Cultural Diversity and Ethnic Minority Psychology*. They found that seven areas dominated cross-cultural counselling research: acculturation, stress and coping, attitudes toward diverse populations and toward counselling, racial/ethnic identity development, multicultural competence and training, vocational and academic issues, and quantitative instrument development. Although this is a very small sample when compared with the field as a whole is still very small, it no doubt leaves us with the feeling that race, culture and counselling will always remain the distant relative when it comes to research and development, and funding priorities.

In this chapter we explore race, culture and research in counselling, generally attempting to highlight some of the newer and emerging themes. We begin with a critique in which current cross-cultural research is being undertaken.

## Critique on cross-cultural counselling research

The discussion and critique on race, culture and research has been well documented, especially by social researchers (see, for example, Ball 1991; Stanfield and Dennis 1993). For example, Stanfield (1993) argues that the research that is often conducted under the guise of objective study is actually ideologically determined. This means that those that fund research often happen to dictate who is researched and by whom. How and where the research is conducted is also inextricably linked to this hegemony. When it comes to research and the black community, Ball (1991) argues for the study of racism and its processes rather than the study of black people. Furthermore, she suggests that researchers should take account of the 'wider social structures that perpetuate and reinforce racial discrimination' (p. 37).

Since black and ethnic minority people have historically always been connected to pseudo-scientific racist ideologies, research endeavours and researchers (white and black) are vulnerable to the pervasive way in which these ideological assumptions can unconsciously interfere. Janet Helms (1993) argues that white researchers are the primary gatekeepers of cross-cultural research and this problematizes the way in which data is conceptualized and interpreted; whilst Sue and Sundberg (1996) suggest that cross-cultural counselling research is primarily shaped by Euro-American culture. These sentiments raise important questions about the complexities surrounding race and culture which professionals (black and white) find themselves in.

Although there is a long history of cross-cultural counselling research in North America and Canada, particularly in the United States, the publications are not reflective of the demographics or the interest in this field. The research agenda appears also to follow the popular preoccupation of notions of race and culture in mainstream society, for example race (meaning black) and culture (meaning ethnicity) was seen as problematic and therefore critical to investigate. A number of people have been responsible for this process from its early days. For example, Heine (1950) was one of the first therapists to call attention to racial and cultural problems in psychotherapy with African Americans. Rosen and Frank (1962) recognized difficulties that white psychiatrists encountered in working with black clients. Burrell and Rayder (1971) reported that black and white students held different attitudes toward white counsellors. Cimbolic (1972) revealed that the race and professional experience of counsellors affected their therapeutic effectiveness with black clients, and Ewing (1974) found that counsellor–client racial similarity was related to client satisfaction.

For many years, psychiatrists and psychologists have pointed out that racism negatively affects the personality and behaviour of racial minorities, especially blacks. Grier and Cobbs (1968), black psychiatrists, described African American clients who manifested 'black rage'. Karon (1975) provided clinical cases of blacks who had been scarred by racism in American society. Cose's (1993) research looked at the rage of middle-class African Americans, many of whom sedate themselves with alcohol and illicit drugs, while Eyerman's (2001) work explained how slavery and years of trauma still impact the personality and behaviour of African Americans. In most cases these research findings were attempting to acknowledge and state the position as it was happening to black and ethnic minority communities. Not much was said about how some of these processes were resistance to racism and class oppression, nor was there much discussion about how some of these behaviours were defence mechanisms to aid a fragmented ego. Vontress and Epp (1997) indicated that historical hostility in African American clients can influence the counselling relationship, diagnosis, prognosis and intervention strategies in counselling blacks – a theme that seems to be consistently present in the literature. For example, Talahite and Moodley (2004) explore the notions of '(mis)trust: I have that history' in their research, *Carl Rogers counsels a Black Client*.

Increasing numbers of researchers are conducting empirical research on multicultural counselling competencies (Holcomb-McCoy 2000; Robinson 2005) and racial identity development (see Cross 1971; Helms 1990; Carter 1995). Vontress and Jackson (2004) argued that the development of the multicultural counselling competencies may go a long way toward finding the best way to merge culture and counselling therapeutically but is problematized by restricting its focus to the four major minority groups in North America (i.e. Native-American, African-American, Asian-American and Latino – and the latter term not even hyphenated with the category American).

Currently, many other issues are still being examined, for example, white therapist–black client interaction (see Watkins and Terrell 1988; Nickerson *et al.* 1994), and black family relationship and dynamics in therapy (Boyd-Franklin 1989). Other emerging research areas are the intersections of multiple identities of race, gender, sexual orientations, class, age, religion and disability, and one that will be the tour de force for the future is research into the

integrating of traditional healing practices into counselling and psychotherapy (Moodley and West 2005). These and other issues will raise methodological problems. We briefly discuss these below.

## Methodology problems

This is the area that poses numerous difficulties for cross-cultural counselling
researchers. As Fernando says:

> The models used in research for analysing emotions, identifying stress
> and evaluating psychological processes are often those developed in a
> Western context, used without any attempt to test their cross-cultural
> validity. The illness categories that emerge may well be artifacts of
> research methodology of ethnoscience.
>
> (Fernando 1988: 63)

On the other hand, Fernando's comments may be an indictment of the profession itself for not being sensitive to ethnic minority needs and experiences.

The research investigation, data collection and the production of new
knowledge/s, whilst evolving in spaces privileged for dominant discourses,
will need to articulate newer meanings on the context of the psycho-social
experiences of ethnic minority clients. In a study of schizophrenia and ethnicity, for example, Sashidharan and Francis remind us that the problem 'is
not whether rates of mental illness or schizophrenia vary across populations
but how such variations are understood and articulated' (Sashidharan and
Francis 1993: 113). It seems that the only time 'race' and ethnicity are given
any consideration at all depends on the ideological motivations of such
research, often with seemingly negative outcomes for the ethnic minority
groups concerned (see Stanfield and Dennis 1993). An example of this is seen
in the numerous studies of schizophrenia and the African-Caribbean community with an emphasis on genetic and biological factors, although there
have been major conceptual and methodological problems with such research
(Sashidharan and Francis 1993).

This raises the question of whether there has been sufficient consideration
given to the way conventional mental (ill) health theory is applied to research
findings and whether explanations take into account socio-cultural and
political factors. Even if socio-cultural and political factors feature as critical
variables in psychotherapy, it is the manner in which they are introduced,
analysed and reported that will make these factors effective in therapeutic
change. The way in which research data and analysis on ethnic minority
clients' therapy are articulated will either reinforce or question cultural and
racial stereotyping that prevails in society today. The repeated emphasis of

culture as a factor tends to create an artificial barrier against 'race'-related ideas, for example racism, black consciousness and racial identity theories, and then placing culture within the location of illness when it suits certain ideological positions. In other words, sometimes culture is seen as exotic and needing exploration and at other times it can be viewed as the basis for psycho-pathology. It seems that the present practice of multicultural psychotherapy and counselling has been constructed in a particular way as a result of this kind of mental (ill) health representation in ethnic minority clients. A specific set of cultural concepts, vocabularies and metaphors, then, seem to evolve and dictate the kind of treatment for this client group. As Sashidharan says, when he critically examines the transcultural approach:

> The transcultural approach emphasises the cultural dependence of clinical problems (of genesis, presentation and management of mental ill-health amongst blacks) and by doing so the political and structural dimensions of contemporary racism are ignored and the model of welfare/treatment provisions is isolated from the day to day struggles of black people in this country.
>
> (Sashidharan 1986: 174)

Sashidharan's point about 'the political and structural dimensions of contemporary racism' being ignored appears to be critical. Although articulated more than a decade ago, it still has relevance today. Cultural dominance of counselling and psychotherapy with ethnic minority clients has limited the discussion of racism in the clinical setting. The inclusion and emphasis of cultural aspects were welcomed against the dominance of the Eurocentric models in which psychiatry and psychotherapy were engaging; however, it led to cultural hegemony and culturalism of the client. The individual client appears to be lost or forgotten in much of the discourse of multicultural counselling. Issues such as racism, anti-semitism, homophobia, sexism and others are not being researched sufficiently. This can become a problem in the therapeutic process eventually as it becomes known to the black and ethnic minority client that the profession has either neglected or intentionally avoided these issues in research and consequently in clinical processes.

The critique of cultural inclusion without 'race' has been growing steadily, particularly by the African-American and Asian-American psychotherapists such as Jones (1984, 1985), Carter (1995) and Sue and Sundberg (1996). They argue that very few studies have incorporated 'race' and ethnicity as explicit variables in psychotherapy. For example, Jones (1984) notes that research of 'race' and ethnicity in psychotherapy appears to be insubstantial compared to the detailed and sophisticated literature in psychotherapy generally. In the UK, Ahmad (1993) notes that some of the available literature in psycho-therapy, psychoanalysis and psychiatry has been heavily skewed, espousing a naive empiricism and cultural reductionism that reflect the interests of the health professional rather than the priorities of ethnic minority communities. Fernando (1988) points out that very few papers on racial issues are published in British psychiatric journals, suggesting that this may reflect the tradition of the journals, the dearth of black editors or the general lack of papers on racial and cultural issues. He adds the concern that some papers that have been published clearly hold racist positions, although written by eminent authors. This is a view shared by Sue and Sue (1990) on the North American position. They acknowledge:

> The profession's preoccupation with pathology tends to encourage the study of personality deficits and weaknesses rather than strengths and assets. Racist attitudes may intensify this view, as minorities may be portrayed in professional journals as neurotic, psychotic, psychopath, parolee.
>
> (Sue and Sue 1990: 21)

## The 'difficult' areas in cross-cultural research

Assessment, diagnosis, demographic recording, that is, the way researchers ascribe racial, ethnic and cultural identities, and the interpretations of social class status, issues of trust and self-disclosure and researchers' own 'counter-transference' awareness and responses are a few of the many areas that present 'difficulties' for research with black and ethnic minority communities. We discuss some of these below.

### Placing individuals in racial or cultural boxes

Perhaps the most glaring shortcoming of much cross-cultural counselling research is the way subjects are selected and racially and culturally described. In general, researchers in multicultural research in North America use undergraduate college students without any attempt to be critical of sampling – the way subjects are categorized by race, ethnicity or cultural heritage. For example, all students from Asia may be placed in a single category as if to suggest that they are culturally similar. Subjects whose native language is Spanish are often grouped together as if to suggest that they too are culturally similar. Blacks, regardless of the complexities and problematics of the varying and changing definition of the African diaspora, are often assumed to be descendants of American slavery. African, African-American, African-Caribbean and black British subjects are homogenized into a single category. The same could be said for Asian and other communities. Even the diversity of cultures which make up the category white is made invisible.

In terms of social class status most black and ethnic minority groups are 'unconsciously' represented as lower middle- or working-class. Moreover, when we consider that most of this quasi research takes place in university settings, where many of the participants could see themselves differently in terms of that kind of class description, this begs questions regarding generalizations and applicability of research findings. In their review of the research literature in cross-cultural counselling Ponterotto *et al.* (2002) note that the samples used in much of the research were 'neither representative or random; they were simply samples of convenience' (p. 412). They offer two suggestions for future research in terms of sampling: if college or university samples are used it is important to use a random sampling technique, and more counselling research needs to be done with non-college and non-adolescent groups. This call for expanding the research sample base arises as a result of their analysis of the journals and the absence of multicultural counselling research on children, the elderly and families.

These are just a few of the flaws in the sampling, design and methodology of many studies in cross-cultural counselling research that often cause their reported results in the prestigious journals to be questionable.

### Assessment and diagnosis

In its role as a critique of western counselling and psychotherapy, multicultural counselling has pointed to the problems that mainstream assessment and diagnosis processes offer. This counter-cultural position is not just limited to the culturally insensitive domains in the *Diagnostic and Statistical Manual of Mental Disorders* (DSM IV), but is highly critical of all forms of assessment that do not take into account race, culture and ethnic variables in black and ethnic minority clients. However, the critique has not generated any new, appropriate and valid diagnostic process. Although assessment and diagnosis are probably the most important aspect of counselling, little or no research has focused on it. An incorrect diagnosis can be dangerous to clients, because it dictates treatment. This is especially true today when psychiatric drugs are often the preferred mode of intervention. Breggin and Breggin (1998) indicate that although white psychiatrists generally are less able to make an accurate diagnosis of black children, they are more inclined to prescribe psychiatric drugs for them than for other clients. Assuming that even in situations where these practices do not occur, there is still the question of finding a common clinical grammar and language within which counselling can meaningfully make sense of the network of meanings of a particular client's personal and sociocultural experience. Here we turn to Arthur Kleinman (1977) and Good and Good (1982), whose research focuses on the network of cultural and personal meanings that illness has individual clients.

## Other neglected areas of research

There are many other areas of cross-cultural counselling research that also appear to be neglected. Not least amongst them are: self-disclosure; resilience and hopefulness; and intersections of race, class, gender, sexual orientations, age, disability and religion. In terms of self-disclosure, Vontress (1971) pointed out that African Americans, especially black men, are reluctant to reveal themselves psychologically to counsellors, because they have been socialized in a society that they perceive to be hostile. Thus, they have learned to 'keep your mouth shut', to stay out of trouble. In other words, many black and ethnic minority clients have learnt to mistrust whites as a healthy defence against racism.

Another topic that deserves research is hopefulness and resilience. In the 1960s Frank (1963, 1968) pointed out that hopelessness was pervasive among blacks and other oppressed groups, and affected all aspects of the person's sense of well-being. In the 1990s we have come to realize that research focused on resilience and hopefulness may help psychotherapeutic professionals understand the positive strategies that black and ethnic minority groups have developed historically through slavery, colonialism, oppression and racism. This understanding may provide therapists with clinical insights and treatment strategies to deal with depression and related maladies peculiar to many minority group clients.

The area that we feel is beginning to show a potential for research in counselling is the examination and investigation of the post-structuralist ideas around plural or multiple identities and how individual clients tend to express these forms of identities in counselling (Moodley 2003a). In other words, if a client is black and gay, in multicultural counselling would race take precedence over being gay? Similarly, if a client is white and disabled, would multicultural counselling privilege being white over being deaf? The intersections and convergence of race, class, gender, sexual orientations, age, disability and religion have been made by many scholars (see for example Pope 1995; Olkin 2002; Reid 2002). However, there appears to be very little development of ideas in relation to how counsellors can understand the complexity of these multiple identities and its relationship to the process of therapy. As Moodley says:

> The specific labeling of race, gender, class, disability and sexual orientation has allowed each of the oppressed groups to find their own socio-political and psycho-cultural voice within the dominant discourse of therapy. But therapy is more than a social, cultural and political strategy ... For many disadvantaged clients, it seems that when it comes to their pain, discomfort, distress and illness, these

tend to disappear . . . and are replaced by the sociology of race, gender, class, disability and sexual orientation.

(Moodley 2003a: 126–7)

Whilst it seems critical to uncover the ideas surrounding multiple identities it is also important for researchers to think about other key themes, such as anorexia nervosa, bulimia, child abuse, alcoholism and depression. The constant emphasis on the sociology of identity of black and ethnic minority groups also moves the focus of researchers away from these key themes of anorexia nervosa, bulimia etc., since there is an implicit notion that these experiences belong to the mainstream culture only. A cyclic pattern begins to evolve; the research remains contained in the politics of identity, which then constructs the theory in a particular way, reinforcing and perpetuating the same patterns of racial, gendered and sexualized stereotypes. Consequently, in the practice the client is seen as black, or gay, or deaf first and then as a person in pain and distress. No wonder many drop out of counselling and therapy.

Clearly, there are many areas of counselling research that need to be explored. Priorities for such research will depend very much on the resources, the context and the needs of the clients within which counselling is practised. Harper and McFadden (2003) outline a number of other areas not mentioned above that also need attention – for example, career counselling, help-seeking orientations, culture and family functioning, the impact of prejudice and injustice on client behaviour and the counselling relationship are few of the many they mention in their review of cross-cultural research. And finally, we feel that it is important that cross-cultural counselling researchers design and carry out studies that can be replicated in many different settings and with diverse client individuals and groups. It also seems critical that counsellors educate and inform those who have an investment and interest in research outcomes, such as health authorities, policy makers and the medical establishments so that research results are received with less resistance.

## Conclusions

In the last two decades, counsellors and psychotherapists have come a long way from the exclusivity of investigating migration, immigration, culture shock and identity problems as major variables of mental (ill) health issues. Many counselling and psychotherapy researchers have also critically examined the methodologies that have been used and the dubious and stereotyped results that have emerged from such studies. Although therapy with black and ethnic minority groups has been limited to the multiple cultural abstractions of multiculturalism and the ambivalent and complex sociopolitical concepts of 'race', culture and ethnicity, it has nevertheless provided theoretical guidelines for research and practice with clients from these groups. Whilst the homogenizing of ethnic minority communities into a single racial, ethnic and cultural group, namely, black and ethnic minority, has led to general developments in research methodologies, it also seems important to distinguish between these groups and acknowledge that different methodologies may be necessary to investigate 'psychological distress' amongst individuals who may or may not identity with the restrictive paradigms of the notions of groups, irrespective of race, gender, sexual orientations, class, age, religion, culture and ethnicity.

Since clinical researchers and counselling and psychotherapy practitioners are engaged in the dynamics of the what, when and how questions regarding the gaze on the psychoanalytic space, it seems reasonable to deduce that not engaging in psychotherapy research with the racial and ethnic 'other' is not a conscious avoidance or a lack of interest in clinical matters of the culturally different client. There seem to be enough tensions already present with the research–practice gap (see Moodley 2001), the scientific–subjective dilemma of psychotherapy research and the complexities surrounding appropriate methodologies for examining and labelling 'psychological distress'.

Yet, others will argue that traditional counselling and psychotherapy has appeared to be less enthusiastic about finding a different voice in the talking cure. It is this different voice that speaks out of a particular history, culture and experience (Hall 1992) and that appears in the representations and presentations of psychological distress in conversations with counsellors and psychotherapists and it is this voice that will necessitate innovate methodologies in research with black and ethnic minority clients. Such methodologies must take account of the historical and socio-political complexities within which black and ethnic minority groups live their lives, whilst at the same time acknowledging that most of the time and in many contexts these groups are outside the cultural and educational sites that produce and reproduce knowledge concerning counselling and psychotherapy theory and practice.

# Appendix: Definitions

## Assimilation

Becoming similar . . . aiming to preserve the presumed cultural homogeneity of existing British society . . . incomers expected to adapt to the existing social environment.

## Black

> The term 'black' is used extensively in the literature and has been used to describe people from South Asian, African and Caribbean backgrounds. (See later definition: 'minority ethnic'.) In the UK, members of Asian groups claim they are not 'black' as part of their struggle to assert their own identity in historical, cultural, ethical and linguistic terms.
>
> (Robinson 2001: 193)

> 'Black' is used as an inclusive political term to counter the divisive aspects of racism.
>
> (Dominelli 1997: xi)

## Culture

Culture is the 'collective mental programming of a people in an environment' (Hofstede 1980b).

> Culture is defined as the transmission of knowledge, skills, attitudes, behaviours and language from one generation to the next . . . culture is a learned behaviour.
>
> (Carter 1995: 12)

> The culture of a particular people or other social body is everything one must learn in order to behave in ways that are recognisable, predictable and understandable to those people.
>
> (Valentine 1968)

The term 'culture' has often been used in the literature as synonymous with 'race' and 'ethnic group'. However, there are clear distinctions between the terms. For example, the white group is made up of many diverse ethnic groups, such as Irish, Polish, Jewish, Italian, Central and Eastern European and so on. Within these ethnic groups lie a diversity of cultures predicated by such factors as length of time living within the USA (UK), socio-economic status, religion, sexual orientation, geographic locale, etc. Given this diversity between and within human groups we prefer the broad definition of culture put forth by Linton (1945): 'The configuration of learned behaviour whose components and elements are shared and transmitted by the members of a particular society' (p. 32).

(Ponterotto and Pedersen 1993: 7)

## Ethnicity

A great deal of confusion surrounds the meaning of the term ethnic or ethnicity.

(Carter 1995: 13)

Smedley (1993, cited in Carter 1995: 13) suggests that 'ethnic or ethnicity be used as an analytic term to refer to a group of people seen by others and themselves as having distinct cultural features and history and a clearly defined sociocultural history'.

The term ethnic group has been used to refer to minority groups within a larger culture.

(Rotherham and Phinney 1987: 12)

Similar to the USA, the term ethnicity (and culture) has been used as a euphemism for race when referring to people 'of colour' and as a non-racial designation for whites.

(Betancourt and Lopez 1993, cited in Carter 1995: 13)

A segment of a larger society whose members are thought, by themselves and/or others, to have a common origin and to share important segments of a common culture and who, in addition, participate in shared activities in which the common origin and culture are significant ingredients.

(Yinger 1976: 200)

## Integration

Some recognition of the presence of black people, but underpinned by concern to maintain existing social order . . . Weak recognition of the existence of racism, but grounded in the belief that it is caused by failure of settlers to assimilate as well as white prejudice.

## Minority ethnic

Belonging to a cultural, racial or religious group that is numerically smaller than the predominant white majority power base in the United Kingdom. This includes groups visible on the basis of their skin colour, as well as others such as Irish, Jewish, Polish, Turkish and Travelling People. Belonging can come either through personal identification with a group or through allocation by others or individuals to it. It is recognised that the use of the terms to describe groups in the community of different ethnic origins is extremely sensitive . . . No single description is totally satisfactory. . . . The term 'minority ethnic group/communities' is taken to encompass the common collective term 'black', as defined by the DoH (1991). People of African, Caribbean and Asian origin widely refer to themselves as 'black', a term which underlines a common shared experience of life in the UK among people whose skin colour is not white but who live in a majority white society.

(Nadirshaw and Goddard 1999)

## Multiculturalism

The goal is a plural society where groups can maintain their own identity while sharing values for social stability. A belief that there is a lack of cultural understanding. (It ignores the notion of a dominant white middle-class culture: it portrays cultures as static and traditional, which can reinforce stereotypical images; it ignores the position of black people in terms of access to resources; it assumes that culture is the primary category of social analysis, neglecting class and gender.) To learn about other cultures is not to learn about the racism of one's own.

(Smith 1999)

## Race

> Race as a social and social scientific construct refers to group charac-
> teristics that in popular ideology (not in fact) are carried in the blood
> (i.e. skin colour).
>
> (Johnson 1990)

> In continuing to use the term race we run the risk of making it real
> and legitimising it as a valid concept. On the other hand, race is
> a social and political reality in the Western world, and is a major
> signifier of power, position and collective experience. In avoiding
> any reference to race, we deny the inescapable effects of racism, and
> collude with the silence about racial inequality and injustice. For
> some writers, this tension is managed by the use of the term 'race' in
> quotation marks as a constant reminder that it is a social construction
> rather than a fixed reality.
>
> (Tuckwell 2002)

> Race is defined as a socio-political designation in which individuals
> are assigned to a particular racial group based on the presumed bio-
> logical or visible characteristics such as skin colour, physical features,
> and in some cases, language . . . Race is a reality created in the human
> mind, not a reflection of objective truths.
>
> (Carter 1995)

Atkinson *et al.* (1989) highlight that the term 'race' has no biological consequences, but what people believe about race has profound social consequences. The concern here is that through subtle socializing influences,
people come to accept as 'social fact' the myriad stereotypes about a group of
people based solely on their skin colour, facial features and so forth.

## Racism

> Any behaviour or pattern of behaviour that systematically tends to
> deny access to opportunities or privilege to one social group while
> perpetuating privilege to members of another group.
>
> (Ridley 1989: 60)

> Racism = prejudice + power.
>
> (Katz 1978: 151)

*Individual racism* consists of personal attitudes of racial superiority, leading to behaviour that is discriminatory in nature.

*Institutional racism* consists of established laws, customs and practices in institutional policies that unfairly restrict the opportunities of defined groups of people, whether or not the individuals maintaining these practices have racist intentions.

Institutional racism has been defined as:

> The collective failure of an organisation to provide an appropriate and professional service to people because of their colour, culture or ethnic origin. It can be seen or detected in the processes, attitudes and behaviour which amount to discrimination, ignorance, thought-lessness and racist stereotyping which disadvantage minority, ethnic people.
>
> (MacPherson 1999: 28)

> *Cultural racism* consists of broad-based beliefs in the superiority of one's cultural heritage, leading to individual and institutional expression of dominant cultural values and practices as reflected in economics, music, art, religious beliefs, traditions and language.
>
> (Jones and Carter 1996)

> Cultural racism is a relatively new form of racism and has been called 'modern racism' (McConahay 1986), 'aversive racism' (Gaertner and Dovidio 1986) and 'symbolic racism' (Sears 1988).
>
> (Robinson 2001: 194)

# Bibliography

Ahmad, W. I. U. (1993) 'Making black people sick: 'race', ideology and health research'. In W. I. U. Ahmad (ed.) *'Race' and Health in Contemporary Britain*. Buckingham: Open University Press.

Akbar, N. (1996) *Breaking the Chains of Psychological Slavery*. Tallahassee, FL: Mind Productions.

Albee, G. W. (1977) The protestant ethic, sex and psychotherapy. *American Psychologist*, 32, 150–61.

Allen, S. (1973) The institutionalisation of racism. *RACE*, XV(1).

Alleyne, A. (1998) Which women? What feminism? In I. B. Seu and M. C. Heenan (eds) *Feminism and Psychotherapy*. London: Sage Publications.

Alleyne, A. (2004) Black identity and workplace oppression. *Counselling and Psychotherapy Research*, 4(1), 4–8.

American Field Services (n.d.) *Orientation Handbook Resource*. AFS Intercultural/International Programmes Inc.

Anthony, K. (2000) Counselling in cyberspace. *Counselling Journal*, 11(10), 625–7.

Anzaldua, G. (1998) To(o) queer the writer – Loca, escritora y chicana. In Trujullo, C. (ed.) *Living Chicana theory* 263–276. Berkeley, CA: Third Woman Press.

Argyle, M. (1975) *Bodily Communication*. London: Methuen.

Atkinson, D. (1985) A meta-review of research on cross-cultural counselling and psychotherapy. *Journal of Multicultural Counselling and Development*, 13, 138–53.

Atkinson, D., Morten, G. and Sue, D. W. (1989) *Counselling American Minorities: A Cross Cultural Perspective*. Dubuque, IA: William C. Brown.

Atkinson, D. R., Morten, G. and Sue, D. W. (1993) *Counseling American Minorities: A cross-cultural perspective* (4th edition). Madison, WI: Brown and Benchmark.

Bachner, D. J. and Rudy, S. K. (1989) Organisational factors in cross-cultural counselling. In D. R. Koslow and E. P. Salett (eds) *Crossing Cultures in Mental Health*. Washington, DC: SIETAR.

BACP (British Association for Counselling and Psychotherapy) (2002) *BACP Ethical Framework for Good Practice*. Rugby: British Association for Counselling and Psychotherapy.

BACP (2004a) *The Age of Therapy: Exploring Attitudes towards Acceptance of Counselling and Psychotherapy in Modern Britain*. Rugby: BACP; London: Futures Foundation.

BACP (2004b) *Exploring Mental Health*. A photocopyable teaching resource for schools – for work with students aged 14–16. Rugby: BACP.

BACP (2005) *Training in Counselling and Psychotherapy Directory*. Rugby: British Association for Counselling and Psychotherapy.

BACP Equality and Diversity Forum (2005) *Definition of Diversity*. Rugby: British Association for Counselling and Psychotherapy.

BACP (website) www.bacp.co.uk/about_bacp/profile.html, Accessed 2 February 2005.

Baker, K. G. (1989) A workshop model for exploring one's cultural identity. In D. R. Koslow and E. P. Salett (eds) *Crossing Cultures in Mental Health*. Washington, DC: SIETAR.

Baldwin, J. A. and Bell, Y. R. (1985) The African Self Consciousness Scale: an Africentric personality questionnaire. *The Western Journal of Counselling and Psychotherapy with Refugees*, 9, 61–8.

Ball, W. (1991) The ethics and politics of doing antiracist research in education: key debates and dilemmas. *European Journal of Intercultural Studies*, 2, 35–49.

Bandura, A. (1969) *Principles of Behaviour Modification*. New York: Wiley.

Banks, N. (1999) *White Counsellors – Black Clients*. Hampshire: Ashgate.

Barbarin, O. A. and Gilbert, R. (1981) Institutional Racism Scale: assessing self and organisational attributes. In O. A. Barbarin, P. R. Good, O. M. Pharr and J. A. Siskind (eds) *Institutional Racism and Community Competence*. (DHSS Publication, No. ADM 81–907, pp. 147–71.) Rockville, MD: National Institute of Mental Health, Center for Minority Group Mental Health Programs.

Beattie, J. (1964) *Other Cultures: Aims, Methods and Achievements in Social Anthropology*. London: Routledge and Kegan Paul.

Becker, E. (1972) *The Birth and Death of Meaning*. Harmondsworth: Penguin.

Becker, H. S. and Gear, B. (1960) Latent culture: a note on the theory of latent social roles. *Administrative Science Quarterly*, 5, 304–13.

Benedict, R. (1968) *Patterns of Culture*. London: Routledge and Kegan Paul.

Ben Tovim, G. and Gabriel, J. (1982) The politics of race in Britain, 1962–79; a review of the major trends and of recent debates. In C. Husband (ed.) *Race in Britain: Continuity and Change*. London: Hutchinson.

Bergerson, A. A. (2003) Critical race theory and white racism: is there room for white scholars in fighting racism in education? *Qualitative Studies in Education*, 16(1), 51–63.

Berne, E. (1968) *Games People Play*. Harmondsworth: Penguin.

Bernstein, B. (1973) *Class Codes and Control*. London: Routledge and Kegan Paul.

Betancourt, H. and Lopez, S. R. (1993) The study of culture, ethnicity and race in American psychology. *American Psychologist*, 48(6), 629–37.

Blackwell, D. (2005) *Counselling and Psychotherapy with Refugees*. London: Jessica Kingsley Publishers.

Bolton, G., Howlett, S., Lago, C. and Wright, J. (2004) *Writing Cures: An*

*Introductory Handbook of Writing in Counselling and Psychotherapy*. Hove: Brunner-Routledge.

Bourdieu, P. (1976) Systems of education and systems of thought. In R. Dale, G. Esland and M. Macdonald (eds) *Schooling and Capitalism*. London: Routledge and Kegan Paul.

Boyd-Franklin, N. (1989) *Black Families in Therapy: A Multisystems Approach*. Guildford: New York.

Bozarth, J. (1998) *Person-Centered Therapy: A Revolutionary Paradigm*. Ross on Wye: PCCS Books.

Bragg, M. (2003) *The Adventure of Black Studies. English: The Biography of a Language*. London: Hodder and Stoughton.

Bram, R. W. (1956) Language and categories. In J. S. Bruner, J. J. Goodnow and G. A. Austin (eds) *A Study in Thinking*. New York: Wiley.

Breggin, P. R. and Breggin, G. R. (1998) *The War against Children of Color*. Monroe, ME: Common Courage Press.

Brislin, R. W., Cushner, K., Cherrie, C. and Yong, M. (1986) *Intercultural Interactions: A Practical Guide*. Beverly Hills: Sage Publications.

Brown, C. (1984) *Black and White Britain: The Third PSI Survey*. Aldershot: Gower.

Buckley, J. (2004) Cross-ethnic therapeutic relationships: a qualitative study of therapists' experiences. Unpublished dissertation. University of Sheffield, Dept of Clinical Psychology.

Burnham, L. (2001) *The Wellspring of Black Feminist Theory*. Oakland, CA: Women of Color Resource Center.

Burrell, L. and Rayder, N. (1971) Black and white students' attitudes toward white counselors. *Journal of Negro Education*, 40, 48–52.

Burstow, B. (1992) *Radical Feminist Theory*. Newbury Park, CA: Sage Publications.

Butler, J. (1990) *Gender Trouble: Feminism and the Subversion of Identity*. New York: Routledge.

Byham, W. C. and Cox, J. (1988) *Zapp, the Lightning of Empowerment*. New York: Fawcett Columbine.

Callender, C. (1997) *Education for Empowerment*. Stoke-on-Trent: Trentham Books.

Carotenuto, A. (1992) *The Difficult Art: A Critical Discourse on Psychotherapy*. Wimetta, IL: Chiron Publications.

Carr, S. C. and Sloan, T. S. (2003) *Poverty and Psychology: Emergent Critical Practice*. New York: Kluwer Academic Publishers.

Carroll, M. (1988) Counselling supervision: the British context. *Counselling Psychology Quarterly*, 1(4).

Carroll, M. and Holloway, E. (1999) *Training Counselling Supervisors*. London: Sage Publications.

Carroll, M. and Walton, M. (1997) *Handbook of Counselling in Organisations*. London: Sage Publications.

Carter, R. (1995) *The Influence of Race and Racial Identity in Psychotherapy: Towards a Racially Inclusive Model*. New York: Wiley and Sons.

Carter, R. T. (1997) Is White a race? Expressions of white racial identity. In M. Fine, L. Weis, L. C. Powell and L. Mun Wong (eds) *Off White: Readings on Race, Power and Society*. New York and London: Routledge.

Casement, P. (1985) *On Learning from the Patient*. London: Tavistock Publications.

Cass, V. C. (1979) Homosexual identity formation: a theoretical model. *Journal of Homosexuality*, 4, 219–35.

Casse, P. (1981) *Training for the Cross Cultural Mind*. Washington, DC: SIETAR.

Chantler, K. and Smailes, S. (2004) Working with differences: issues for research and counselling practice. *Counselling and Psychotherapy Research*, 4(2), 34–9.

Charleton, M. (1996) *Self-directed Learning in Counsellor Training*. London: Cassell.

Chen, C. (1963) Some psychopathological thoughts in the Book of Tso Chuen. *Acta Psychologica Sinica*, 2, 156–64.

Chertok, L. (1984) 200 years of psychotherapy: the curative elements in suggestion and affect. *Psychoanalytic Psychology*, 1(3), 173–91.

Cimbolic, P. (1972) Counselor race and experience effects on Black clients. *Journal of Consulting and Clinical Psychology*, 39, 328–32.

Clare, E. (2001) Stolen bodies, reclaimed bodies: disability and queerness, *Public Culture*, 13(3), 359–65.

Clark, J. (1982) Change is boundaries dissolved: person-centred approaches in a multi-racial society. In S. A. Segrera (ed.) *Proceedings of the First International Forum on the Person-Centred Approach*. Mexico City: Universidad Iberoamericana.

Clark, J. and Lago, C. O. (1981) *Multi-racial Videoscenes*. Leicester: Educational Technology Department, De Montfort University.

Clark, R. W. (1980) *Freud: The Man and the Cause*. London: Cape and Weidenfeld and Nicolson.

Clarkson, P. and Nippoda, Y. (1998) Cross-cultural issues in counselling practice: a qualitative study of one multicultural training organisation. In P. Clarkson (ed.) *Integrating Theory Research and Supervised Practice*. London: Routledge.

Cleminson, D. (1997/98) Attitudes and prejudice in the education of counsellors/supervisors. *Race and Cultural Education In Counselling*. 15(Winter), 26–7.

Coldridge, L. and Mickelborough, P. (2003). Who's counting? Access to UK counsellor training: a demographic profile of trainees on four courses. *Counselling and Psychotherapy Research*, 3(1), 72–5.

Coleman, E. (1982) Developmental stages of the coming out process. *Journal of Homosexuality*, 7, 31–43.

Collinson, L. (1984) Transactional analysis. In W. Dryden (ed.) *Individual Therapy in Britain*. London: Harper and Row.

Combahee River Collective (2000) A black feminist statement. In W. Kolmar and F. Bartkowski (eds) *Feminist Theory: A Reader*. California: Mayfield.

Connor, M. (1994) *Training the Counsellor – An integrative model*. London: Routledge.

Cook, D. (1983) A survey of ethnic minority clinical and counselling graduate student perceptions of their cross-cultural supervision experience. Unpublished doctoral dissertation, Southern Illinois University.

Cooper, C. (1984) Individual therapies: limitations. In W. Dryden (ed.) *Individual Therapy in Britain*. London: Harper and Row.

Cooper, M., Mearns, D., Stiles, W. B., Warner, M. and Elliot, R. (2004) Developing self-pluralistic perspectives within the person centered and experiential approaches: a round table dialogue. *Person Centered and Experiential Psycho-therapies*, 3(3), 176–91.

Cose, E. (1993) *The Rage of a Privileged Class*. New York: HarperCollins.

Cotter, J., Cymbala, R., Heap, B. *et al.* (1992) Late capitalist culture and culture critique: Part I. Multiculturalism and culture critique. *The Alternative Orange 2*. http://www.etext.org/Politics/AlternativeOrange/2/v2n1_lccc.html. Accessed 17 February 2005.

Cox, C. (1988) Acculturative stress and world view. Unpublished doctoral dissertation, Ohio State University, Columbus.

Cox, C. I. (1982) *Outcome Research in Cross-Cultural Counselling*. Unpublished manuscript. Cited in Speight *et al.* (1991) A redefinition. *Journal of Counselling and Development*, 70 (September/October), 29–36.

Cox, J. L. (ed.) (1986) *Transcultural Psychiatry*. London: Croom Helm.

Crandel, D. L. and Dohrenwend, B. P. (1967) Some relations among psychiatric symptoms, organic illness and social class. *American Journal of Psychiatry*, 123, 527–38.

CRE (Commission for Racial Equality) (1999) *Ethnic Minorities in Britain*, Factsheet, revised edition. (Available in electronic form at: http://www.cre.gov.uk).

CRE (2004) *Ethnic Diversity*. London: CRE (http://www.cre.gov.uk/ethdiv/ethdiv.html).

Cross, W. E. (1971) Towards a psychology of liberation: the negro-to-black conversion experience. *Black World*, 20, 13–27.

Cross, W. E. (1978) The Thomas and Cross models of psychological nigrescence: a review, *Journal of Book Psychology*, 5, 13–31.

Cross, W. E. (1991) *Shades of Black*. Philadelphia, PA: Temple University Press.

Cross, W. E. (1995) The psychology of nigrescence: revising the Cross model. In J. G. Ponterotto, J. M. Casas, L. A. Suzuki and C. M. Alexander (eds) *Handbook of Multicultural Counseling*. Thousand Oaks, CA: Sage Publications.

D'Andrea, M. and Daniels, J. (1992) The structure of racism and implications for Higher Education. In T. Hilgers *et al.* (eds) *Academic Literacies in Multicultural Higher Education: Selected Essays*. Manoa, HI: Center for Studies of Multicultural Higher Education, University of Hawaii.

D'Andrea, M., Daniels, J. and Beck, R. (1991) Evaluating the impact of multicultural counsellor training. *Journal of Counselling and Development*, 70, 143–50.

D'Ardenne, P. and Mahtani, A. (1989) *Transcultural Counselling in Action*. London: Sage Publications.

D'Ardenne, P. and Mahtani, A. (1999) *Transcultural Counselling in Action*, 2nd edition. London: Sage Publication.

De Marre, P. (1975) The politics of large groups. In L. Kreeger (ed.) *The Large Group: Dynamics and Therapy*. London: Constable.

Derrida, J. (1976) *of Grammatology*. Baltimore, MD: Johns Hopkins University Press.

Dhillon, K. and Ubhi, M. (2003) Acculturation and ethnic identity in marginal immigrant South Asian men in Britain: a psychotherapeutic perspective. *Counselling and Psychotherapy Research*, 3(1), 42–8.

Dhillon-Stevens, H. (2004a) Healing inside and outside: an examination of dialogic encounters in the area of anti-oppressive practice in counselling and psychotherapy. PhD thesis, Middlesex University.

Dhillon-Stevens, H. (2004b) Personal and professional integration of anti-oppressive practice and the multiple oppression model in psychotherapeutic education. *British Journal of Psychotherapy Integration*, 1(2), December.

Dhillon-Stevens, H. (2004c) *DVD Programmes on Anti Oppressive Practice*. Enquiries to: Dhillon-Stevens Ltd., PO BOX 120, Chertsey, Surrey, KT16 9YS.

Dhillon-Stevens, H. (2005) Personal and professional integration of anti-oppressive practice and the Multiple Oppression Model in psychotherapeutic education. *The British Journal of Psychotherapy Integration*, 1(2), 47–62.

Dhingra, S. (n.d.) Unpublished course handout materials: 'Some suggestions for cross cultural supervision'; 'Issues for white supervisors', 'Issues for black supervisees'.

Diamond, S. (2005) Towards an examination of diversity education in clinical and counselling psychology programmes. MA thesis, University of Toronto.

Dominelli, L. (1997) *Anti-racist Social Work*, 2nd edition. London: Macmillan.

Douglas, C. (1998) *From Surviving To Thriving: Black Women Managers in Britain*. PhD thesis, University of Bath.

Downing, N. and Roush, K. (1985) From passive acceptance to active commitment: a model of feminist identity development for women. *The Counseling Psychologist*, 13, 695–709.

Dryden, W. (1984) *Individual Therapy in Britain*. London: Harper and Row.

Dryden, W. (1990) Counselling under apartheid: an interview with Andrew Swart. *British Journal of Guidance and Counselling*, 18(3), September.

Dryden, W. (ed.) (1996) *Research in Counselling and Psychotherapy*. London: Sage Publications.

Dryden, W. and Spurling, L. (1989) *On Becoming A Psychotherapist*. London: Tavistock/ Routledge.

Dryden, W. and Thorne, B. (eds) (1991) *Training and Supervision for Counselling in Action*. London: Sage Publications.

Dudley, J. (2004) *Home Office Statistical Bulletin – Control of Immigration: UK Statistics 2003*. London: Home Office.

DuPont, J. A. (1997) Working with issues of race in counselling. *Counselling*, 8(4), 282–4.

Dyer, R. (1997) *White*. London: Routledge.

Edwards, D. (1991) Categories are for talking: on the cognitive and discursive basis of categorization, *Theory and Society*, 1: 515–42.

Eibl-Eibesfeldt, I. (1972) Similarities and differences between cultures in expressive movements. In R. A. Hinde (ed.) *Non-Verbal Communication*. Cambridge: Royal Society and Cambridge University Press.

Eleftheriadou, Z. (1994) *Transcultural Counselling*. London: Central Book Publishing.

Ellenberger, H. F. (1970) *The Discovery of the Unconscious: The History and Evolution of Dynamic Psychiatry*. London: Allen Lane.

Ellis, B. (2004) Racial politics and therapy, *Counselling and Psychotherapy Journal*, 15(8), 40–1.

Ellsworth, E. (1989) Why doesn't this feel empowering? Working through the repressive myths of critical pedagogy. *Harvard Educational Review*, 50, 297–324.

Ewing, T. N. (1974) Racial similarity of client and counselor and client satisfaction in counseling. *Journal of Counseling Psychology*, 21, 446–9.

Eyerman, R. (2001) *Cultural Trauma: Slavery and the Formation of African American Identity*. Cambridge, MA: Cambridge University Press.

Ezeilo, B. (1994) Western psychological therapies and the African client. *Changes: An International Journal of Psychology and Psychotherapy*, 12(1), 11–17.

Fanon, F. (1967) *Black Skin, White Masks*. New York: Grove Press; London: Pluto Press.

Feltham, C. (1997) Challenging the core theoretical model. *Counselling. The Journal of the British Association for Counselling*, 8(2), 121–5.

Feltham, C. and Dryden, W. (1993) *Dictionary of Counselling*. London: Whurr.

Fernando, S. (1988) *Race and Culture in Psychiatry*. London: Croom Helm.

Fernando, S. (1996) Counselling minorities: aspects of race and culture. *RACE Newsletter* (BACP), 10, 8.

Fernando, S. (2001) *Mental Health, Race and Culture*. London: Palgrave/Macmillan.

Fernando, S. (2003) *Cultural Diversity, Mental Health and Psychiatry*. Hove: Brunner-Routledge.

Flew, A. (1972) *An Introduction to Western Philosophy: Ideas and Argument from Plato to Sartre*. London: Thames and Hudson.

Foucault, M. (1978) *The History of Sexuality*. New York: Vintage Books.

Fowler, S. M. and Mumford, M. G. (1995) *Intercultural Source Book: Cross Cultural Training Methods*. Yarmouth, ME: Intercultural Press.

France, M. H., Rodriguez, M. D. C. and Hett, G. G. (2004) *Diversity, Culture and Counselling: A Canadian Perspective*. Calgary: Detselig Enterprises Ltd.

Frank, J. D. (1963) *Persuasion and Healing*. New York: Schocken Books.

Frank, J. D. (1968) The role of hope in psychotherapy. *International Journal of Psychiatry*, 5, 383–95.

Frank, J. D. (1973) *Persuasion and Healing: A Comparative Study of Psychotherapy*. Baltimore, MD: Johns Hopkins University Press.

Frankenberg, R. (1993) *White Women, Race Matters: The Social Construction of Whiteness*. Minneapolis, MN: University of Minnesota Press.

Fransella, F. (1984) Personal construct therapy. In W. Dryden (ed.) *Individual Therapy In Britain*. London: Harper and Row.

Freire, P. (1972) *Pedagogy of the Oppressed*. Harmondsworth: Penguin.

Frey, S. and Heslett, B. (1975) *Existential Theory for Counselors* Boston, MA: Houghton Mifflin.

Frijda, N. and Johoda, G. (1969) On the scope and methods of cross-cultural research. In D. R. Price-Williams (ed.) *Cross-Cultural Studies*. Harmondsworth: Penguin.

Fryer, P. (1984) *Staying Power: The History of Black People in Britain*. London: Pluto.

Furnham, A. and Bochner, S. (1986) *Culture Shock: Psychological Reactions to Unfamiliar Environments*. London: Methuen.

Future Foundation (2004) *The Age of Therapy: Exploring Attitudes Towards the Acceptance of Counselling and Psychotherapy in Modern Britain*. London: The Future Foundation.

Gaertner, S. L. and Dovidio, J. F. (1986) The aversive form of racism. In J. F. Dovidio and S. L. Gaertner (eds) *Prejudice, Discrimination and Racism*. New York: Academic Press.

Galway, J. (1989) *Counselling Skills for Immigrant Workers: A Training Guide*. Toronto: Ontario Council of Agencies Serving Immigrants.

Garfield, S. and Kurtz, R. (1976) Clinical psychologists in the 1970s. *American Psychologist*, 31, 1–9.

Gilbert, M. and Evans, K. (2000) *Psychotherapy Supervision in Context: An Integrative Approach*. Buckingham: Open University Press.

Gill, C. J. (1997) Four types of integration in disability identity development. *Journal of Vocational Rehabilitation*, 9, 39–46.

Gillis, J. R. (2003) The marginalization of sexual orientation and gender identity in multicultural psychology: cause for concern? Paper presented at the Critical Multicultural Practice, Toronto, June.

Gillon, E. (2002) Counselling training and social exclusion. *Counselling and Psychotherapy Journal*, 13(3), 24–7.

Good, B. J. and Good, M.-J. D. (1982) Towards a meaning-centred analysis of popular illness categories: 'fright-illness' and 'heat distress' in Iran. In A. J. Marsella and G. M. White (eds) *Cultural Conceptions of Mental Health and Therapy*. Dordrecht: Reidel.

Gopaul-McNicol, S. A. (1993) *Working with West Indian Families*: New York: Guildford Press.

Gore, J. (1993) *The Struggle for Pedagogies*. London: Routledge.

Goss, S. P., Anthony, K., Palmer, S. and Jamieson, A. (2001) *BACP Guidelines for Online Counselling and Psychotherapy*. Rugby: BACP.

Grier, W. H. and Cobbs, P. M. (1968) *Black Rage*. New York: Basic Books.

*Guardian* (1994) Labour figures show rise in reported race attacks, 18 March.

Gudykunst, W. B. (1994) *Bridging Differences: Effective Intergroup Communication*, 2nd edition. London: Sage Publications.

Guitterez, F. (1982) Working with minority counsellor education students. *Counsellor Education and Supervision*, 21, 218–26.

Gumperz, J. J., Jupp, T. C. and Roberts, C. (1981) *'Cross-talk' – The Wider Perspective* (Pamphlet). Southall, Middlesex: Industrial Language Training Laboratory.

Gurnah, A. (1992) On the specificity of racism. In M. Arnot and L. Barton (eds) *Voicing Concerns*, 2nd edition. Oxford: Triangle Books.

Hall, B. and Moodley, R. (2001) Using an African world view in therapy with Black clients. *Counselling and Psychotherapy Journal*, 12(3), 10–13.

Hall, E. T. (1959) *The Silent Language*. New York: Anchor Press/Doubleday.

Hall, E. T. (1966) *The Hidden Dimension*. New York: Anchor Press/Doubleday.

Hall, E. T. (1976a) *Beyond Culture*. New York: Anchor Press/Doubleday.

Hall, E. T. (1976b) How cultures collide. *Psychology Today*, July, 66–74.

Hall, E. T. (1983) *The Dance of Life*. New York: Anchor Press/Doubleday.

Hall, S. (1992) New ethnicities. In J. Donald and A. Rattansi (eds) *'Race', Culture and Difference*. Buckingham: Open University Press.

Hall, S. (1996) New ethnicities. In H. A. Baker Jr., M. Diawara and R. H. Lindeborg (eds) *Black British Cultural Studies*. Chicago, IL: University of Chicago Press.

Hammon, D. and Jablow, A. (1970) *The Africa That Never Was: Four Centuries of British Writing about Africa*. New York: Twange Publishers.

Hardiman, R. (1982). White identity development: a process oriented model for describing the racial consciousness of White Americans. *Dissertation Abstracts International*, 43, 104A (University Microfilms No. 82–10330).

Harner, M. (1990) *The Way of the Shaman*. San Fransisco, CA: Harper and Row.

Harper, F. D. and McFadden, J. (2003) *Culture and Counseling: New Approaches*. Boston, MA: Allyn and Bacon.

Hartmann, P. and Husband, C. (1974) *Racism and the Mass-Media*. London: Davis-Pointer.

Hawkins, P. and Shohet, R. (1989) *Supervision in the Helping Professions*. Milton Keynes: Open University Press.

Heath, T., Jeffries, R. and Purcell, J. (2004) *Asylum Statistics, UK 2003*, 2nd edition. Home Office Statistical Bulletin. London: Home Office.

Heine, R. W. (1950) Negro client in psychotherapy. *Journal of Clinical Psychology*, 6, 373–6.

Helms, J. (1982) Differential evaluations of minority and majority counselling trainees practicum performance. Unpublished manuscript, University of Maryland.

Helms, J. (1995) An update of Helms' white and people of color racial identity models. In J. G. Ponterotto, J. M. Casas, L. Suzuki and C. Alexander (eds) *Handbook of Multicultural Counseling*. Thousand Oaks, CA: Sage Publications.

Helms, J. E. (1984) Towards a theoretical model of the effects of race on counselling: a black and white model. *The Counselling Psychologist*, 12, 153–65.

Helms, J. E. (ed.) (1990) *Black and White Racial Identity: Theory, Research and Practice*. Westport, CT: Greenwood Press.

Helms, J. E. (1992) *A Race Is a Nice Thing to Have: A Guide to Being a White Person or Understanding the White Persons in your Life*. Topeka, KS: Content Communications.

Helms, J. E. (1993) I also said, White racial identity influences White researchers. *The Counseling Psychologist*, 21, 240–3.

Helms, J. E. and Richardson, T. Q. (1997) How 'multiculturalism' obscures race and culture as differential aspects of counseling competency. In D. B. Pope-Davis and H. L. K. Coleman (eds) *Multicultural Counseling Competencies: Assessment, Education and Training and Supervision*. Thousand Oaks, CA: Sage Publications.

Herr, E. L. (1987) Cultural diversity from an international perspective. *Journal of Multicultural Counselling and Development*, 15, 99–109.

Hess, A. (ed.) (1982) *Psychotherapy Supervision: Theory, Research and Practice*. New York: Witney.

Hesse, H. (1979) *The Glass Bead Game*. Harmondsworth: Penguin.

Heyes, C. (2002) *Identity Politics*. http://plato.stanford.edu/archives/fall2002/entries/identity-politics/. Accessed 31 August 2004.

Hillmann, J. and Ventura, M. (1992) *We've Had 100 Years of Psychotherapy and the World is Getting Worse*. San Francisco, CA: Harper.

Hills, H. I. and Strozier, A. L. (in press) Multicultural training in APA approval counselling psychology programmes: a survey. *Professional Psychology*.

Hiro, D. (1971) *Black British, White British*. Harmondsworth: Penguin.

Hobbs, G. (1993) White magic: in South Africa a growing number of white people are being initiated as witch doctors. *Observer Magazine*, 29 August.

Hofstede, G. (1980a) Motivation, leadership and organisation. Do American theories apply abroad? *Organisational Dynamics*, 9(1), 42–63.

Hofstede, G. (1980b) *Culture's Consequences: International Differences in Work Related Values*. Beverly Hills: Sage Publications.

Hofstede, G. (1994) *Uncommon Sense About Organisations: Cases, Studies and Field Observations*. London: Sage Publications.

Holcomb-McCoy, C. C. (2000) Multicultural counseling competencies: An exploratory factor analysis. *Journal of Multicultural Counseling and Development*, 28, 83–97.

Holloway, E. and Hosford, R. (1983) Towards developing a prescriptive technology of counsellor supervision. *The Counselling Psychologist*, 11(1), 73–7.

Home Affairs Committee (1983) *Ethnic and Racial Questions in the Census: Report and Minutes of Evidence*, 2 (HC 33). London: HMSO.

Home Affairs Committee (1986) *Racial Attacks and Harassment*. London: HMSO.

Home Office (2001) Race Relations (Amendment) Act 2000. New Laws for Successful Multi-Racial Britain. Proposals for implementation. London: Home Office.

Home Office (2002) Secure Borders, Safe Haven. Integration with Diversity in Modern Britain. CM 5387. London: The Stationery Office.

Hooks, B. (1982) *Ain't I a Woman? Black Women and Feminism*. London: Pluto Press.

Hunt, P. (1987) Black client: implications for supervision of trainees. *Psychotherapy*, 24(1), 61–4.

Ibrahim, F. A. (1985) Effective cross-cultural counselling and psychotherapy: a framework. *The Counselling Psychologist*, 13, 625–38.

Institute of Race Relations (2002) *IRR News: Fact File on Racial Violence*. (www.irr.org.uk).

Ivey, A. E. (1982) *International Interviewing and Counselling*. Monterey, CA: Brooke-Cole.

Jackson, A. P. and Meadows, F. B. (1991) Getting to the bottom to understand the top. *Journal of Counselling and Development*, September/October, 70.

Jacobs, M. (1984) Psychodynamic therapy: the Freudian approach. In W. Dryden (ed.) *Individual Therapy in Britain*. London: Harper and Row.

Jacobs, M. (1992) *Sigmund Freud*. London: Sage Publications.

Jacobson, C. K. (1985) Resistance to affirmative action: self interest or racism? *Journal of Conflict Resolution*, 29, 306–29.

Jahoda, G. (1999) *Images of Savages: Ancient Roots of Modern Prejudice in Western Culture*. London: Routledge.

James, W. (1890/1951) *The Principles of Psychology*. New York: Dover.

Jamieson, A. (2005) The challenges of diversity to organisations. A presentation to the BACP regional consultation held in Bristol, January.

Jewel, P. (1994) Multicultural counselling research: an evaluation with proposals for future research. *Counselling Psychology Review*, 9(2).

Jilek, W. G. (1989) Therapeutic use of altered states of consciousness in contemporary North American dance ceremonials. In C. A. Ward (ed.) *Altered States of Consciousness and Mental Health: A Cross Cultural Perspective*. London: Sage Publications.

Johns, H. (1998) On the tightrope. In H. Johns, *Balancing Acts: Studies in Counselling Training*. London: Routledge.

Johnson, S. D. (1990) Toward clarifying culture, race and ethnicity in the context of multicultural counselling. *Journal of Multicultural Counseling and Development*, 18(1), 41–50.

Jones, C. (2001) Black women in ivory towers: racism and sexism in the academy. In P. Anderson and J. Williams (eds) *Identity and Difference in Higher Education: Outsiders Within*. Aldershot: Ashgate.

Jones, E. (ed.) (1959) *Sigmund Freud: Collected Papers*, Vol. 1. New York: Basic Books.

Jones, E. E. (1984) Some reflections on the black patient and psychotherapy. *Clinical Psychology*, 37, 62–8.

Jones, E. E. (1985) Psychotherapy and counseling with black clients. In P. Pedersen (ed.) *Handbook of Cross-Cultural Counseling and Therapy*. New York: Praeger.

Jones, J. M. and Carter, R. T. (1996) Racism and white racial identity: merging realities. In B. P. Bowser and R. G. Hunt (eds) *Impacts of Racism on White Americans*, 2nd edition. Thousand Oaks, CA: Sage Publications.

Jordan, E. M. (2004) The professional is personal: an evaluative enquiry into the experience of setting up a university counselling service. Unpublished PhD thesis, University of Middlesex in collaboration with Metanoia Training Institute.

Jordan, W. D. (1982) First impressions: initial English confrontations with Africans. In C. Husband (ed.) *Race in Britain: Continuity and Change*. London: Harmondsworth.

Jowell, R., Witherspoon, S. and Brook, L. (1984) *British Social Attitudes: The 1984 Report*. Aldershot: Gower/Social and Community Planning Research.

Jumaa, M. (1993) From the chair. *RACE Newsletter*, (BACP), 3.

Kanfer, F. H. and Phillips, J. W. (1970) *Learning Foundations of Behavior Therapy*. New York: Wiley.

Karasu, T. *et al.* (1984) *The Psychological Therapies*. Washington, DC: American Psychiatric Press.

Kardiner, A. (1959) *The Psychological Fortunes of Society*. New York: Columbia University Press.

Kardiner, A. and Linton, R. (1947) *The Individual and This Society*. New York: Columbia University Press.

Kareem, J. (1978) Conflicting concepts of mental health in multi-cultural society. *Psychiatrica Clinica*, 11, 90–5.

Kareem, J. and Littlewood, R. (1992) *Intercultural Therapy: Themes, Interpretations and Practice*. Oxford: Blackwell Scientific Publications.

Karon, B. P. (1975) *Black Scars*. New York: Springer.

Karpman, S. (1968) Fairy tales and script drama analysis. *Transactional Analysis Bulletin*. Selected articles from Vols 1–9, 51–6.

Katz, J. H. (1978) *White Awareness: Handbook for Anti-Racism Training*. Norman, OK: University of Oklahoma Press.

Katz, J. H. (1985) The sociopolitical nature of counselling. *The Counselling Psychologist*, 13, 615–24.

Katz, J. H. (1989a) The challenge of diversity. In C. Woolbright (ed.) *College Unions at Work*, Monograph, No. 11, 1–17. Bloomington, IA: Associations of College Unions.

Katz, R. (1989b) Healing and transformation: perspectives from !Kung hunter-gatherers. In C. A. Ward (ed.) *Altered States of Consciousness and Mental Health: A Cross Cultural Perspective*. New Park, CA: Sage Publications.

Kearney, A. (2003) Class and counselling. In C. Lago and B. Smith (eds), *Anti-discriminatory Counselling Practice*. London: Sage Publications.

Kemal, A. (1994) Sufism: a prevention and cure. *Changes: An International Journal of Psychology and Psychotherapy*, 12(2), 87–91.

Kerwin, C. and Ponterotto, J. (1995) Biracial identity development. In J. G. Ponterotto, J. M. Casas, L. A. Suzuki and C. M. Alexander (eds) *Handbook of Multicultural Counseling*. Thousand Oaks, CA: Sage Publications.

Kincheloe, J. L., Steinberg, S. R., Rodriguez, N. M. and Chennault, R. E. (eds)

(1998) *White Reign: Deploying Whiteness in America*. New York: St. Martin's Press.

Kirschenbaum, H. (1979) *On Becoming Carl Rogers*. New York: Delacort.

Kleinman, A. (1977) Depression, somatisation and the new 'cross cultural psychiatry', *Social Science and Medicine*, 11, 3–10.

Kluckholm, C. and Murray, H. A. (1953) Personality formation: the determinants. In C. Kluckholm, H. A. Murray and D. M. Schneider (eds) *Personality in Nature, Society and Culture*. New York: Random House.

Kohls, R. L. (1981) *Developing Intercultural Awareness: A Learning Module Complete with Lesson Plan, Content, Exercises and Handouts*. Washington, DC: Society for Intercultural Education, Training and Research.

Kolko, D. J. (1987) Simplified inpatient treatment of nocturnal enureses in psychiatrically disturbed children. *Behaviour Therapy*, 2, 99–112.

Koslow, D. R. and Salett, E. P. (eds) (1989) *Crossing Cultures in Mental Health*. Washington, DC: SIETAR.

Kreeger, L. (1975) *The Large Group: Dynamics and Therapy*. London: Karnac Books.

Kuhn, T. (1962) *The Structure of Scientific Revolutions*. Chicago, IL: University of Chicago Press.

La Barre, W. (1964) Paralinguistics, kinesics and cultural anthropology. In T.A. Sebeok, (ed.) *Approaches to Semiotics*. The Hague: Moulton.

LaFramboise, T. D., Coleman, H. L. K. and Hernandez, A. (1991) Development and factor structure of the cross cultural counselling inventory – revised. *Professional Psychology: Research and Practice*, 22, 380–8.

Lago, C. O. (1990) *Working with Overseas Students: A Staff Development Training Manual*. Huddersfield: Huddersfield University and British Council.

Lago, C. O. (1992) Some complexities in counselling international students. *Journal of International Education*, Spring.

Lago, C. O. (1994) Therapy for a masturbatory society: the need for connectedness. *Counselling*, 5(2).

Lago, C. O. (2005) You're a white therapist: have you noticed? *Counselling and Psychotherapy Journal*, 16(3), 35–7.

Lago, C. O. and Barty, A. (2003) *Working with International Students: A Cross Cultural Training Manual*, 2nd edition of Lago 1990. London: United Kingdom Council for Overseas Student Affairs.

Lago, C. O., Baughan, R., Copinger-Binns, P., Brice, A., Caleb, R., Goss, S. P. and Lindeman, P. (1999) *Counselling Online: Opportunities and Risks in Counselling Clients via the Internet*. Rugby: BACP.

Lago, C. O. and Kitchin, D. (1998) The *Management of Counselling and Psychotherapy Agencies*. London: Sage Publications.

Lago, C. O. and Smith, B. (eds) (2003) *Anti-Discriminatory Counselling Practice*. London: Sage Publications.

Lago, C. O. and Thompson, J. (1989a) Counselling and race. In W. Dryden,

D. Charles-Edwards and R. Wolfe (eds) *Handbook of Counselling in Britain*. London: Tavistock-Routledge.

Lago, C. O. and Thompson, J. (1989b) *Issues of Race and Culture in Counselling Settings*, Video and Training Manual. Leicester: Leicester University, AVA Department (video); (1991) London: Barr Publications (manual).

Lago, C. O. and Thompson, J. (1996) *Race, Culture and Counselling*. Buckingham: Open University Press.

Lago, C. O. and Thompson, J. (2002) Counselling and race. In S. Palmer (ed.) *Multicultural Counselling*. London: Sage Publications.

Lago, H. M. (1994) The implications of empowerment with respect to accountability, training, costs, benefits and problems and the effect on management's role. Unpublished MBA essay, University of Surrey.

Lamm, N. (1995) It's a big fat revolution. In B. Findlen (ed.) *Listen Up: Voices from the Next Feminist Generation*. Emeryville, CA: Seal Press.

Langs, R. (1994) *Doing Supervision and Being Supervised*. London: Karnac Books.

Larson, P. C. (1982) Counselling special populations. *Professional Psychology*, 12(6), 843–58.

Laungani, P. (1999) Culture and identity: implications for counselling. In S. Palmer and P. Laungani (eds) *Counselling in a Multicultural Society*. London: Sage Publications.

Lawrence, D. (2003) Racial and cultural issues in counselling training. In A. Dupont-Joshua (ed.) *Working Inter-culturally in Counselling Settings*. Hove: Brunner-Routledge.

Lazurus, A. A. (1989) *The Practice of Multimodal Therapy*. Baltimore, MD: Johns Hopkins University Press.

Lazurus, A. A. (1995) 'Foreword'. In S. Palmer and W. Dryden, *Counselling for Stress Problems*. London: Sage Publications.

Lee, C. (1994) Introductory lecture to a conference on race, culture and counselling, University of Sheffield, July.

Lee, C. C. and Kurilla, V. (1993) Ethics and multi-culturalism: the challenge of diversity. *Ethical Issues in Professional Counselling*, 1(3), 1–11.

Lee, C. C., Oh, M. Y. and Mountcastle, A. R. (1992) Indigenous models of helping in non-western countries: implications for multicultural counselling. *Journal of Multicultural Counselling and Development*, 20 (January), 3–10.

Lee, C. C. and Richardson, B. L. (1991) *Multicultural Issues in Counselling: New Approaches to Diversity*. Alexandria: American Association for Counselling and Development.

Leff, J. P. (1973) Culture and the differentiation of emotional states. *British Journal of Psychiatry*, 123, 299–306.

Lehmann, P. (1994) Progressive psychiatry: publisher J. F. Lehmann as promoter of social psychiatry under fascism. *Changes: The Journal of the Psychology and Psychotherapy Association*, 12(1).

Le Page, R. B. (1968) Problems of description in multi-lingual communities. *Transactions of the Philological Society Journal*, 189–212.

Linton, R. (ed) (1945) *The Science of Man in World Crisis*. New York: Columbia University Press.

Lipsky, S. (1987) *Internalized Racism*. Seattle, WA: Rational Island Publishers.

Loganbill, C., Hardy, C. and Delworth, U. (1982) Supervision: a conceptual model. *The Counselling Psychologist*, 10(1), 3–42.

Lyons, C. H. (1975) *To Wash an Aethiop White: British Ideas about Black African Educability, 1530–1860*. New York: Teachers College Press.

McCarn, S. R. and Fassinger, R. E. (1996) Revisioning sexual minority identity formation: a new model of lesbian identity and its implications for counseling and research. *The Counseling Psychologist*, 24, 508–34.

McCarthy, P., Debell, C., Kanuha, V. and McLeod, J. (1988) Myths of supervision: identifying the gaps between theory and practice. *Counsellor Education and Supervision*, 28, 22–8.

McConahay, J. B. (1986) Modern racism, ambivalence, and the modern racism scale. In J. F. Dovidio and S. L. Gaertner (eds) *Prejudice, Discrimination and Racism*. New York: Academic Press.

McDevitt, C. (1994) Countertransference issues in working with students from other European cultures. Paper presented to the FEDORA (European Association of Guidance and Counselling) Conference, Barcelona.

McGrath, P. and Axelson, J. A. (1993) *Accessing Awareness and Developing Knowledge: Foundations for Skills in a Multicultural Society*. Monterey, CA: Brooks/Cole.

McInnis, E. (2002) Institutional racism in the NHS and clinical psychology? Taking note of MacPherson. *The Journal of Critical Psychology, Counselling and Psychotherapy*, 2(3), 164–70.

McIntosh, P. (1988) 'White privilege and male privilege: A personal account of coming to see correspondences through work in women's studies.' Wellesley College Center for Research on Women Working Papers Series 189. (Reprinted in Andersen, Margaret and Collins, Patricia Hill (eds) *Race, Class and Gender: An Anthology*. Belmont, CA: Wadsworth, 1992, 70–82.)

McIntosh, P. (1989) White privilege: unpacking the invisible knapsack. *Peace and Freedom*, 2, 10–12.

Mackay, D. (1984) Behavioural psychotherapy. In W. Dryden (ed.). *Individual Therapy in Britain*. London: Harper and Row.

McKenzie-Mavinga, I. (2003) Linking social history and the therapeutic process in research and practice on black issues. *Counselling and Psychotherapy Research*, 3(2), 103–6.

McLeod, J. (1993) *An Introduction to Counselling*. Buckingham: Open University Press.

McLeod, J. (1994) Issues in the organisation of counselling: learning from NMGC. *British Journal of Guidance and Counselling*, 22(2), 163–74.

McLeod, J. (2003) *An Introduction to Counselling*, 3rd edition. Maidenhead: Open University Press.

MacPherson, W. (1999) *The Stephen Lawrence Inquiry: Report of an Inquiry by Sir William MacPherson of Cluny, advised by Tom Cook, the Right Reverend Dr John Sentamu, Dr Richard Stone*. London: HMSO.

Mactaggart, F. and Gostin, L. (1983) Letter to the *Guardian* (reporting findings by the Joint Council for the Welfare of Immigrants and the National Council for Civil Liberties).

Mahrer, A. (1989) *The Integration of Psychotherapies: A Guide for Practising Therapists*. New York: Human Science Press.

Malik, K. (1996) *The Meaning of Race: Race, History and Culture in Western Society*. London: Macmillan.

Mandelbaum, D. G. (1940) (ed.) *Selected Writings of Edward Sapir*. London: Cambridge University Press.

Marszalek, J. F. and Cashwell, C. S. (1999) The gay and lesbian affirmative development (GLAD) model: facilitationg positive gay identity development. *Adultspan Journal*, 1, 13–31.

Maw, Dr J. (1980) Lecture on the experience of African students in the United Kingdom, University of London, June.

Mearns, D. (1994) *Developing Person-Centred Counselling*. London: Sage Publications.

Merry, T. (with Lusty, B.) (1999) *Learning and Being in Person-centred Counselling*. Ross-on-Wye: PCCS Books.

Migration Watch UK (2001) A nation of emigrants – emigration from the UK. Briefing Paper, 10 August (www.migrationwatchuk.org/briefingpapers/history/nationemigrants.asp). Accessed 6 January 2005.

Migration Watch UK (2004) An overview of UK migration. Briefing Paper (Revised) January (www.migrationwatchuk.co.uk/overview.asp). Accessed 6 January 2005.

Milliones, J. (1980) Construction of a Black consciousness measure: psychotherapeutic implications. *Psychotherapy: Theory, Research and Practice*, 17, 175–82.

Mohr, J. (2002) Proposal for a diversity course requirement. www.loyola.edu/diversityproposals. Accessed 2 July 2003.

Monach, J. (2004) Supervised practice. Privately circulated essay to the author.

Moodley, R. (1991) Interpreting the 'I' in counselling and guidance: an anti-racist approach. Text of lecture privately circulated to the authors.

Moodley, R. (2000a) Counselling and psychotherapy in a multicultural context: some training issues, Part 1. *Counselling: The Journal of the British Association for Counselling*, 11(3), 154–7.

Moodley, R. (2000b) Counselling and psychotherapy in a multicultural context, Part 2. *Counselling: The Journal of the British Association for Counselling*, 11(4), 221–4.

Moodley, R. (2001) (Re)Searching for a client in two different worlds: mind the research–practice gap. *Counselling and Psychotherapy Research*, 1(1), 18–23.

Moodley, R. (2003a) Double, triple, multiple jeopardy. In C. Lago and B. Smith (eds) *Anti-Discriminatory Counselling Practice*. London. Sage Publications.

Moodley, R. (2003b) Matrices in black and white: implications of cultural multiplicity for research in counselling and psychotherapy. *Counselling and Psychotherapy Research*, 3(2), 115–22.

Moodley, R. and Dhingra, S. (1998) Cross-cultural/racial matching in counselling and therapy: white clients and Black counsellors. *Counselling: The Journal of the British Association for Counselling*, 9(4), 295–9.

Moodley, R., Lago, C. and Talahite, A. (eds) (2004) *Carl Rogers Counsels a Black Client*. Ross-on-Wye: PCCS Books.

Moodley, R. and West, W. (eds) (2005) *Integrating Traditional Healing Practices into Counseling and Psychotherapy*. Thousand Oaks, CA: Sage Publications.

Morgan, H. (1998) Between fear and blindness: the white therapist and the black patient. *Journal of the British Association of Psychotherapists*, 31(1), 48–61.

Morgan, W. J. and Bo, J. (1993) Why should overseas students return to their home countries? *Journal of International Education*, 4(2): 66–70.

Murphy, H. B. M. (1986) The mental health impact of British cultural traditions. In J. L.Cox (ed.) *Transcultural Psychiatry*. London: Croom Helm.

Myers, L. (1988) *Understanding an Afrocentric World View: Introduction to an Optimal Psychology*. Dubuque, IA: Kendall/Hunt.

Nadirshaw, Z. and Goddard, S. (1999) *Rethinking Clinical Psychology: A Race Against Time for Minority Ethnic Communities in Mental Health Settings*. A research report into the views of black and minority people towards clinical psychology conducted with the support of the Department of Health and the Division of Clinical Psychology within the British Psychological Society.

National Statistics (2004) *National Statistics [online]*. Available at: http://www.statistics.gov/uk/downloads/themecompendia/foe2004/Ethnicitty.pdf. Accessed 8 June 2004.

NCVO (National Council for Voluntary Organizations) (2003) *Managing Diversity in the Workplace*. London: NCVO.

Neely, K. (1995) Suicide on the Net, *Guardian*, 6 January.

Nelson-Jones, R. (1988) *The Theory and Practice of Counselling Psychology*. London: Cassell.

Neville, B. (1994) Five kinds of empathy. Paper presented to the Third International Conference on Client-Centred and Experiential Psychotherapy, Gmunden, Austria.

Nickerson, K. J., Helms, J. E. and Terrell, F. (1994) Cultural mistrust, opinions about mental illness and black students' attitudes towards seeking psychological help from white counselors. *Journal of Counseling Psychology*, 41, 378–85.

*Observer* (2001) Race in Britain 2001. Special Edition, 25 November.

Olkin, R. (2002) Could you hold the door for me? Including disability in diversity. *Cultural Diversity and Ethnic Minority Psychology*, 8(2), 130–7.

Orbach, S. (1993) Behind the political psyche. *Weekend Guardian*, November.

Osler, A. (1997) *The Education and Careers of Black Teachers*. Buckingham: Open University Press.

Ossana, S. M., Helms, J. E. and Leonard, M. M. (1992) Do 'womanist' identity attitudes influence college women's self-esteem and perceptions of environmental bias? *Journal of Counseling and Development*, 70, 402–8.

Ouseley, H. (2004) Forget this phoney debate, we need to confront racism. *Guardian*, 10 April.

Owen, D. (1992–95) *1991 Census Statistical Papers 1–9*, Coventry: Centre for Research in Ethnic Relations, University of Warwick/Commission for Racial Equality.

Owen, D. (1993) *Analysis of the 1992 Census*. Coventry: Centre for Research in Ethnic Relations, University of Warwick.

Palmer, M. (1991) *The Elements of Taoism*. London: Element.

Palmer, S. (1999) In search of effective counselling across cultures. In S. Palmer and P. Laungani (eds) *Counselling in a Multicultural Society*. London: Sage Publications.

Palmer, S. (2002) *Multicultural Counselling: A Reader*. London: Sage Publications.

Palmer, S. and Laungani, P. (1999) *Counselling in a Multicultural Society*. London: Sage Publications.

Palmer, S. and Satoru, S. (eds) (2000) *Introduction to Counselling and Psychotherapy*. London: Sage Publications.

Paniagua, F. A. (1994) *Assessing and Treating Culturally Diverse Clients: A Practical Guide*. London: Sage Publications.

Parekh, B. (2000) *Rethinking Multiculturalism: Cultural Diversity and Political Theory*. London: Palgrave/Macmillan.

Parham, T. A. and Helms, J. (1981) The influence of black students' racial identity attitudes on preferences for counsellor's race. *Journal of Counseling Psychology*, 28, 250–7.

Park, L. C. and Covi, L. (1965) Nonblind placebo trial. *Archives of General Psychiatry*, 12 April, 336–45.

Patel, N., Bennett, E., Dennis, M. *et al*. *Clinical Psychology, 'Race' and Culture: A Training Manual*. Leicester: British Psychological Society.

Pattison, S. (2003) Cultural diversity: mapping the experiences of students on an international counsellor-training programme. *Counselling and Psychotherapy Research*, 3(2), 107–14.

Pedersen, P. B. (1977) The triad model and cross cultural counsellor training. *Personnel and Guidance Journal*, 56, 410–18.

Pedersen, P. (1985) *The Handbook of Cross Cultural Counseling and Therapy*. Westport, CT: Greenwood.

Pedersen, P. B. (1987a) Ten frequent assumptions of cultural bias in counselling. *Journal of Multicultural Counselling and Development*, January, 16–24.

Pedersen, P. B. (1987b) *Handbook of Cross-Cultural Counselling and Therapy*. New York: Praeger.

Pedersen, P. B. (1988) *Handbook for Developing Multicultural Awareness*. Alexandria, VA: American Counseling Association.

Pedersen, P. B. (1991) Multiculturalism as a generic approach to counselling. *Journal of Counselling and Development*, September/October, 70.

Pedersen, P. B., Draguns, J. G., Lonner, W. J. and Trimble, J. E. (1981) *Counselling Across Cultures*. Honolulu, HI: East-West Center, University of Hawaii.

Persaud, R. (1996) The wisest counsel? *Counselling: The Journal of the British Association for Counselling*, 7(3), 199–201.

Phoenix, A. (1994) Research: positioned differently? Issues of race, difference and commonality. *Changes*, 12(4).

Phung, T. C. (1995) An experience of inter-cultural counselling: views from a black client. *Counselling*, 6(1): 61–2.

Pilgrim, D. (1992) Psychotherapy and political evasions. In W. Dryden and C. Feltham (eds) *Psychotherapy and its Discontents*. Buckingham: Open University Press.

Pinker, S. (1994) *The Language Instinct: The New Science of Language and Mind*. London: Allen Lane.

Ponterotto, J. G. (1987) Counseling Mexican Americans: a multimodal approach. *Journal of Counseling and Development*, 65(6), 308–12.

Ponterotto, J. G., Burkard, A., D'Onofiro, A. A. *et al.* (1993) Development and validation of the Quick Discrimination Index (QDI). Unpublished manuscript.

Ponterotto, J. G., Costa, C. I. and Werner-Lin, A. (2002) Research perspectives in cross-cultural counseling. In P. B. Pederson, J. G. Draguns, W. J. Lonner and J. E. Trimble (eds) *Counseling across Cultures*, 5th edition. Thousand Oaks, CA: Sage Publications.

Ponterotto, J. G. and Pedersen, P. B. (1993) *Preventing Prejudice: A Guide for Counsellors and Educators*. Newbury Park, CA: Sage Publications.

Ponterotto, J. G., Sanchez, C. M. and Magids, D. M. (1991) Initial development and validation of the Multicultural Counseling Awareness Scale (MCAS). Paper presented at the annual meeting of the American Psychological Association, San Francisco, August.

Pope, M. (1995) The 'salad bowl' is big enough for us all: an argument for the inclusion of lesbians and gay men in any definition of multiculturalism. *Journal of Counseling and Development*, 73, 301–4.

Pope-Davis, D. B. and Coleman, H. L. K. (eds) (1997) *Multicultural Counselling Competencies: Assessment, Education and Training, and Supervision*. Thousand Oaks, CA: Sage Publications.

Poston, W. S. C. (1990) The biracial identity development model: a needed addition. *Journal of Counseling and Development*, 69, 152–5.

Power, G. (1981) The language of ethnic minority groups with special reference to education. Paper given at a conference on education and cultural diversity, Homerton College, Cambridge, June.

Prilleltensky, I. (1994) *The Morals and Politics of Psychology: Psychological Discourse and the Status One*. Albany, NY: State University of New York Press.

Proctor, B. (1989) *Supervision: A Working Alliance*. London: Alexia Publications.

Proctor, G. (2002) *The Dynamics of Power in Counselling and Psychotherapy: Ethics, Politics and Practice*. Ross-on-Wye: PCCS Books.

Raboteau, A. J. (1986) The Afro-American traditions. In R. L. Numbers and D. W. Amundsen (eds) *Caring and Curing: Health and Medicine in the Western Religious Traditions*. New York: Macmillan.

*RACE* Newletter (1993) Editorial: report on national survey. Rugby: British Association for Counselling and Psychotherapy.

Rees, T. (1982) Immigration policies in the United Kingdom. In C. Husband (ed.) *Race in Britain: Continuity and Change*. London: Hutchinson.

Reid, P. T. (2002) Multicultural psychology: bringing together gender and ethnicity. *Cultural Diversity and Ethnic Minority Psychology*, 8(2), 103–14.

Relate (1992) *History of the National Marriage Guidance Council, Now Known as Relate*. Information paper. Rugby: Herbert Gray College.

Ridley, C. (1984) Clinical treatment of the nondisclosing black client: a therapeutic paradox. *American Psychologist*, 39(11): 1234–44.

Ridley, C. R. (1989) Racism in counselling as an adverse behavioural process. In P. B. Pedersen, J. G. Draguns, W. L. Lonner and J. E. Trimble (eds) *Counseling Across Cultures*, 3rd edition. Honolulu, HI: University of Hawaii Press.

Ridley, C. R. (1995) *Overcoming Unintentional Racism in Counselling and Therapy: A Practitioners' Guide to Intentional Intervention*. Thousand Oaks, CA; London: Sage Publications.

Robinson, L. (2001) Intercultural communication in a therapeutic setting. In N. Coker (ed.) *Racism in Medicine: An Agenda for Change*. London: King's Fund Publishing.

Robinson, T. L. (2005) *The Convergence of Race, Ethnicity and Gender: Multiple Identities in Counseling*, 2nd edition. New Jersey, NJ: Pearson, Merrill Prentice Hall.

Rogers, C. R. ([1951] 1987) *Client-Centred Therapy*. London: Constable.

Rogers, C. R. (1959) A theory of therapy, personality and interpersonal relationships as developed in the client-centred framework. In S. Koch (ed.) *Psychology: A Study of Science*. New York: McGraw-Hill.

Rogers, C. R. (1961) *On Becoming a Person: A Therapist's View of Psychotherapy*. Boston, MA: Houghton-Mifflin.

Rogers, C. R. (1978) *Carl Rogers on Personal Power: Inner Strength and its Revolutionary Impact*. London: Constable.

Rogers, C. R. (1980) *A Way of Being*. Boston, MA: Houghton Mifflin.

Rogers-Saliu, F. and Lipman, A. (2005) African emotional support: A new direction for counselling. *Counselling and Psychotherapy Journal*. 16(3), 38–9.

Romaine, S. (1994) *Language in Society: An Introduction to Sociolinguistics*. Oxford: Oxford University Press.

Root, M. P. P. (2000) Multiracial Asians: models of ethnic identity. In R. D. Torres, L. F. Mirón and J. X. Inda (eds) *Race, Identity and Citizenship: A Reader*. Oxford: Blackwell.

Rosen, H. and Frank, J. D. (1962) Negroes in psychotherapy. *The American Journal of Psychiatry*, 10, 456–60.

Roth, A. and Fonagy, P. (eds) (1996) *What Works for Whom? A Critical Review of Psychotherapy Research*. New York: Guilford Press.

Rotherham, M. J. and Phinney, J. S. (1987) Ethnic behaviour patterns as an aspect of identity. In J. S. Phinney and M. J. Rotherham (eds) *Children's Ethnic Socialisation: Pluralism and Development*. Newbury Park, CA: Sage Publications.

Rowe, W., Bennett, S. and Atkinson, D. R. (1994) White racial identity models: a critique and alternative proposal. *The Counseling Psychologist*, 22, 120–46.

Runnymede Trust (1991) *Race and Immigration*, Bulletin 247. London: Runnymede Trust.

Ryde, J. (2000) Supervising across difference. *International Journal of Psychotherapy*, 5(1), 37–48.

Sabnani, H. B., Ponterotto, J. G. and Borodousky, L. G. (1991) White racial identity development and cross-cultural counselor training: a stage model, *The Counseling Psychologist*, 19: 76–102.

Sampson, E. E. (1993) Identity politics: challenges to psychology's understanding, *American Psychologist*, 48(12): 1219–30.

Samuels, A. (1985) *Jung and the Post-Jungians*. London: Tavistock/Routledge.

Samuels, A. (1993) *The Political Psyche*. London: Routledge.

Sanders, C. (1994) Most immigrants are white. *Times Higher Education Supplement*, 21 January: 5.

Sapir, E. (1931) Conceptual categories of primitive languages. *Science*, 74.

Sarup, M. (1978) *Marxism and Education*. London: Routledge and Kegan Paul.

Sashidharan, S. and Francis, E. (1993) Epidemiology, ethnicity and schizophrenia. In W. I. U. Ahmad (ed.) *'Race' and Health in Contemporary Britain*. Buckingham: Open University Press.

Sashidharan, S. P. (1986) Ideology and politics in transcultural psychiatry. In J. L. Cox (ed.) *Transcultural Psychiatry*. London: Croom Helm.

Scaife, J. M. (2001) *Supervision in Psychological Health Care*. London: Routledge.

Scheutz, A. (1944) The stranger: an essay in social psychology. *American Journal of Sociology*, 49, 499–507.

Schwartz, R. C. and Parker, W. M. (2002) On the experience of shame in multicultural counselling: implications for white counsellors-in-training. *British Journal of Guidance and Counselling*, 30(3), 311–18.

Scull, A. (1975) From madness to mental illness: medical men as moral entrepreneurs. *European Journal of Sociology*, 16, 218–61.

Scull, A. (1979) *Museums of Madness: The Social Organisation of Insanity in Nineteenth Century England*. London: Allen Lane.

Sears, D. (1988) Symbolic racism. In P. A. Katz and D. A. Taylor (eds) *Eliminating Racism: Profiles in Controversy*. New York: Plenum.

Sedlacek, W. E. and Brooks, G. C. Jr (1970) Measuring racial attitudes in a situational context. *Psychological Reports*, 27, 971–80.

Sharrock, W. W. and Anderson, D. C. (1981) Language, thought and reality, again. *Journal of British Sociological Association*, 15(2), 287–93.

Shipton, G. (ed.) (1997) *Supervision of Psychotherapy and Counselling: Making a Place to Think*. Buckingham: Open University Press.

Shoaib, K. and Peel, J. (2003) Kashmiri women's perceptions of their emotional and psychological needs, and access to counselling. *Counselling and Psychotherapy Reseach*, 3(2), 87–94.

Skellington, R. and Morris, P. (1992) *Race in Britain Today*. London: Sage Publications and Open University.

Smedley, A. (1993) *Race in North America: Origin and Evolution of a World View*. Boulder, CO: Westview Press.

Smith, B. (1999) Potency, permission, protection and politics. *ITA News*, 55 (Autumn), 17–20.

Smith, D. J. (1977) *Racial Disadvantage in Britain: The PEP Report*. Harmondsworth: Penguin.

Sodowsky, G. R., Taffe, R. C., Gutkin, T. and Wise, S. L. (1992) Development and applications of the Multicultural Counseling Inventory. Unpublished manuscript.

Speight, S. L., Myers, L. J., Cox, C. I. and Highlen, P. S. (1991) A redefinition. *Journal of Counseling and Development*. 70 (September/October), 29–36.

Stanfield, J. H. (1993) Epistemological considerations. In J. H. Stanfield and R. M. Dennis (eds) *Race and Ethnicity in Research Methods*. Thousand Oaks, CA: Sage Publications.

Stanfield, J. H. and Dennis, R. M. (eds) (1993) *Race and Ethnicity in Research Methods*. Thousand Oaks, CA: Sage Publications.

Staub, E. (1993) The psychology of bystanders, perpetrators and heroic helpers. *International Journal of Intercultural Relations*, 17(3), 315–41.

Stringer, S. (1992) Home is where the heart is. *Counselling News*, 8 (December).

Sue, D. and Sundberg, N. D. (1996) Research and research hypotheses about effectiveness of intercultural counseling. In P. B. Pedersen, J. G. Draguns, W. J. Lonner and J. E. Trimble (eds) *Counseling Across Cultures*, 3rd edition. Honolulu, HI: University of Hawaii Press.

Sue, D. W. (1981) *Counselling the Culturally Different: Theory and Practice*. New York: Wiley.

Sue, D. W. (2001) The superordinate nature of cultural competence. *Counselling Psychologist*, 29(6), 850–7.

Sue, D. W., Arrendondo, P. and McDavis, R. J. (1992) Multicultural counselling competencies and standards: a call to the profession. *Journal of Counselling and Development*, 7 (March–April).

Sue, D. W., Bernie, J. E., Durran, A. *et al.* (1982) Position paper: cross cultural competencies. *The Counselling Psychologist,* 10, 1–8.

Sue, D. W., Ivey, A. E. and Pedersen, P. B. (1996) *A Theory Of Multicultural Counseling And Therapy*. Pacific Grove, CA: Brooks/Cole Publishing Co.

Sue, D. W. and Sue, D. (1990) *Counselling the Culturally Different: Theory and Practice,* 2nd edition. New York: John Wiley and Sons.

Sue, D. W. and Sue, D. (1999) *Counseling the Culturally Different: Theory and Practice,* 3rd edition. New York: John Wiley and Sons.

Sue, D. W. and Sue, D. (2003) *Counseling the Culturally Different: Theory and Practice,* 4th edition. Indianapolis, IN: Wiley.

Sue, S. (1988) Psychotherapist service for ethnic minorities. *American Psychologist,* 43(4), 301–8.

Sullivan, N. (2003) *A Critical Introduction to Queer Theory*. New York: New York University Press.

Sutton, C. (1987) *Handbook of Research for the Helping Professions*. London: Routledge and Kegan Paul.

Szasz, T. (1970) *The Manufacture of Madness: A Comparative Study of the Inquisition and the Mental Health Movement*. New York: Harper and Row.

Szasz, T. (1971) The sane slave. *American Journal of Psychotherapy,* 25 (April), 228–39.

Talahite, A. and Moodley, R. (2004) Therapist's faces, client's masks: racial enactments through pain, anger and hurt. In R. Moodley, C. Lago and A. Talahite (eds) *Carl Rogers Counsels a Black Client: Race and Culture in Person-Centred Counselling*. Ross-on-Wye: PCCS Books.

Thomas, A. (1998) The stresses of being a counselling trainer. In H. Johns (ed.) *Balancing Acts: Studies in Counselling Training*. London: Routledge.

Thomas, A. and Sillen, S. (1972) *Racism and Psychiatry*. New York: Bruner and Mazell Inc.

Thomas, L. (1992) Racism and psychotherapy. Working with racism in the consulting room: an analytical view. In J. Kareem and R. Littlewood (eds) *Intercultural Therapy: Themes, Interpretations and Practice*. Oxford: Blackwell.

Thompson, A. (2003) Tiffany, friend of people of color: white investments in antiracism. *Qualitative Studies in Education,* 16(1), 7–29.

Thompson, C. E. and Jenal, S. T. (1994) Interracial and intraracial quasi counseling interactions. When counselors avoid discussing race. *Journal of Counseling Psychology,* 41(4), 484–91.

Thompson, H. (1992) The context of abuse and deprivation. *Counselling,* 3(4), 225–8.

Thompson, J. (1991) Issues of race and culture in counselling supervision training courses. Unpublished MSc thesis, Polytechnic of East London.

Thorne, B. (1984) Person-centred therapy. In W. Dryden (ed.) *Individual Therapy in Britain*. London: Harper and Row.

Torrey, E. F. (1972) *The Mind Game: Witch Doctors and Psychiatrists*. New York: Emerson-Hall.

Toukmanian, S. G. and Rennie, D. L. (eds) (1992) *Psychotherapy Process Research: Paradigmatic and Narrative Approach*. Newbury Park, CA: Sage Publications.

Triandis (1975) *Culture Training, Cognitive Complexity and Interpersonal Attitudes. Cross Cultural Perspectives in Learning*. New York: Wiley.

Troiden, R. (1988) Homosexual identity development. *Journal of Adolescent Health Care*, 9, 105–13.

Troyna, B. (1981) *Public Awareness and the Media: A Study of Reporting on Race*. London: Commission for Racial Equality.

Troyna, B. (1993) *Racism and Education: Research Perspectives*. Buckingham: Open University Press.

Troyna, B. (1994) Blind faith? Empowerment and educational research. Paper presented to the International Sociology of Education Conference, Sheffield University, 4–6 January.

Tseng, W. and Hsu, J. (1979) Culture and psychotherapy. In A. J. Marsella, R. Thorp and T. Ciborowski (eds) *Perspectives on Cross-Cultural Psychology*. New York: Academic Press.

Tseng, W. S. (1986) Chinese psychiatry: development and characteristics. In J. L. Cox (ed.) *Transcultural Psychiatry*. London: Croom Helm.

Tuckwell, G. M. (2002) *Racial Identity, White Counsellors and Therapists*. Buckingham: Open University Press.

Turner, V. (1967) *The Forest of Symbols: Aspects of Ndembu Ritual*. Ithaca, NY: Cornell University Press.

Turner, V. W. (1964) An Ndembu doctor in practice. In A. Kiev (ed.) *Magic, Faith and Healing: Studies in Primitive Psychiatry Today*. London: The Free Press of Glencoe/Collier-Macmillan.

Usher, C. H. (1989) Recognizing cultural bias in counselling theory and practice: the case of Rogers. *Journal of Multicultural Counseling and Development*, 17(2), 62–71.

Uwahemu, A. (2004) The proxy self – a more acceptable version of me. *Counselling and Psychotherapy Journal*, 14(1), 44–5.

Valentine, C. A. (1968) *Culture and Poverty*. Chicago, IL: University of Chicago Press.

Valla, J. P. and Prince, R. H. (1989) Religious experiences as self-healing mechanisms. In C. A. Ward (ed.) *Altered States of Consciousness and Mental Health: A Cross Cultural Perspective*. London: Sage Publications.

Vandervolk, C. (1974) The relationship of personality, values and race to anticipation of the supervisory relationship. *Rehabilitation Counselling Bulletin*, 18, 41–6.

Van Dijk, T. A. (1993) *Elite Discourse and Racism*. London: Sage Publications.

Van Duerzen-Smith, E. (1984) Existential therapy, in W. Dryden (ed.) *Individual Therapy in Britain*. London: Harper and Row.

Vash, C. L. (1981) *The Psychology of Disability*. Springer Series on Rehabilitation – Vol. 1. New York: Springer Publishing Co.

Vaughan, M. (1977) Overseas students: some cultural clues. *UKCOSA NEWS*, 9, 1.

Venkoba Rao, A. (1986) Indian and Western psychiatry: a comparison. In J. L. Cox (ed.) *Transcultural Psychiatry*, London: Croom Helm.

Vera, E. M. and Speight, S. L. (2003) Multicultural competence, social justice, and counseling psychology: expanding our roles, *The Counseling Psychologist*, 31(3): 253–72.

Vera, H., Feagin, J. R. and Gordon, A. (1995) Superior intellect? Sincere fictions of the white self. *Journal of Negro Education*, 64(3), 295–306.

Vontress, C. E. (1971) *Counseling Negroes*. Boston, MA: Houghton Mifflin.

Vontress, C. E. and Epp, L. R. (1997) Historical hostility in the African American client: implications for counseling. *Journal of Multicultural Counseling and Development*, 25, 170–84.

Vontress, C. E. and Jackson, M. L. (2004) Reactions to the multicultural counseling competencies debate. *Journal of Mental Health Counseling*, 26, 74–80.

Walcott, R. (2003) Multiculturally crazy. Paper presented at the Critical Multicultural Practice, Toronto, June.

Walker, R. D. and La Rue, R. (1986) An integrative approach to American Indian mental health. In C. R. Wilkinson (ed.) *Ethnic Psychiatry*. New York: Plenum.

Ward, C. A. (ed.) (1989) *Altered States of Consciousness and Mental Health: A Cross-Cultural Perspective*. London: Sage Publications.

Watkins, C. E. and Terrell, F. (1988) Mistrust level and its effects on counseling expectations in black client–white counselor relationship: an analogue study. *Journal of Counseling Psychology*, 35, 194–7.

Watson, J. and Rayner, R. (1920) Conditional emotional reactions. *Journal of Experimental Psychology*, 3, 1–14.

Watson, V. V. V. (2004) The training experiences of black counsellors. PhD thesis, University of Nottingham.

Webb Johnson, A. (1993) Cultural divide. *Counselling News*, 9 March, 26–7.

West, C. (1993) *Race Matters*. Boston, MA: Beacon Press.

West, W. and Abu Talib, M. (2002) Hearing what research participants are really saying: the influence of researcher cultural identity. *Counselling and Psychotherapy Research*, 2(4), 253–8.

Westwood, M. J. (1990) Identification of human problems and methods of help seeking: a cross cultural study. Paper presented to the Comparative and International Education Society, Anaheim, California, 29 March–1 April.

Westwood, S., Conlohte, J., Desai, S., Mathew, P. and Piper, A. (1989) *Sadness in My Heart: Racism and Mental Health. A Research Report*. Leicester: University of Leicester.

Whorf, B. L. (1956) Language, mind and reality. In J. Carroll and B. Carroll (eds) *Language, Thought and Reality*. Cambridge, MA: MIT Press.

Wikipedia (2005) *Metanarrative*. http://en.wikipedia.org/wiki/metanarrative. Accessed 11 March 2005.

Wilchins, R. (2004) *Queer Theory, Gender Theory: An Instant Primer*. Los Angeles: Alyson Books.

Williams, R. (2004) *Queer Theory, Gender Theory: An Instant Primer*. Los Angeles, CA: Alyson Books.

Williams, R. (1983) *Keywords: A Vocabulary of Culture and Society*. London: Fontana.

Winnicott, D. W. (1965) *Maturational Processes and the Facilitating Environment*. London: Hogarth.

Wittkower, E. D. (1970) Trance and possession states. *International Journal of Social Psychiatry*, 16, 153–60.

Wolpe, J. (1958) *Psychotherapy by Reciprocal Inhibition*. Stamford, NY: Stamford University Press.

Wood, J. K. (1990) *Everything and Nothing: Client-Centred Therapy, the Person-Centred Approach and Beyond*. Brazil: privately published document.

Yeaxlee, B. A. (1925) *Spiritual Values in Adult Education*. London: Oxford University Press.

Yinger, J. M. (1976) Ethnicity in complex societies. In L. A. Coser and O. N. Larsen (eds) *The Uses of Controversy in Sociology*. New York: Free Press.

Yui, L. (1978) Degree of assimilation and its effect on the preference of counselling style and of self-disclosure among Chinese Americans in Hawaii. Unpublished doctoral dissertation, Indiana University.

# Index